KREMLIN TARGET: U.S.A.

DONALD DUNHAM

KREMLIN TARGET: U.S.A.

Conquest by Propaganda

IVES WASHBURN, INC.
New York

FOR

ROBERT ROSS

by whom this book may one day
be rewritten.

PREFACE

ELEVEN and one-half years have passed since the Kremlin-imposed regime in Romania closed my office and forced me to leave the country. And twelve years have passed since my Romanian secretary was thrown into jail and given a sentence of fifteen years of hard labor for treason because she worked for the Americans.

My professional life was changed by this experience. I found that accommodation with the Russians was impossible and cultural relations for purposes of good will were futile. The USSR was dedicated to world domination through the imposition of dictatorial totalitarianism on one free country after another. I found, too, that—as pointed out by De Tocqueville one hundred and twenty-six years ago—the basis for this dedication lay in the traditional, historical Russian relationship between the ruler and the ruled, rather than in communism which is simply one, recently created, outlet of national expansion used as a façade for propaganda aggression.

So I was forced to switch from cultural-information representative of the United States to propagandist, from a person trying to cultivate cordial relations for my country to a competitor in a new arena of international conflict. This shift was accomplished during the first year of my assignment in Bucharest, when my staff tried to compete, like David, against the Goliath of the Kremlin propaganda apparatus.

Kremlin Target: U.S.A.—Conquest by Propaganda was written in an effort to alert American men and women, inside and outside the government, to what we are losing to the USSR in a war which we have not really been fighting. I have tried to bring together a substantial amount of evidence to portray the threat posed by Kremlin propaganda to the security of our country and that of the entire world. I have also tried to make some modest suggestions about what we all can do to counter this threat and turn a propaganda attack against the USSR.

In the writing of this book I ran into two problems. The first was to find a word in the English language which would adequately convey the meaning of "political activation" as it is practiced by the USSR. The fact is that no such word exists because until now the civilized Western world has not gone in for psychological warfare in peacetime. Consequently, I was forced to choose a word from the Russian vocabulary which carried a partial intimation to Westerners of the Russian concept, and to translate it into its approximate English equivalent. *Propaganda* in the hands of the Kremlin covers all action necessary to induce a person to act in the way the Kremlin wishes him to act. It covers all forms of agitation up to the point of all-out war.

The second problem was the handling of the subject matter in the light of a rapidly changing situation. And how it did change from the moment I went to work on this venture in May 1960. First, there was the Eisenhower administration's turning of the other cheek after Khrushchev's slap in Paris. Then we had the prospect of vigorous action against our opponents by either of the two young, pragmatic, energetic candidates for the presidency. Next, we found the new administration proclaiming its intention of pursuing a policy of "quiet diplomacy" in its dealings with the USSR. And, finally, we witnessed the break-through of April 20, 1961, when President Kennedy made his declaration of propaganda war on world communism.

No doubt more changes will come after the book goes to press, but that is a small matter now that we have entered the fray. From this point on the only question will be: how fast and how effectively can the President's declaration of propaganda war against world communism be implemented against the USSR?

DONALD DUNHAM

May 7, 1961
New York

CONTENTS

THERE are, at the present time, two great nations in the world, which seem to tend toward the same end, although they started from different points; I allude to the Russians and the Americans:

The American struggles against the natural obstacles which oppose him; the adversaries of the Russian are men: the former combats the wilderness and savage life; the latter, civilization with all its weapons and its arts; the conquests of the one are therefore gained by the ploughshare; those of the other, by the sword. The Anglo-American relies upon personal interest to accomplish his ends, and gives free scope to the unguided exertions and common sense of the citizens; the Russian centers all the authority of society in a single arm: the principal instrument of the former is freedom; of the latter, servitude. Their starting-point is different, and their courses are not the same; yet each of them seems to be marked out by the will of Heaven to sway the destinies of half the globe.

ALEXIS CHARLES HENRI MAURICE CLEREL DE TOCQUEVILLE

The Republic of the United States of America, and Its Political Institutions, Reviewed and Examined, 1835

The United States is one of the very rare guiltless powers. America has set free territories that were under its jurisdiction; it has assisted in the liberation of many nations; it has helped almost every country you can name to save its independence and to restore its economy. In one way or another the United States has displayed a generosity that is without parallel in history.

Now let us look at Soviet Russia. That country has set at nought every treaty it has ever signed; it has violated every principle of international law; it has never ceased working by subversive means

xiii

to overturn the political order and to destroy the independence of other countries; it has, most notably of all, subjugated by force nine countries of Europe, each of which has an impressive record of freedom and independence. It can be asserted without hesitation that Soviet Russia's aggressions are unmatched both in number and in scope.

And yet the United States is criticized and suspected throughout the greater part of the world, whereas Soviet Russia has become the champion—if you please—of anti-imperialism and anti-colonialism, and the defender of the independence of states.

> CONSTANTIN VISOIANU, Former Minister of Foreign Affairs of Romania
>
> *Address to the Assembly of Captive European Nations,* September 24, 1958

PART I

THE CRITICAL CHALLENGE

My tongue is my secret weapon.

KHRUSHCHEV, July 4th Reception, 1961
American Embassy, Moscow

Words are one thing, actions another. Good words are a mask for concealment of deeds.

STALIN, 1913

CHAPTER 1.

The Scope of Kremlin Propaganda

... it is clear that the forces of communism are not to be underestimated in Cuba or anywhere else in the world. The advantages of a police state, its use of mass terror and arrest to prevent the spread of free dissent, cannot be overlooked by those who expect the fall of every fanatic tyrant.

If the self-discipline of the free cannot match the iron discipline of the mailed fist in economic, political, scientific, and all the other kinds of struggle as well as the military, then the peril to freedom will continue to rise.

... it is clearer than ever that we face a relentless struggle in every corner of the globe that goes far beyond the clash of armies or even nuclear armaments.

... We dare not fail to see the insidious nature of this new and deeper struggle. We dare not fail to grasp the new concept, the new tools, the new sense of urgency we will need to combat it. . . . And we dare not fail to realize that this struggle is taking place every day without fanfare in thousands of villages and markets day and night and in classrooms all over the globe.

... Too long we have fixed our eyes on traditional military needs; on armies prepared to cross borders; on missiles poised for flight. Now it should be clear that this is no longer enough; that our security may be lost piece by piece, country by country, without the firing of a single missile or the crossing of a single border.

We intend to profit from this lesson. We intend to re-examine and reorient our forces of all kinds; our tactics and our institutions here in this community. We intend to intensify our efforts for a struggle in many ways more difficult than war ...

PRESIDENT JOHN F. KENNEDY,
to the American Society of
Newspaper Editors
Washington, D. C.
April 20, 1961

THE above statement is the first top official recognition of the significance of the propaganda war being waged against us since it started some sixteen years ago. It is also the first official declaration of intention to enter that war for the purpose of safeguarding our security. This declaration has historic import, and may well mark the turning point in the tides of political affairs among the nations of the world since the end of World War II.

This decision of President Kennedy's to enter fully into the propaganda war has profound implications for the future of the United States because Kremlin propaganda poses the greatest threat to our security of any single force arrayed against us today. Kremlin propaganda outranks nuclear and space weapons because in the military field there is a stalemate. It rises above the USSR brand of communism because this ism constitutes only one of the propaganda's operational parts. And perhaps its greatest danger for us lies in our failure to understand it.

The Kremlin has fashioned out of propaganda the most powerful nonmilitary weapon of national aggression the world has ever known. By blending the recruiting techniques for its communist agents with methods of psychological warfare to include political activation, agitation, infiltration, incitement to revolution, delusion and subversion in political, trade, ideological, and cultural fields, the Kremlin has added a new dimension to the conduct of international relations. Consequently Kremlin propaganda has become synonymous, and interchangeable, with USSR foreign policy in forwarding the centuries-old Russian attempt to extend her power beyond her borders.

Since the United States is the strongest obstacle in her path to world conquest, we have been singled out as the chief USSR propaganda target and labeled "The Enemy." The vast Kremlin propaganda machine has been put to work to slander us abroad in order to cut down the respect and trust other peoples have in us, and thus reduce the effect of our foreign-policy actions. As subversion it has been directed to our own people to undermine our faith in our institutions and to confuse the issues in our relations with the USSR. And, finally, it has been turned on the captive audiences inside the USSR—and inside the captive nations of eastern Europe—to inoculate them against the effects of any Free World ideas which seep into their closed, totalitarian societies.

To the USSR goes the distinction of being the first to assault nations with the help of all-pervading *political* propaganda. The atheist leaders of the Kremlin imitated in the field of politics what the leaders of the Roman Catholic Church, for instance, had been doing in the spiritual realm of religious faith. The definition of the Latin word *propagandum* shows that the Kremlin has managed to find a common base in semantics with the Church of Rome and a common point of historical reference as well.

"Any organized . . . group . . . to spread a . . . system of . . . principles" is the first definition given by Webster to the word *propagandum*. It mentions the College of Propaganda, "a college instituted by Urban VIII (1623–44) to educate priests for missions."

It is evident that the Kremlin regime looked back nearly three hundred years to find a model for its own "missions." It had been quick to grasp the vital importance of one ingredient in the organization of the Church of Rome which enabled it to cross national borders: proselytizing through specially selected citizens of foreign countries. Having established its own "colleges of propaganda," the Kremlin is continuously training and "educating" foreign nationals for the purpose of political activation and subversion once they have returned to their native lands. Since these "missionary workers" of the Kremlin creed hold on to their citizenship, they cannot be kept out, and their activities can be curbed only with considerable difficulty in free societies.

But the Kremlin's use of "communism" as an instrument of propaganda and a façade for aggression is only part of the operational picture. The USSR has also used diplomacy as a channel and has corrupted the traditional and civilized practice of diplomatic courtesy and immunity.

The entire USSR diplomatic and consular services—plus special representatives—are meshed in propaganda operations with those of international "front" organizations, local "front" groups, and local Kremlin "communist" parties. The combination is a felicitous one. The diplomatic immunity and free and unchecked customs entry of goods accorded the overt Kremlin representatives is added to the freedom of political action accorded the covert Kremlin agents because of their citizenship status.

These two coordinated networks are directed by, and report back to, a remarkable two-headed Kremlin creation: the USSR Foreign Office and the organization of world communism. The overt forms of the latter were called the Communist International (Comintern) until 1943, and the Communist Information Bureau (Cominform) from 1947 until 1956. Both heads are subject to propaganda direction by the Section of Propaganda and Agitation (Agitprop), which, in turn, is controlled by the current dictator and the Presidium of the Central Committee of the Kremlin communist party. Today, in the absence of a large formal staff headquarters for its world propaganda effort, the USSR holds periodic conferences—as it did in 1957 and 1961—to hand down "the word" to representatives from subordinate Kremlin "communist parties" in other countries.

Most probably, in the early years, before the USSR had pretensions as a world power, these two governmental units were separate and competed with one another for bureaucratic precedence. In the past history of the worldwide network organization, when Kremlin communism was the only communism and the USSR had a monopoly on the ism, the regime may have treated it as a real faith and may have given the nod to the Comintern over the Foreign Office. However, by the time Stalin formally disbanded the Comintern in 1943, in a deceptively pacifying gesture to his newly found allies, it would appear that the Foreign Office and USSR foreign policy had taken the lead.

Under current direction, embassies, legations, consulates, commercial and cultural offices of the USSR—as well as those of the captive nations of eastern Europe—are used as guidance centers for propaganda under their safeguard of diplomatic immunity. They receive propaganda materials and money from the Kremlin which they pass on to the "front" and "party" groups. Their personnel are careful not to be caught meddling too directly in domestic affairs of the country of their assignment for fear of being declared *persona non grata* and requested to leave.

Top USSR government representatives are among its principal agents of propaganda. Khrushchev, on his highly publicized visits and in his frequent news-making declarations, Foreign Office representatives in their dramatic presentations at the United Nations, and diplomats in their "personal" contacts and occasional appearances, all have the primary objective of swaying public opinion and gathering allegiances.

These representatives, like the local Kremlin agents, are given thorough and expert training in propaganda at various stages of their careers. Special courses and schools have been set up for just this purpose. Large sums of money are invested in this enterprise, but of course the specific figures are kept secret. For the various forms of Kremlin propaganda outside the USSR involving "front" and "communist party" groups, it has been roughly estimated in 1960 that the total expenditures approximated $2 billion, and the total personnel, paid and voluntary, numbered about 500,000. For purposes of comparison, it is noted that the Kremlin (with slight aid from Peking) spends $2.00 per year per free man to be subjugated, as against two cents per person per year for the world propaganda put forth by all free countries, of which the United States contributes 1½ cents.

No criteria—number of schools and courses, amount of money or degree of indoctrination—can be found to estimate the national investment in propaganda the USSR makes when she sends her subjects abroad. For every citizen who is permitted to travel beyond the heavily guarded frontiers is charged with one of two duties, or perhaps with both: to project propaganda or to collect information.

Just as no activity in the USSR may be pursued as an end in itself but must have in it a political "line," or serve a political objective, so no performing artist, no scholar, no engineer traveling abroad may consider himself simply a professional man; he is a propaganda or intelligence agent of the state. Comparison with the Eisenhower effort to make every American traveler an ambassador of good will provides an illustration of the difficulty our country has had and still has in coming to understand the meaning and significance of Kremlin propaganda. Only a politically naïve people could hope to pit good will effectively against propaganda with a built-in political line and objective.

To the majority of our citizens, the very idea of propaganda is repugnant. We mix it up with espionage, and because we disapprove of spying we feel we personally should not stoop to it. If our government must indulge in espionage as a means of survival in order to counter the espionage of other countries, then we condone the practice. But gathering information is for special government agents and does not touch those of us who are average citizens.

We are inclined to accept the second definition of *propagandum* offered by Webster, "... secret or clandestine dissemination of ideas, information, gossip or the like, for the purpose of helping or injuring a person, an institution, a cause." Thus, we assume all propaganda is "black," that it is disseminated in a clandestine, underhanded manner, and we tend to dismiss it as dishonest and dishonorable. And because we disdain propaganda in general we do not take the pains to analyze and understand Kremlin propaganda in particular. If we did so we would discover how far beyond Webster's definitions it has been developed and how effectively it is being used against our national interests. This national tendency has been characterized as "hiding behind our finger."

Our history fails to equip us with the experience we need to understand the significance of propaganda in today's world of military peace and political war. We have developed a nation of workers, of contenders with the forces of nature, not of politicians, of manipulators of the relations between man and man. But if we are to come to exert the influence in the world which our society, our national character, our intentions and purposes merit, we must change and educate ourselves in propaganda. Human nature being what it is, letting the facts speak for themselves is not enough; the truth objectively set forth is no match for lies or half-truths vigorously projected. We have been aware of this foible for a long time in the merchandising of detergents in a highly competitive market. It is time for us to recognize it in the conduct of our relations abroad.

To get down to terms, we can even save our sensibilities from the taint of the clandestine and the underhanded in Kremlin propaganda if we will only analyze it closely. Not all of it is disseminated covertly. In fact, today by far the greatest proportion is sent forth openly and directly from the Kremlin, from TASS, the USSR monopoly news agency, from Radio Moscow, the USSR state radio station, or is published officially in many magazines of many languages and distributed abroad with a Moscow date line. It is this "white" propaganda which is acknowledged, which is open and aboveboard in dissemination, that we must deal with first. If we manage to penetrate its fraud and expose it to the world, much of the effect of the "black" brand of Kremlin propaganda will be nullified, and we will have taken a long step toward destroying this vast weapon of total aggression.

CHAPTER 2.

Kremlin Propaganda Defined

KREMLIN propaganda succeeds in deluding many intelligent Americans on a number of strategic counts: the objectives of the USSR toward world conquest, the character of propaganda in the Kremlin sense, and the kind of methods used in applying it to our society.

On the international scene the hearts and minds of some well-informed Americans are beguiled by the image of a phony world disarmament or by the advantages of doing business with Khrushchev. They are led to feel that the USSR, through its façade of a worldwide "party," can or will bring about the realization of these ideals. Until the Kremlin repudiates its proclaimed basic aim of world domination these worthy Western American idealists and "wishful thinkers" will be traded upon cynically for the purpose of USSR political expansion.

On the domestic scene, some of our citizens—regardless of political persuasion, from the far left to the far right—are manipulated by the Kremlin to compete politically in terms of communism as a social doctrine. This action brings communism as an instrument of aggression into domestic politics, has it contended over in terms of *American* interests, identifies the interests of an American group with the interests of the USSR, and thus creates an American political party out of an organization of Kremlin agents.

Perhaps we are gullible and are too prone to assume everyone is honest until he proves himself otherwise, are too ready to overlook past lies, in our compulsion to feel that everyone in the world is basically "good." Perhaps our predominantly European stock with its openness and directness makes us an easy, open target for the Kremlin propagandists with their oriental admixture. Perhaps it is this admixture which makes them able to think on two planes at once. Certainly, we frequently get lost in trying to follow the Russian mentality, with its simultaneous grasp and treatment of the actual and the theoretical.

Whatever the explanation for our failure to understand this, we have no excuse for not familiarizing ourselves with what they frankly state about themselves, their intentions, and their methods of propaganda operations.

Their intentions toward world conquest were set forth officially at the Second and Sixth Congresses of the Communist International in 1920 and 1928. It is obvious that the Kremlin hierarchy originated the project of world conquest, has been pursuing this goal ever since, and is determined to remain the dictator of dictatorships (of the proletariat).

Let the Kremlin speak for itself from the 1920's:

"The Russian Soviet Republic . . . is grouping around itself the soviet movements . . . of the workers of all countries, and all national liberation movements of the colonial and subject countries . . ."

". . . the USSR . . . becomes . . . the center of international revolution. . . ."

"In the event of the imperialist states declaring war upon and attacking the USSR, the international proletariat must retaliate . . . by mass action . . . and overthrow . . . the imperialist governments with the slogan of: 'Dictatorship of the Proletariat and Alliance with the USSR.' "

". . . the international proletariat must be bound by . . . the strictest international discipline in the communist ranks . . . (which) must find expression in the subordination of local interest . . . to . . . the decisions passed by the leading bodies of the Communist International."

Then, with special reference to propaganda targets in the underdeveloped areas, these proclamations state boldly:

"It is the duty of the Communist International to support the

revolution in its first stages. But if from the outset the leadership
is in the hands of a communist vanguard, the revolutionary masses
will not be led astray, but may go ahead through the successive
periods of development of revolutionary experience."

Finally, the following two points taken from these writings are
worth noting. They hold in effect that the multinational socialist
state—the USSR—will serve as a model for the future socialist
world state; and that bourgeois ideology is forever trying to cor-
rupt the citizens of the USSR so it must be combated by revolutionary vigilance.

The proclamations of these congresses constitute the bible of
the Kremlin system, which is followed today just as scrupulously
as it was in the 1920's. From reading them we learn three most
important facts. First, "communism"—the applied, not the theoretical, version—is Kremlin communism, not Yugoslav, nor even
Polish. The propaganda in its name, or on its behalf, is designed to
benefit only the USSR. Second, as early as the 1920's the Russian
leaders in the Communist International decreed that all "communists" would owe primary allegiance in time of war to the
Russian Soviet Republic, and only secondarily to their own country. Thus, every communist working for Kremlin communism
is an agent of the USSR. Third, social doctrine has long since
been abandoned as the principal issue of Kremlin proselytizing,
although it has been retained as a major talking point in the
more advanced societies. The real objective now is the organization of people in the noncommunist world into a vanguard of
agents.

In the light of these statements and USSR actions over the past
fifty-odd years it is almost inconceivable that anyone should believe in her peaceful intentions, trust her word, or expect to make
gains for the security of the world through negotiation or accommodation. The fact that these statements and actions have not
had the effect they deserve on the thinking of the peoples of the
Free World, especially the Americans, is a tribute to the ingenuity
of the Kremlin propagandists. They have managed to so confuse

issues that inconsistencies, contradictions, and outright fraud are not fully understood, exposed, or penalized.

To appreciate the character of Kremlin propaganda we must get rid of our own conception of propaganda. We must not dismiss it with the observation: "Oh, it is just words." All contacts among men are "just words" until people begin fighting and killing each other.

Instead, we would come much nearer the mark by considering it what has been termed a "total system of semantics, a multi-level apparatus of psychological warfare which demoralizes as it disorients."

We must realize that the Kremlin has gone far beyond Goebbels in using falsified statistics, the "smear," and the "big lie." Propaganda is no longer "that branch of lying which succeeds in confusing your friends without quite deceiving your enemies." In the hands of the Kremlin, propaganda has taken on more attributes and is directed to deeper ends than we in the Free World ever dreamed. It can be judged best from what the USSR really considers propaganda, agitation, and political activation to be. Her definitions throw light not only on the character of the total Kremlin operation called "propaganda" but on its mechanics and the USSR foreign political objective and practices as well.

The *Soviet Political Dictionary* (1958) gives the following definitions:

> *PROPAGANDA*—The dissemination and elucidation of certain ideas, doctrines, and political theories. Propaganda is of a class and party character. Unlike agitation, propaganda engages in the dissemination of a broader body of ideas and in their more profound and thorough elucidation among a comparatively narrower circle of people.
> *AGITATION*—A way of political influence over the masses by means of talks, reports, and speeches at meetings, through newspapers, books, brochures, leaflets, the radio, and motion pictures, etc. Agitation is distinctly on

a mass scale and consists in the dissemination among the broad masses of a body of ideas and knowledge narrower in scope and content than in propaganda.

Thus we may conclude that *propaganda* is used largely for recruiting party members and fellow travelers, while *agitation* is what, strictly speaking, is projected to the mass public in the Free World. The two processes are considered inseparable as indicated by the name in USSR bureaucracy given the unit charged with these functions: *Agitprop*.

If these two definitions appear imprecise, the impression has not been left to chance. The regime wishes to keep these activities in a fluid, elastic state in order to respond to the changing demands of the times and to developing situations. Propaganda—agitation in the West is a living action as suggested by the description of *agitation* in the *Large Soviet Encyclopedia* (1949-58). It reads:

> In the capitalist countries, the arsenal of the imperialist bourgeoisie is a supplement to the means of state action upon the masses (police, courts, prisons, etc.) with the aim of strengthening and broadening the rule of the bourgeoisie and the enslavement of the laborers. Having at their disposal completely the sold press, owning printing establishments, paper, cinema, radio, lecture halls, the bourgeois parties and their government from day to day sow lies among the workers and peasants. The imperialist bourgeoisie does not stop short of the most infamous means for psychological working over of public opinion, for deceiving and subverting the masses. In the United States, England, and other capitalist countries agitation by the reactionary bourgeoisie is directed against the USSR, against the countries of people's democracies, against the communist parties, mass popular progressive organizations, the leading figures in science, culture and the arts, fighting for peace and democracy.

The American and English imperialists have unleashed the ideological preparation for a new aggressive war. By the paths of lying and humanity-hating agitation and propaganda, the imperialist aggressors seek to disrupt the will of the freedom-loving peoples for counteraction against the encroachment by the Anglo-American imperialists upon the national sovereignty and freedom of peoples.

But even this combination of definition, description, incitement to agents, and self-justification does not quite confer upon *agitation* the leverage and potential in the political field which I witnessed in Romania, for instance. There the agents had another name for their activities—*political activation,* and they endeavored to infiltrate and spread political activation into every field of human activity in the country.

The Romanians, who were being introduced to Kremlin totalitarianism, found need for a more explicit connotation, but subjects of the Kremlin have long since passed the primary "education" stage. The *Political Dictionary* does not even address itself to the word "political" when defining *political activation.* It is simply "precipitation of action, transference from a static condition to a moving one"; also, "adding acceleration to an already-moving one." The assumption in the USSR is, of course, that every action has a political character as well as purpose and result.

Application and Conditioned Reflexes

With the intentions and the objectives of the USSR and the nature of its propaganda spelled out in its own terms, it is now pertinent to investigate the basis of the application of its propaganda to Free World audiences. Whenever the Kremlin propagandists launch a propaganda campaign outside the frontiers of their own heavily guarded territory, they draw upon their experiences with captive audiences and recruits to Kremlin communism. They draw upon the findings of the great Russian physiologist, Ivan Petrovich Pavlov, the father of the "conditioned reflex" theory of behavior. According to an outstanding American authority on this subject, we in the Free World are treated like the dogs in Professor Pavlov's experiments.

In these well-known experiments the professor would ring a bell a few moments before feeding his dogs and repeat this practice until the dogs would salivate as soon as they heard the ring. Thus he induced them to respond to the sound of the bell just as they did to the sight of the food, to associate the bell with their hunger.

Later in the experiments Pavlov changed the pitch or frequency of the bell signal or followed up with an electric shock instead of the expected food. He found out that he could bring on a neurotic condition in the dogs by scrambling the signals and by mixing the positive and negative cues. Once confused and neurotic, the dogs were easily susceptible to suggestion, and it was relatively simple to direct their behavior. Pavlov related this to the direction of behavior of humans by saying, "The [spoken] word is tied up, thanks to the whole previous life of a grown-up man, with all his internal and external stimuli ... and may cause all the actions and reactions of the organism which are conditioned by these stimuli."

Proceeding from this position, Dr. George F. Sutherland, an American authority on Pavlov, holds that if the "statistical anticipation" of the future is interfered with, human beings will be deprived of the ability to deal realistically with their environment. Applying this theory to international affairs, Dr. Sutherland states that Kremlin propagandists are deliberately trying to bring on neuroses among noncommunist countries by means of manipulating positive and negative signals.

From 1955 until 1959 he clipped headlines from newspapers which related to both Kremlin and Western activities on the diplomatic front. The collection, containing some five thousand clippings, was separated into two sections, "for us" and "against us." At first he thought that the Kremlin propaganda and political actions were themselves simply neurotic, but in the end he was convinced there was a definite pattern to their moves. "The seemingly erratic measures and countermeasures of the Soviet world powers in conducting their diplomatic affairs first suggested the possibility of a plan to create neurosis on a global scale.... On one occasion it inclined toward peaceful settlement of world affairs, whereas on another objections were raised that made this impossible...."

He found that the Western world, like the animals in the experiments, showed little external effect and the "latent possibilities" were disarmingly hidden from the victims. By 1957 the "blowing hot and cold tactics" of the Kremlin propagandists had created enough uncertainty and tension to induce the Western world to consider elements of political compromise with the USSR. Simultaneously, faith abroad in the leadership of the United States started to waver.

Then came Sputnik! Dr. Sutherland reports that by noon of the day it was launched, American commentators were levying charges against their country of political and administrative incompetence, inadequacy of educational facilities, and ineptitude of research.

"The resultant change in mass attitude betrays its neurotic origin by its implied anxiety, self-deprecation, and disavowal of responsibility for what has been permitted to take place. Such emotional immaturity is a well-recognized characteristic of the psychoneurosis and often hinders the patient from making a realistic appraisal of these difficulties and what he should do about them. Unfortunately, neuroses have a tendency to become self-perpetuating, and so are to be resistant to corrective action." Then he added, "Such a lightning-like transformation in mass attitude is probably without parallel. This glaring illustration of a laboratory technique applied on a universal scale should alert us to the dangers ahead."

One need not believe that reflexes can be conditioned beyond a point or brains washed completely when the victim is a captive, much less if he is living in a free society. One need not believe either that the neurosis produced can last beyond the period that the victim is subject to conditioning.

However, if the conditioning partly disorients thoughts and emotions and values, influences opinion and directs action in the Free World, its effects are dangerous to our continued security.

The conclusion is inescapable that the Kremlin believes this theory does work. The "carrot and stick" statements of Khrushchev, the alternating of sweet talk with bellicose threats to exploit the Free World's hope for peace and fear of war is but one indication. Others are to be found in Kremlin campaigns of slander against us, of subversion of our people, and in the multiple slogans and propaganda tricks it performs with experienced dexterity.

CHAPTER 3.

Conquest by Propaganda

KREMLIN propaganda helped produce the situation in Cuba which forced President Kennedy to make his declaration of April 20, 1961. It created for the United States a Pearl Harbor of the Cold War, a propaganda defeat we suffered only ninety miles from our own shores. However, like Pearl Harbor, such a dramatic battering from our enemy on territory close to our homes may be essential to alert us to the dangers of the aggression by propaganda—agitation of the USSR.

A prototype, which could have served as a warning to us, occurred in 1947 and 1948 in the countries of eastern Europe. Romania, as one example, fell under the domination of the Kremlin in very much the same manner that Cuba has been doing. Reviewing what the USSR accomplished in that remote country in that remote time gives a clear indication of what the Kremlin has been accomplishing by its propaganda-agitation operations with varying degrees of success in all corners of the globe ever since. It also suggests what the future holds for our dealings with Cuba's Castro and with other Kremlin agents, both witting and unwitting in other Kremlin-exploited trouble spots.

The Kremlin propaganda-agitation take over of all countries follows a standard routine regardless of fundamental political, geographic, and cultural differences. Some of the minor propaganda techniques are given different emphasis, but beyond that there is little variation. This routine has been spelled out in a specialized blueprint of great value to revolutionary leaders such as Castro. For it and for key personnel to help implement it they pay a high price—in all instances, eventually too high a price. With respect to Cuba one point is certain: if the Kremlin continues at its present rate of absorption of the country, Cuba will become as tightly integrated into the empire of the USSR as Romania or any other captive eastern European nation is now.

The social and political backgrounds of both Cuba and Romania, prior to the take over, were similar. Both were agricultural and were organized in large estates. Both had a type of military dictatorship which favored the landowners. A revolt unseated the dictator in Cuba and World War II put an end to the Antonescu Iron Guard regime in Romania. Each country was ripe for some system which would really give a better break to more people. However, the past experiences of the two countries with the USSR held major differences. The Romanians knew and distrusted the Russians while the Cubans neither know nor distrust them—yet. The Kremlin gained military control first in Romania by occupying the country with its armed forces at the end of World War II. Then it was able easily to operate indirectly, to work through propaganda—agitation, infiltration, and subversion. In Cuba the Kremlin was obliged to rely on propaganda—agitation alone without the presence or threat of military force.

The political deal was made in Romania through strong-arm methods in 1945 and 1946 by Vishinsky, and in Cuba with barter and persuasion in 1959 by Mikoyan.

The early months in 1947 in Romania and until King Michael was forced out at Christmas time were similar politically to the days in Cuba down to the United Nations meeting in September 1960. The parties leading the country were not called communist, in fact it was officially denied in Romania that they were communist, just as Castro has been doing. Romania's prime minister, installed by Vishinsky, was the leader of a small group called the Plowman's Front. Emphasis was on agrarian reform as it is in Cuba.

In both countries the Communist party used its energies to recruit members and to build up the reputation of championing the interests of the oppressed and unpossessing. Party members—

and agitators—went tieless in Romania for identification; Castro's group affects fatigues and beards.

In 1947 direct propaganda in the name of the USSR was carried on through the cultural and press attachés of the USSR embassy as well as by the head diplomatic commissar himself. The major supporting organization in the "direct" category was called the "Association for Strengthening Romanian-Soviet Relations" or ARLUS, and it spread its tentacles over the entire country at all educational levels.

In Cuba this type of propaganda organization had to wait until the establishment of diplomatic relations which occurred in May 1960. But not so the wholesale infiltration of local institutions by Kremlin crypto-communists or auxiliaries who took their propaganda to the trade-unions, to the agrarian reform organizations, and to the army. They have operated through a network of international and national "fronts" just as had been done in Romania. According to C. P. Cabell, deputy director of the Central Intelligence Agency in a *New York Times* story of August 22, 1959, it was then that a Kremlin intelligence officer arrived in Cuba to take over the training and directing of infiltrators into the Castro government.

Assurances were generously proclaimed in both Romania and Cuba that the governments were not "communist," that free, secret, democratic elections would take place in the foreseeable future, that civil rights would be respected. The timing of the surfacing of direct Kremlin control in Romania was carefully and subtly worked out in advance. The stages of exposure were related specifically to the success of infiltration and organization by Kremlin agents of the key government institutions: the military, the interior departments or police, the legal apparatus, the media of communications, the financial organization, and so on. The fact that there were reportedly only 12,000 Communists in Cuba when Castro assumed power and an estimated 1,000 in Romania at the end of her participation in World War II was unimportant: this nucleus was organized and disciplined and part of The System, the Kremlin System.

It is interesting to recall that the head of the communist party in Romania at the time of the take over lasted only as long as he acted directly in the Kremlin's interest. He was a lawyer of standing even among noncommunists, and he was appointed minister of justice. But when his sense of Romanian justice made him insist that the dispossessed be given the chance to put their talents to work for the country, he was removed—and later executed. The Kremlin principle of reducing the people of education and talent to impotence and keeping them there under rigid control was adamant. It was and is part of the formula for keeping entire countries under control.

It is also interesting to recall that Fidel Castro was reported ill and for a time was not expected to attend the United Nations meeting in New York in the summer of 1960. At the last moment he was cured and was able to make this trip. He, too, like the admitted Kremlin communist Romanian leader is essentially a nationalist without indoctrination training in the USSR, but for all practical purposes an agent of the Kremlin—and is expendable.

Perhaps the most significant similarity in the take over of these two countries from the United States' point of view is that we were (and are) singled out as the straw man to shout at, as Public Enemy No. 1, the role we play today in all Kremlin propaganda. Until 1947 in Romania their propagandists had a difficult time making this image stick. The Romanians moved to our side as they withdrew from the war; we had no territorial—nor extraterritorial—designs upon their country and we were offering postwar economic relief which was incorporated in the Marshall Plan. Also, on the whole we were not very well known by the people. At that time we were not quite yet "imperialists" or "colonialists" in our own right in the Kremlin propaganda galaxy of epithets but were closely associated with the British who were.

In Cuba the Yankee has long since been a symbol of power, therefore also an object of envy, fear, and dislike to the point of hate. Not only was there a revolution already made for the Kremlin to barter for but there was a built-in profitable propaganda image to draw upon. A century ago Uncle Sam exchanged affection for respect in Latin America, just as is now happening in the world as a whole.

Both dictatorships—in Cuba and Romania—like dictatorships everywhere, require a focal point for public attention, a straw man to shoot at. Hitler chose the Jews and the Kremlin has chosen the United States. By concentrating on the fears and animosities of the masses, the dictators divert attention from shortcomings in their totalitarian type of government and succeed in uniting their people in the first instance, and in uniting them behind their regime in the second instance, because they feature the regime as champion of the security and interests of the people.

The acquisition of Romania and progressive take over of Cuba by the USSR have been made possible by propaganda techniques in two fairly distinct phases of operation: the first lasts until the gradually shifting balance of political control of the country tips the scales over to 51 per cent in favor of the Kremlin agents; and the second lasts until the proclamation of a Kremlin communist government is undertaken.

In both phases the primary purpose is to induce people to act on behalf of this process. All stimuli necessary to induce action are employed: threats and terror, bribery of the leaders with money and promises of power, bribery of the masses with promises of better living conditions and higher social status, strikes, demonstrations, riots. Victims need to be persuaded— not necessarily convinced—of the infallibility of The System.

Also, in both phases disorientation or conditioning reflexes play a large role to induce action. The regimes in Romania and Cuba both sought to gain control of the thinking of their subjects because this control is basic to the control of their actions—more fundamental than control by coercion. The first step was the acquisition of a monopoly of the communications media and the sources of information upon which the people could draw.

The position taken by the Romanian communist officials on control of information was practically the same as that proclaimed by Castro and his leaders. In 1947 it was held that the persistence of a pro-fascist mentality made it inexpedient for the Romanian press to have absolute freedom. The organ of the USSR occupation army in Bucharest wrote that complete freedom of the press in Romania would be tantamount to pleading "for fascism's right to take a share in Romania's political life." Hence freedom of expression could not be granted. Identical ideas were expressed by the then minister of information, who said the government was in favor of complete freedom of the press for the people, for the masses, but that this freedom must be supervised by the government lest it be misunderstood and be placed in the service of "antidemocratic" forces.

Castro's views on freedom of thought and expression were stated in his speech of May 1. 1960.

"Democracy is that which guarantees to man not the right to freedom of thought, but rather the right to know how to think, the right to know how to write what he thinks, the right to know how to read what he or others think."

This statement by Castro was augmented by his minister of education, who said that "impartiality is a myth of civilization" and press reporters are conditioned by "personal bias" or are dominated by "determined interests and ideologies." He announced that "the only true basis for objectivity rests on alignment with public opinion," and the only "true" expression of public opinion comes from Castro. Therefore, when Castro spoke he spoke for the people and thus expressed public opinion. He concluded that if the press did not attune itself to public opinion so described it "defended the interests of oligarchy."

In Romania prior to publication newspapers, periodicals, pamphlets, books, and other reading matter first had to receive the approval of the Ministry of Information, which employed direct censorship through the Press Bureau, Office of the Censorship. The Office of the Censorship had a domestic press section, which not only edited material but also wrote in passages as it saw fit, and a foreign press section which censored foreign publications. Actually direct, like indirect, censorship was supervised by the head of the Political Education Section of the Romanian communist party—also head of the local Agitprop—who placed his own personnel in key positions in the government and the trade-unions.

In addition to direct censorship, the Kremlin-dominated Romanian government used various indirect methods to promote the dissemination of approved views. Some of these methods were: monopoly of news agencies and the radio industry and partial or complete ownership of newspapers and periodicals; government subsidies or direct contributions by trade-unions to newspapers and book-publishing houses which followed the Kremlin communist party line; withholding legal authorization from all but pro-government printing firms; strict, but one-sided, observance of the laws of libel and slander; preferential allotment of raw materials; preferential allocation of credits by the nationalized National Bank of Romania; editorial interference by the Printers' Union, and control of personnel through the Romanian Union of Writers, Journalists, and Artists; intimidation of workers employed by opposition or independent publishing plants; and control of distribution.

All of the above methods were used against opposition and independent publications from the advent of the Kremlin-dominated government in March 1945 until December 1947, by which time all such publications had been completely eliminated. By February 1, 1948, the press expressed but one point of view: that of the Kremlin and the Romanian communist.

Dissemination of news from abroad was also a state monopoly: all foreign news was distributed by the two government-controlled news agencies. On September 30, 1947, the Associated Press and the regime's Agerpress signed an agreement under which the latter was to get the AP news file and distribute it to the local press, but the majority of the AP reports selected for distribution under this arrangement were without political significance.

In Havana, of the sixteen Spanish-language newspapers in existence when Castro took over, only three were still under their original owners a year and a half later, and two of these were trade papers. Traditionally, as in Romania, almost no news-

papers were self-supporting financially, but were subsidized orig-
inally by various political parties. As these parties were gradually
turned into "government" parties, subsidy was withdrawn by the
regime to force the paper out of business, or backing was continued if the paper put out the required Kremlin line.

Where this direct method was not considered thorough or fast
enough, an indirect suppression was employed. In Bucharest, the
head of the printers' or typesetters' union invaded the newspaper,
seized the premises, and expelled the publishers. In Havana, it
was the head of the Union of Graphic Arts who led the ex-
propriation.

With a monopoly of the communications media by the regime,
the blacking out of most sources of news and information and the
conditioning of thought for more than two years, it is small
wonder that the people in Cuba were not prepared psychologically
for the abortive attempt at invasion in April 1961. Added to this
was the usual Kremlin organization of terror under a secret
agent police system, spying and reporting on neighbors for
tangible rewards and an iron discipline of control from the top.

Under these circumstances one could hardly expect the masses
of Cubans even to realize that they were being given a chance at
liberty. They do not yet know—as a mass—they are victims of
the totalitarianism of the USSR. They still have the illusion that
the regime belongs to them, that Castro is first a Cuban and later
a pro-Kremlin communist, that he is not a captive of the USSR.
And a great deal of reagitation and reorientation will be required
before they realize they have been captured, along with Castro,
before the USSR is exposed, before Cuba finds herself responding
to the oppression of the USSR the way in which another captive
nation of eastern Europe did five years ago—Hungary—in all-out
revolution.

PART II

TARGET: U.S.A.

FOR every country in the world the Kremlin has a plan of propaganda action, and the one for the United States is the most strategic and comprehensive in its portfolio. The reason is that in terms of propaganda our country is the most important to the USSR. Our society, our government organization, our treatment of other countries, and our power must be changed, defeated, or frustrated before the USSR can be successful in completing its drive for world conquest.

The Kremlin plan of propaganda action—U.S.A. breaks down into three sections. The first is a well-defined campaign of slander against us in third countries. The labels the Kremlin propagandists endeavor to attach to the image of the United States are principally: imperialists, spreaders of lies, spies, war criminals, colonialist oppressors, inciters to revolution, and warmongers. The fraudulent accusations hurled at us under these titles are stepped up and toned down as any particular political situation is believed to require. I have watched their development and application in three countries abroad and in New York City, particularly at the United Nations.

The second section consists of a blueprint for subverting the people of the United States by whatever delusion the Kremlin propagandists can manage. While the propaganda is aimed mainly at the general public, so that it may bring pressure on the legislative and executive branches of our government, it also aspires to take in government leaders and officials as well. Three very important targets for undermining us are our military policy, our foreign policy, and our federal government organization, including the presidency.

Finally, the third section lays down a definite image of Uncle Sam and of our citizens which is to be injected into the minds of the subject peoples inside the USSR. Along with this image—in gross misrepresentation—goes a vast machinery of communications control which screens practically all impressions of the United States its subjects are likely to pick up, and filters out those aspects which might inspire challenge to dictatorial rule.

These three sections in the Kremlin propaganda plan for the United States are dealt with in the form of case histories.

CHAPTER 1.

Combat by Slander

Hurl your calumnies boldly, something is sure to stick.

FRANCIS BACON, *The Dignity and Growth of the Sciences*

The Assembly has witnessed over the last weeks how historical truth is established; once an allegation has been repeated a few times, it is no longer an allegation, it is an established fact, even if no evidence has been brought out in order to support it. However, facts are facts, and the true facts are there for whosoever cares for truth. Those who invoke history will certainly be heard by history. And they will have to accept its verdict as it will be pronounced on the basis of the facts by men free of mind and firm in their conviction that only on a scrutiny of truth can a future of peace be built.

From text of Hammarskjold's reply to Khrushchev, Monday, October 3, 1960.

IMPERIALISTS

WHEN I arrived in Romania in the spring of 1947 the local Kremlin communist regime propagandists were lumping the United States and Great Britain together and referring to them as "those Anglo-American imperialists." The two-headed image, however, proved to be too diffuse for effective propaganda purposes with the local population. Clarification and concentration were urgently needed. And by the time I was transferred three years later the situation had been more than remedied. Then there was only one Public Enemy No. 1: Uncle Sam.

31

In 1947 the puppet head of the Romanian government was a rich landowner named Petru Groza, whose principal qualification was his Balkan political acumen, which had made him turn toward Stalin instead of the allies at the end of World War II. But for the Kremlin, Groza lacked the militant temperament necessary to push with enough force and speed The System's program of regimentation and colonialization. It was not until Stalin's handmaiden, the Kremlin-indoctrinated Ana Pauker, took over on November 12 the position of foreign minister that militancy was injected into the regime. She went to work immediately to apply the formula of The System which called for the creation of a bogeyman outside the country who is a threat to the security of the subjects of the dictatorship. The attacks on the "Anglo-American imperialists" were stepped up even before the Americans and the British withdrew their representations on the Allied Control Commission.

Actually the use of the United States as bogeyman and the sticking of the label of "imperialist" on us presented the propagandists with a challenge. We had no past reputation comparable to that of the strong man of the East, and we had not been much of an enemy during the war. We were far away, little known, and were not suspected of having territorial designs on this much-occupied country, or of acting as oppressors if we should become interested. Consequently, the local propagandists had to work against a double handicap in branding us "imperialists" because they had to play down the same image of their employer that they had to play up for us. The USSR had come, over the years, to represent to the Romanians an ogre to be greatly feared.

In 1947, the United States made their task even more difficult by setting up large foreign economic-aid programs and offering assistance to countries with economies riven by the war. The prospect was so attractive, even to the local communist regime, that it might well have declared its independence from colonial status to the USSR—just as Tito did the following year—if there had been no USSR military occupation of the country.

These American offers of assistance gave the lie to the slander of us as "imperialists." The Kremlin propagandists—and their facsimiles in Romania—had to be more than nimble-witted to rationalize away for the public the fact that we had made a truly humanitarian offer.

Our aid to Greece and Turkey had recently been announced, and hopes were high with all Romanians but the outright Kremlin representatives like Pauker that some of this dollar supply would be stretched to extend to their country. One "opposition" party even went so far as to predict seriously that the aid would be forthcoming.

To discourage these enthusiasts and blacken the United States as "imperialists," a local Kremlin communist rag took a back-handed slap at us in a footnote to a quote from Walter Lippmann. He was reported as advocating granting credits and reparations from Germany's current production direct to Stalin "because the Truman Doctrine might be construed as anti-USSR." The caustic Kremlin observation attached was: even the "advocates of expansion and intervention" were beginning to realize that peace and prosperity could be obtained only by a "loyal and sincere understanding with the USSR."

A few days later the newspaper of the USSR military forces, *Red Army,* was more explicit in calling us "imperialists." This organ was usually first and strongest in announcing to the people of Romania the propaganda line which had been laid down by the Kremlin. The article in *Red Army* said that people in sore need of help and anxious to get it know how to differentiate "between help that conceals imperialistic plans" and the "real support they get in order to overcome the difficulties with which they have to contend." It went on to say that it is the duty of the members of the United Nations to prevent the realization of the "scoundrelly aims of the imperialists who do not hesitate to make a political weapon of their food and goods reserve by trying to impose their will and domination on the countries suffering from famine and difficulties."

The Kremlin propagandists then called upon author Ilya Ehrenburg, who was well known in Romania, to enter the campaign to calumniate us. A 3,500-word article by him was reprinted in a local Kremlin communist paper in which he vehemently attacked the United States on a number of scores. He lambasted our newspapers for stating daily that "the Russians are imperialists," that "the USSR tends toward expansionism." The fact was that Undersecretary of State Acheson had characterized them in just those words and the newspapers had reported his statements.

"It is an old adage," declared Ehrenburg, "for the thief to run off shouting 'catch the thief!' " Then he listed a number of actions we had taken to "prove" it was we who were "imperialistic" and "expansionistic." Since I was watching the day-by-day absorption of Romania into the colonial empire of the USSR, I appreciated the enormity of the misrepresentation by this top Kremlin propagandist.

In the next blast at the Truman Doctrine the Kremlin propagandists outdid themselves. They attributed to us probably the most ambitious plan of "imperialism" we have ever been accused of. In *Pravda* they wrote an article under the title "The Capitalist Monopolies of the United States—the Basis of Imperialistic Expansion." It was reproduced in a local paper and ended thus:

"... The American monopolies which accumulated untold wealth during the war are doing all they can to monopolize the financing of all the countries in the world. They hope, by that means, not only to enslave the economic and financial life of a great many countries but also to influence powerfully the internal and foreign policies of those countries...." Here was slander which more than flattered our policy planners.

For a few weeks there was a respite—until the Marshall Plan extended the Truman Doctrine to all countries of Europe. This was the moment when the resistance by Romanians such as Groza to direct Kremlin representatives like Ana Pauker came briefly and hesitantly out in the open. It created a furore in all the countries of eastern Europe. Consequently the Kremlin not only had to call on its propagandists to step up its slander of the United States but even had to apply political pressure on some of its own agents in the various local Kremlin communist parties.

The propaganda line at the moment of announcement was cautious and mild. *Pravda* simply called the Marshall Plan a repetition of the Truman Plan "for political pressure with the help of dollars."

The *Red Army* stated that the United States had the ulterior purpose of finding markets for its products to avert an economic crisis, while the USSR "is fighting for effective help for the countries in Europe . . ." but "doesn't believe in using economic aid as a means of political pressure." They really didn't need to do so since they were already using an army of occupation for this purpose.

At that time one of the Party papers printed a lively cartoon. In it Secretary of State Marshall, dressed as a farmer's wife, trying to lure a scattering of scared baby chickens with feed held in her apron, was calling "chickie, chickie, chickie!" Behind his back President Truman was sharpening two huge knives. The caption ran: "Marshall's appeal and the Truman Doctrine."

In an effort to outdo the Kremlin propagandists, a local communist paper took up the cudgels in really purple language. It characterized the Truman Doctrine as the "most rapacious usury" and declared the United States falsely made itself out as a "magnanimous savior" who tomorrow, presumably under the Marshall Plan, would reveal "the bony fingers of a usurer to whom you have made over even the fire in your hearth while gratefully kissing his hand to the last."

All this slanderous propaganda did not succeed in preventing the Romanian puppet regime from speaking up for some of the Marshall dollars. In an official announcement, after declaring conservatively that the Marshall Plan was not "a philanthropic action," a government spokesman stated that if this "fact" could be borne in mind, "it will be possible to reach an agreement which will be useful to both the European States and to the United States."

Unhappily for this captive nation Stalin decreed "no" on United States aid, and sent the Kremlin propagandists into action. In Romania *Red Army* declared that the resulting relationship of the United States and Romania would be "collaboration between the wolf and the lamb," and that "on no condition" would the USSR "be a party to an action which would force peoples to jeopardize their future and sell their freedom. . . ."

When the local regime formally announced that it had turned down the invitation to join, the local communist party again rather piteously reported that Romania was willing to collaborate, but that it considered no European economic recovery plan could work without USSR participation.

Immediately following the near controversy an editorial in a communist paper tied up the activities of the United States Information Service with our government's "imperialistic" aims. It attacked a bulletin board set up in the front window of a leading café, which displayed photographs of leading Americans in the news. It declared the same window a few years ago had been full of Hitlerite propaganda and was now presenting "eminent" personalities of the famous "Atlantic lie" dispensary. It added that "those people who smile at us from the show window are the ones who daily curse Romania and the Romanian people and try to instigate a war against our country." We were forced to withdraw the display.

From then on our activities were systematically cut down by the regime. Fewer and fewer people dared to come to our building. Our staff, which then included twenty-one Romanians, refused to give up their jobs, even though the shadowing and harassment by the secret police and the discrimination against them on housing and ration cards began in earnest.

During the next few months the press called the United States "imperialistic" in a routine manner. There was no campaign, no outstanding dramatic blast. Yevgeni Varga, the Kremlin's expert on economics, predicted our country would collapse economically before the Marshall Plan was completed. *Red Army* accused "United States imperialists" of wishing to transform Greece into a bridgehead from which to dominate the Near East, and carried a cartoon depicting the Marshall Plan as a Trojan horse.

On the occasion of the signing of the Romanian peace treaty, a local communist party paper ran an editorial proclaiming that Romanian democracy had gained valuable friendship and support from the USSR and that its value could be appreciated by looking at the present woes of other countries which had been given dollar loans. It observed that USSR friendship aimed neither at "controlling resources of other countries nor at subjecting them to semi-colonial exploitation."

The continued misrepresentation of our humanitarian move, plus the constant slander, by that time had just about used up the initial store of good will with which I had approached my job. I had the editorial clipped and filed against the day we would turn on a full-scale attack on the regime over the Voice of America Romanian language program. VOA programs came in daily; they were the only means of communication with which the regime could not interfere. In the ensuing months I found my contacts falling off sharply; the entire staff became increasingly restricted to our USIS building in carrying out their activities.

My switch toward frankly anti-Kremlin propaganda occurred in reaction to an article in the local party newspaper which announced the production by a factory in Brasov of the one thousandth tractor since the end of the war.

I called for the earlier clipping, cabled VOA the facts about production in Brasov, and suggested they broadcast a feature based on it. The idea was to open the program by congratulating the Brasov factory workers on their fine achievement, then give them a run-down on the achievements over the same period of a comparable factory in Italy, which had benefited by help from the Marshall Plan. No comment was necessary.

After the program was broadcast, it was passed all over the country by the Romanian word-of-mouth news service (which had been born under the Turks and more recently improved under the Nazis). There was no question that the Romanian agents of the Kremlin had been hit where it hurt as was shown by a long front-page article printed in the same party paper.

Under the title "Your Flattery Does Not Deceive Us—Gentlemen of the Voice of America," the article started off with: "So

they have congratulated you! . . . after swearing at you and mock-
ing you . . . month after month." It told its readers that the
Romanian tractors were not manufactured with the congratula-
tions of the Voice of America but were inspired by the glorious
experience of the USSR. It accused us of wanting to stop the
manufacture of tractors in Romania just as the Marshall Plan
wanted to destroy both industry and agriculture in France and
Italy in order to force the consumers in those countries to buy
more American products.

The article ended by saying that the Romanian workers knew
their achievements resulted from their rejection of the Marshall
Plan—"That trap set by the imperialists."

SPREADERS OF LIES

One of the few instances in those early days in which an American official went beyond counterpropaganda and took an aggressive initiative against the Kremlin occurred less than a year after
I had arrived in Bucharest. It was brought off by William Benton,
then former assistant secretary of state, later senator from Con-
necticut, who headed the United States delegation to the United
Nations Conference on the Freedom of Information at Geneva.
I was called in as an advisor to the delegation, thanks to my
office's reporting to Washington on press conditions in Romania.

As a matter of fact, I wondered then, and have wondered ever
since, just how much "Washington" can be credited with Mr.
Benton's enlightened stand and how much really came from his
own substantial grasp of propaganda realities. Since this one effort
stands out as a rare beacon through the ensuing years, it is probable that Mr. Benton is the one to be praised.

On the opening day Mr. Benton set forth certain aspirations of
the Free World for freedom of expression and communication,
which, on rereading today, sound remarkably contemporary.

He said that freedom of expression and information was essential to peace and security in the world, because a free press
means a free and informed public, which in turn helps to insure

liberty within countries, and such free countries all make for a universal peace. He ended by pointing out that the then recent "tragic death" of the republic of Czechoslovakia had struck terror to the hearts of all people throughout the world who valued the dignity and freedom of their persons, the freedom of their consciences, and the independence of their country.

Mr. Benton expressed the hope that the conference would produce an agreement among the participating delegations. He said that the American people wanted to learn the truth about what was happening in other countries and wanted the people there to hear the truth about what was happening in the United States.

One paragraph in particular, which summarized the sequence of events in the previous thirty years in the world, hit home with the USSR representative and with his subordinates, the delegates from the USSR's growing colonial empire. It suggested compactly just what was currently being engineered by the USSR. What was . . . and still is:

> Seizure of power within a nation by a minority group, the creation of a police state; institution of speech control, press control, thought control; erection of censorship walls; liquidation of all opposition. Then an all-out armament program, accompanied by a vicious propaganda campaign of hate and fear against other countries, carried on behind self-created walls of ignorance; and, finally, the marching of armies, the roar of guns, and the sudden death of men and states.

This was the kind of talk that the Kremlin feared most—and still does fear in reference to the massacre of Hungary. Its propaganda mill went immediately to work and distorted the speech to such an extent that in some aspects it attributed precisely the opposite meaning to the words Mr. Benton had used.

TASS alleged the chief United States delegate had urged the conference to give up the principle of freedom and independence of the press. Radio Moscow broadcast the accusation that American political leaders suppressed freedom of the press at home but talked at international conferences about equality of freedom. The Polish News Agency, like TASS a government monopoly, reported that Mr. Benton discussed the events of the last thirty years that "bear the stigma" of control of speech and opinions and contrasted them, along with conditions in countries in eastern Europe, with the press freedoms that were "supposed" to exist in America; and that he had ended his speech by a brutal attack against the Czechoslovakian republic.

However, it was not until later, when the chief USSR delegate took the rostrum, that the key line of slander against us was laid down. He stated simply, "Mr. Benton argued against the responsibility of those who are inciters to war and also propagate false news." Then he proceeded to indict the United States on both counts. The immediate occasion for the "false news" was the reporting of the truth about the suppression of freedom of expression behind the Iron Curtain. He had not been lured by Mr. Benton's address into discussing the principles or methods of achieving information freedoms, nor did he defend or explain attempts at world conquest through propaganda.

From this moment on the Russian stood out as the ringleader of the delegates from the captive nations. Seated at their desks in the hall, they never failed to glance in his direction before voting, or to look for his nod before requesting the chair for a chance to speak.

The Polish delegate, a former newspaperman with a real gift for invective, spoke against the official United States radio, Voice of America, for "lying" in its broadcasts about conditions in Poland and against American correspondents for fabricating "all sorts of slander and false facts" about his country.

The Ukrainian condemned the "monopoly" press in the United States and quoted instances by which he claimed he proved how our press was "fanning a war hysteria and spreading lies and slander."

And the Hungarian added: [The Voice of America] "has always considered the truth as beneath its notice and has never deigned to correct a mistake, rectify a lie, withdraw a slander, or sacrifice itself on behalf of accuracy."

Other puppets echoed these accusations of lying. Then the turn came for the Romanian delegate, Grigore Preoteasa, who was minister of information at the time. In manner he was the most fanatical of all; his high voice frequently reached a screech. He was one of the least important of the band and seemed determined to make an impression on the chief USSR delegate by outperforming all the others.

After a long dissertation on the existence of a fascist press in the United States, on the subversive activities of United States press correspondents in Romania, on our continued "warmongering," he made a very curious observation about truth:

> The United States representative has urged the widest possible dissemination of truth about each country. What is there to prevent that? United States correspondents in Romania enjoy the greatest possible freedom, although that has not prevented reports both in the *New York Herald Tribune* and the *New York Times* from being unsympathetic to the Romanian point of view.

This could only mean that our correspondents were free to write what they wanted about conditions in Romania, but that when they were unsympathetic or critical, they were lying. To normal people this kind of reasoning seems at least spurious and probably deliberately dishonest. However, as I was to learn later, Preoteasa was quite sincere. He, like so many other "convinced" Kremlin communists, had been conditioned to believe that The System supports the only legitimate "social doctrine," offering the solution of all the problems of mankind, and that any ideas interfering with this solution would, of necessity, have to be lies.

Prior to my trip to Geneva I had met Preoteasa formally and briefly three or four times and got absolutely nothing out of him. When he shook hands, he did so with such delicacy that I felt he considered me a special sort of leper.

I had been struck by a kind of messianic quality, a dedicated—almost possessed—gleam in the black eyes of this slight, sallow-faced young man. I learned that his indoctrination had been administered by Ana Pauker herself, whom Stalin had tutored in the black art of his brand of communism. Preoteasa had come under her influence while he was still a college student and later became her private secretary; it was no wonder his emotions were so obviously invested in his dedication.

If the young minister of information had considered me a leper before we left Bucharest, I wondered what he was going to consider me after he heard the American delegation's indictment of his dictatorial oppression of the freedom of speech and the press—an indictment which had been documented carefully in our delegation's "position papers" and which we in Bucharest had helped to prepare. Against me he could do very little (or so I thought at the time) because I enjoyed diplomatic immunity, but the Romanian citizens on my staff were not so fortunate. They would be subject to reprisals.

After firing its opening broadside of slander, the Kremlin bloc settled down to go through the motions of negotiation. Their initial purpose had been served. They had turned the conference into a propaganda free-for-all and were feeding back their charges as "truth" or "facts" through their propaganda machine. This well-oiled instrument produced a rich fare for the captive audiences behind the Iron Curtain, a more bland diet for the Free World.

There was never any intention on the part of these delegates to deal with the problems of freedom of expression and information, and it was naïve to expect them to do otherwise. But in 1948 many Westerners, particularly Americans, did not understand that the Kremlin operated on the basis that the systems of the countries under its control and those of the Free World were incompatible, and that consequently no common ground could be found for compromise and agreement.

The USSR bloc representatives made a few propaganda sallies in the special committees but reserved their major offensive until the end in full assembly. The Pole summed up the conference with this statement among others: "In the face of the whole world, the United States, Great Britain, France, and a number of other countries voted against equal rights for all races and nations, against the subduing of warmongers, against fighting down false and slanderous news in the press."

The Czech, whose country had come in for the severest criticism from the Free World delegates, pronounced the conference the "first postwar battle of ideologies between the United Nations." He claimed that the Kremlin bloc had won, that the "battle ended with victory of truth over hypocrisy," and that on their side they had "truth without any deviations, unity of opinion, a more aggressive spirit, and more capable fighters. . . ."

In Moscow the government newspaper *Izvestia* asked this question in evaluating the results of the conference, "Is it not evident that the United States delegation was trying to create a situation under which false reports emanating from the U.S.A. could not be refuted by that state against which the lie was directed in the first place?"

From my point of view the Czech was right. The Kremlin team had won this engagement not as a triumph of "truth over hypocrisy" but as a victory of propaganda over negotiation, calculated subversion over straightforward honesty. Except for Mr. Benton in his opening address, as well as in another one which he flew to Paris to deliver, our delegation behaved as if it did not realize it was in a battle. And the fact is that few members of the delegation really did. Apparently, too, some of them were reluctant to take up the cudgels without specific State Department instruction.

They, perhaps, should not be held too firmly to account although all of them were professionals of one sort or another in the fields of news and communications. However, Washington (and London and Paris) did know that this conference could not extend the freedom of information in those captive nations of the world where there was no freedom of any kind. The officials also knew that the Kremlin would use the conference as a propaganda platform. They might have followed up the opening address of Mr. Benton with extensive treatment of the conference by the Voice of America and other official or sympathetic radio stations, with press briefings and releases supplying background information that would draw the world's attention to the gravity of Kremlin abuses, and with systematically prepared speeches for delegates to expose the dictators and their dictatorial systems. This campaign could have been just as vigorous, and, of course, would have been more sound than that of the Kremlin against us.

On the day before the closing of the conference, when there was practically nothing left but the formalities of leave-taking, the United States delegation gave a farewell reception to all the other delegations. This was protocol, diplomacy—and hypocrisy—but it was observed by both sides, even by the Czech. In diplomacy one offers hospitality to enemies—accepts it from them—after the battle, before the wounds are bandaged, and nobody gives the hypocrisy a second thought.

Mr. Benton assigned each of us to serve as individual host to one member of another delegation. "I am afraid you will have to take over Preoteasa," he said to me, and glanced away quickly. I was waiting with a dutiful smile at the ballroom door of the Hôtel des Bergues when the wraith-like Kremlin agent materialized. He was alone, and stared furtively from side to side. I advanced to greet him.

Although introductions were not necessary, some common ground was. I saw two comfortable armchairs in a corner at the near end of the impressive cream-and-gold room and escorted him with punctilious politeness across the thick red carpeting under the multi-tiered chandeliers to his place. I wondered how this bourgeois "luxury" agreed with his Kremlin communist tastes.

As we sat down, we remarked in unison, each in rather poor French, that it was a relief the conference was over. Our conversation then moved to the weather, which was generally fine, when a waiter stopped by. He was carrying a tray filled with scotches, martinis, Manhattans, and fruit juices. I knew the hard-core Communists had a strict code for behavior in public, and I expected

Preoteasa to choose a fruit juice. However, I took a chance and asked him if he had ever tasted a Manhattan; it was the strongest drink available.

He replied that he hadn't but would like to become acquainted with American customs, since he expected soon to be assigned to Washington as counselor of legation. He tossed off the cocktail with such relish that I guessed the puritanical attitude was reserved for behavior in the home country.

So, when the waiter passed by again, I did not hesitate to ask Preoteasa if he would have a second. He would, and did. We both relaxed a bit, and he put a number of practical questions to me about setting up housekeeping in our nation's capital. On such subjects he was both rational and calm.

As the third round made its appearance my guest had lost some of his reticence and nodded to the waiter himself. We settled back in our chairs and talked about the technical details of the conference and were studiously careful to avoid its political implications. As we talked we drank, and when he had finished his third Manhattan he put the glass on the table in front of us and turned to look directly at me. The messianic expression seemed to have evaporated, and he dropped his play-acting manner. Then he made, in the form of a question, the clearest observation about the conference I heard from any of the delegates.

He asked, "What difference does it make what conclusions we reach at the information level, if the decisions have not already been taken at the top political level?"

As I marveled over his frank admission that negotiation was useless, that the conference had never been taken seriously by the Kremlin, Preoteasa reached for his fourth Manhattan. I began wondering whether I was drinking this prospective resident of Washington, D.C., under the table, or whether he was doing that to me.

The talk then turned to the more philosophical—no polemics, no controversy, just speculating on where discussions such as those at the conference could be expected to lead. As he drained his last cocktail, he asked me another question—me a representative of the "spreaders of lies"—which revealed the dilemma of his indoctrination and hardly qualified him as a judge of another country's veracity.

"Isn't it awfully difficult"—he was gazing far across the ballroom and spoke in a distant voice—"isn't it awfully difficult," he asked, "to know just what the truth really is?"

SPIES

All dictatorships—whether of the left or the right—use the threat of "spies" inside the country as hirelings of an outside bogeyman to arouse their subjects' patriotism and make them easier to consolidate. In Romania, we Americans, the proclaimed enemies of the people, became "imperialist spies." We were associated in crime with the political parties of the country which opposed the totalitarianism inflicted on the country by the USSR. These parties were eliminated one by one and the strongest and largest, the Peasant party, was the victim of a strong propaganda attack. As demonstration to the public that all opposition had been wiped out, the local Kremlin agents produced a "spy" trial of the Peasant party leader, Iuliu Maniu, and some of his party colleagues. They were accused of high treason, of being in league with the "imperialist spies," with Washington.

This trial was a Kremlin spectacular, the grandest in Romania's history as a Kremlin colony. It used all the props, all the memorized lines, the "conditioning" of the victims by tried Pavlovian methods, the mental and physical torture which have been refined since 1917.

Iuliu Maniu was immensely popular, the greatest statesman the Romanians perhaps ever had; even the Nazis had not dared touch him. His arrest shook the population, and the Kremlin propagandists took full advantage of the popular concern over his fate; it was, of course, identified with that of the country. Anticipation was cultivated in the press and over the air for three months in advance to heighten the impact of the trial.

During the entire week of the trial, which I watched from the gallery, the elderly statesman stood straight as a ramrod. The results of physical torture were not apparent, but he was very thin, and his neck looked scrawny inside a wide, stiff white collar. He failed to attack his tormentors, although he knew he personally was doomed, his country was betrayed, and his party vilified. I could not help wondering whether this remarkable and politically wise parliamentarian had been subtly "persuaded" by his captors that the cause of Romania would not be helped by a public condemnation of the USSR.

From the day of Dr. Maniu's arrest until sentence on him was pronounced, the Kremlin propagandists implicated the Americans as "spies" in a plot against the state. In newspaper editorials they reached back to a trial the year before to repeat spy charges against two young military officers of the United States Military Mission who had been transferred to another country.

A communist newspaper referred to "another fifth column of treason and espionage . . . which American . . . imperialism maneuvers in order to bring about the great conspiracy . . . against the liberty and independence of our peoples." But for the USSR, according to this piece, Romania would have become a semicolony and the fate of the people and their children would have been in the hands of the two young leaders of "the American espionage service in Romania and their agent, Iuliu Maniu."

Next they created two incidents as a further alert to the public that "American spy" slander was planned for the Maniu trial. First there was a suggestion in the press that the Rockefeller Foundation, which had contributed so much in financing, equipment, and instruction in scientific and health work to Romania, was training its overseas personnel as spies for our government. Then a Romanian was picked up as "an American spy" and thrown in jail for having "collaborated" with Reuben Markham, the *Christian Science Monitor* correspondent who had reported the Kremlin-rigged elections of a year and a half before.

During the two-week period just prior to the opening of the trial, "American spies" were denounced in conjunction with the Romanian Foreign Office. Its officials, who belonged to the Liberal party, were publicly castigated for working against the interests of Romania by collaborating with a group which "proved to be an Anglo-American espionage agency."

Then Preoteasa himself wrote in a communist weekly that this high-treason trial had attracted the attention of world opinion. He observed that the trial came as a grievous blow to the spies' masters in Washington where imperialist propagandists had misrepresented the true nature of this spying activity. They had described it as the manifestation of local, national opposition when in reality it was the action of "reactionary" groups in a truly "democratic" country.

In the hundred-page indictment Dr. Maniu and members of the Peasant party were charged with conspiracy, high treason, attempt to undermine public order, rebellion, and armed insurrection. American diplomatic and military personnel, past and present, were mentioned prominently as co-conspirators, as "spies."

The Peasant party "culprits" were accused of selling out their country to the Americans. Three days after the trial opened two editorials appeared in communist newspapers which indicated what our involvement would be. One declared the Peasant party leaders were "merely vile spies" who worked in cooperation with the American "spies" in carrying out foreign orders against the peace, freedom, and future of the Romanian people. The other was more lurid. It described the Peasant party "plot" as the "last drop overflowing the cup of public opprobrium" regarding "the most odious act of betrayal" ever known in Romanian history. Maniu's party was said to have handed over to foreign powers military information aimed at provoking civil war, to have asked for dollar subsidies, requested political and military intervention of foreign powers in Romania's internal life (the United States was one of the "foreign powers"), and desired the outbreak of another world war.

After the verdict was rendered by the Bucharest court and Dr. Maniu was condemned to life imprisonment, a local Kremlin communist paper ran a lead editorial under the heading "The Twentieth Accused," which referred to the "Anglo-Saxon powers," and asked, "who could have imagined, before World War I, that diplomatic envoys openly practiced espionage and prepared civil wars in free and independent states?"

The Romanian propaganda agents of the Kremlin moved against several of the American officials and concentrated their fire on the one American diplomat, our experienced political officer, who had closely observed the Kremlin annexation since 1944. He was accused of acting as liaison between the "conspirators" and Washington in forwarding secret documents and information. Then the question was asked, "But how can proper diplomatic activity be distinguished from this gross and open interference in the domestic affairs of an independent state, from espionage and conspiracy against the legal regime of this country?"

If there had been any opportunity left for our political officer to carry on his contacts in the country, this slander as a "spy" would have discredited him to the point of destroying his usefulness. But the contacts of all American representatives began to dry up anyway, as the regime became quickly totalitarian; its subjects were frightened into seclusion.

The next "spying" charge involved four young members of the legation clerical staff. It was a frame-up. A group of younger employees had gone off on a holiday excursion to the Danube. While they were driving in the dock area they were stopped by a local motorcycle policeman. He accused the two young women and two young men of entering a restricted zone and of taking photographs of secret installations. The four were led to the police station and held overnight.

The next morning our new minister paid a call upon the Foreign Office to protest in high diplomatic language. He had expected to be received by Foreign Minister Ana Pauker—but she was on a pilgrimage to Moscow. So he spoke to one of her deputies; he demanded an apology, but instead was handed an ultimatum. Ana Pauker's assistant told him that the "guilty" four were *persona non grata* and had to leave Romania at once.

This action, I suspected with some reason at the time, had been planned in advance. The resulting anti-American propaganda was certainly considered well worth the effort. A communist paper declared that "the members of the American Legation who were caught in the act of committing espionage illustrate the new diplomacy inaugurated by the State Department which is indulging in provocation in all countries and climes. . . ."

The young people involved had positions of no particular diplomatic consequence, but the next two American officials to be declared *persona non grata* held top positions. One was our counselor of legation and the other our military attaché. These two were listed along with a number of additional staff members, including myself, in another show-case trial of Peasant party "conspirators" being tried for high treason. That trial, too, had the familiar format. It was held just about a year after the Maniu trial.

My part of the indictment connected me with one Mr. Popp. It stated that "from the documents in the files" it was obvious that "the accused member of the Peasant party", Mr. Popp, had transmitted to the United States Legation "through the cultural officer, Donald Dunham, the complete information referring to":

> The convention with the Soviet Union.
> The manufacturing of the Romanian tractor PMT of Brasov.
> The armament and equipment requirements of the Romanian army.
> The munitions-manufacturing possibilities in Romania.
> The production plans of the country.
> Import needs.

The fact that Mr. Popp had been clapped into jail before I arrived in Romania, and consequently had never met me, did not deter the propagandists from their character assassination.

The reference to the tractor plant at Brasov showed that the local propagandists were still embarrassed by the Voice of America broadcast which suggested the kind of loss the country sustained by being forbidden to join the Marshall Plan. "The munitions manufacturing possibilities in Romania" was the subject of a document which a little rat-faced Romanian visitor had held out to me across my desk in the USIS office three weeks earlier. It was the most obvious "plant" I ran into while in the country. I had told him he could take his "document" wherever he wanted to, but that I could not accept it, and then had him shown abruptly to the door.

When the trial was over, the Ministry of Foreign Affairs of the "People's Republic" of Romania sent a formal note to the United States government, which said "in view of the facts revealed during the trial of a group of plotters, spies, and saboteurs ... the Romanian government ... no longer desires the presence in the country [of the counselor and military attaché] and desires their recall to be effected in the shortest possible time."

The State Department moved fast in this case. Within three days it returned a note acceding to the recall of the two officials but adding that the United States government "rejects as ridiculous and entirely contrary to fact the ground upon which the Romanian government presumes to base its request for their recall."

But that was not all. The State Department retaliated. It expelled without explanation two ranking diplomats in the Romanian legation in Washington. And one of them was my old acquaintance, Grigore Preoteasa, who was serving as chargé d'affaires and presumably had not been caught violating any laws of our land. He was returned to Bucharest to a most strategic position as far as I was concerned. He was named deputy foreign minister to Ana Pauker and eventually presided over the liquidation of our USIS office.

As it happened I was in Rome attending a meeting of USIS directors from eastern and southern Europe when the second Peasant party trial took place. Our meeting was given some publicity in the Italian press and some one of the Kremlin agents must have reported my attendance to the home office in Bucharest. No use was made of this fact for propaganda purposes for a few months, but when the attack came there was no mistaking my identification as "the representative of the USIS branch in Romania."

An editorial written in a Kremlin communist newspaper read:

> Lately, many things have been revealed about American espionage. One of the causes was the fact that espionage is even practiced by certain American diplomats who seemingly are not sufficiently "experienced" in these activities. Trials of odious spies and saboteurs in the people's democracies showed the extent to which certain employees of the American missions confused their role with that of spies and instigators. . . .
>
> Three months ago a secret meeting of heads of the European branches of the U. S. Information Service—USIS—was held in Rome. The meeting was convoked at the initiative of the U. S. Central Espionage Service and was held under the leadership of the former head of the American espionage service in Europe. . . .
>
> USIS activity in eastern European countries was examined. In these countries the population is anti-American, so USIS collaborators cannot obtain the necessary information through pro-American sympathizers. That is why USIS heads in eastern European countries must pay special attention to illegal activities.
>
> The representatives of the USIS branch in Romania pointed out that members of the espionage service in Bucharest have succeeded in using the American libraries in order to recruit agents. At the beginning, members of the American espionage service studied the Romanians who took American books and then established tacit contact with them. Thus they have already succeeded in recruiting some persons who are dissatisfied with the regime in Romania.
>
> Lately the USIS branch in Romania had begun to give illegal film shows. This measure, according to the representative of the branch, has greatly facilitated re-

cruiting activities, as those who come in secret to see these films proved their pro-American sympathies.

In conclusion, the assembly was informed regarding the intention of the Central Information Directorate to supply all USIS branches in Europe with experienced informers.

This means that the intensity of this activity—as we have seen—is inversely proportionate to the decrease of American influence in European countries.

This editorial was the signal that the regime intended to force us out of business completely. After its appearance only the most fearless Romanians dared visit our library or would allow themselves to be seen talking with any of our personnel.

I was seriously worried about the Romanian staff members and called a meeting to urge them to report freely and precisely anything that happened in our office if they were questioned by the secret police. The one person whose security I felt most in danger was my secretary-public relations assistant. For my predecessor who set up the office, and for me, she organized and managed our large receptions and celebrations. This work brought her in contact with the leading personalities in Bucharest and focused the social spotlight on her. The resulting prominence made her appear to be an important leader of our "spying" and gave her job political overtones which it did not actually possess.

As it turned out my apprehension on her behalf was justified. During the summer of 1949 while my wife and I were on home leave she was picked up in the middle of the night and carted off to the Ministry of the Interior. She was held there in a sub-basement cell without trial for seven months.

By the time we returned to Bucharest the campaign against our meager counterpropaganda effort was being stepped up with increasing intensity. It reached its climax around five o'clock on the dismal rainy afternoon of March 2, 1950. At this hour Preoteasa, substituting for Ana Pauker, summoned the American minister to the Foreign Office. He told him that the Romanian

government demanded that the United States Information Service
Office be closed immediately, as of that very minute. As soon as
he finished, he turned his back and the chief American representative was dismissed.

Our minister called me over to the chancellery. He was visibly
shaken and white with anger over the treatment he had received
at the hands of a mere deputy. Later it was learned that the
chiefs of the British, French, and Italian missions had also been
summoned, treated with the same grim rudeness, and instructed
to close the press and cultural sections of their legations.

That night I took care to send all the Romanian staff home in
official cars and no one was picked up. The next day the streets
around our office were dotted with plain-clothes men of the secret
police, some lounging about on foot and others nonchalantly
reading newspapers in parked cars. A number of visitors who
came to our library to return books were trailed when they left
the building and led off to jail.

Again that evening I tried to send the staff home in official cars
but several refused with resigned fatalism. "If they want to get
us they will—we can't avoid them forever." The display artist and
one of the young women librarians were picked up immediately, and three others within the following four days. All were
carrying articles they thought they would need in jail. The men
had sweaters and books and the women took soap, combs, tooth-
brushes, large handkerchiefs, and vitamin tablets.

Five days after the office was closed our minister had an official
note delivered to the Foreign Office which observed that the "free
and frank exchange of information among peoples of the world
... so essential to international understanding and peace" had
been "seriously impeded" by the Romanian government. No re-
taliatory steps were taken.

The very afternoon my wife and I departed from Romania
was the time the regime chose to open the trial of my secretary-
assistant. It was the occasion of another fanfare of anti-American
"spy" slander. She was sentenced to fifteen years of hard labor

for treason because she had worked for the United States government. In the summer of 1961 she completed her twelfth year of incarceration.

WAR CRIMINALS

Liberation from the concentration-camp atmosphere of Romania was almost too abrupt. It took me four weeks of sunshine in the south of Austria to begin to relax and regain a sense of balance in free society. And even then the adjustment was only partial. In fact, it was many years before I could look back on my experiences from 1947–50 with any measure of objectivity.

My main reaction in arriving at my new post in Bern, Switzerland, was incredulity that any country in a world which included the USSR menace could seriously maintain a position of neutrality. However, by the time I was transferred to my next post, I had gained the deepest respect for the way the Swiss deal with anti-American slander. I can only wish that my own country would learn from their example.

Their talents for judgment and exposure of the fraud of Kremlin communist claims were demonstrated strikingly in connection with the libel of us as "war criminals." In 1952 the Kremlin mounted a short-range propaganda campaign against us focused on our participation in the Korean War which is significant not only in the propaganda techniques employed by the Kremlin, but also in how the Swiss exposed it.

The propaganda principle involved in short-term subversion undertakings of this sort is to manufacture an accusation from one situation shocking enough to attract world attention quickly, persuade a few people, and cause doubts, or at least raise questions in the minds of many, and broadcast the slander intensively. When the falseness of the charge is about to be disclosed, the trick is to slacken off the massive campaign, turn your back on the issue, repeat the charges, and not answer the countercharge of lying. By this time considerable damage will have been done, a lingering doubt will have been left in many minds about the moral responsibility of the accused, and later evidence to the contrary can never wipe the slate clean.

This was the technique the Kremlin propagandists employed during the Korean War when they accused our Air Force of dropping bombs containing bacteria, which reportedly caused epidemics in North Korea and China: "The United States aggressor has sought to utilize Korea as a proving ground for the effectiveness of death-dealing bacteria." The anti-American slander was projected on a vast scale. The diplomatic and consular offices of the USSR, of captive eastern European governments, and of China were put to work along with the local communist parties, the international "front," and national "front" organizations. They took their line from TASS and Radio Moscow for short-term tactical directives and from the Cominform journal for "theoretical" detailed instructions and arguments. The overt lead was given to the World Peace Council with its network of "national" affiliates.

The campaign had been launched with an article in *Red Fleet,* the newspaper of the USSR Navy, charging us with bacteriological warfare and pinning the blame squarely on General MacArthur who had just been withdrawn from the Far East. It charged him with developing "the wide production of bacteriological weapons for the purpose of using them against the heroic Korean people."

Red Fleet accused us of testing these weapons in the summer of 1949 against Canadian Eskimos and of causing an epidemic of plague. The newspaper claimed General MacArthur's interest in this type of weapon went back to 1946 when, it said, he sent eighteen Japanese specialists in germ warfare to this country to undertake experiments in "numerous laboratories and institutes of America."

Since that time, *Red Fleet* wrote, General MacArthur had set up experimental stations in bacteriological warfare in Japan and staffed them with Japanese war criminals who were especially guarded by American military police.

Until the "germ warfare" issue was raised, there was no opportunity in Switzerland to put the USIS operation to work on direct or counterpropaganda against the USSR. For Switzerland was no Romania, and there could not have been a greater contrast between our activities in this tough little mountain republic, fortified against the "ideological" onslaughts of the moment, and those in the unfortunate Balkan country.

Switzerland had a free press, while Romania had no freedom of expression of any sort; Switzerland outlawed the political extremists—Communists and Nazis alike—and Romania permitted only the Kremlin agents to be active; Switzerland had access to press services, newspapers, magazines, books, and films from all over the world, but Romania was restricted to what the Kremlin allowed her to see; there was no Voice of America program to Switzerland, while the VOA became the only medium of communication with Romanians left to the United States. Our activities in Switzerland were just as low keyed as they were highly pitched in Romania; the Swiss government, a democracy like our own, was conducting no combat by slander and was scrupulously careful that no foreign representatives should disseminate propaganda which would prejudice the Swiss position of neutrality. Its methods of checking on foreign diplomatic missions suspected of trying to engage in such activities had been developed to a high degree of efficiency during World War II while fending off the propaganda blasts of Goebbels. Their supervision could be both efficient and discreet, since the total population of the country was just over a third that of greater New York City.

Perhaps I should have been professionally satisfied with this situation because it presented the most serene atmosphere imaginable for pursuing a mission of good will. But my experience in Romania had placed the propaganda interests of my country against the USSR considerably ahead of good will as an objective. I felt as if we were preaching to the converted.

What made this frustration worse was to watch from the side lines while the unofficial Kremlin propagandists in "front" groups all around us carried on their subversive work for the USSR. Their propaganda activities were not contained by the Swiss government as those of the USSR legation were, because their groups

were made up of Swiss citizens. Also, their efforts were not obvious, since they operated largely through personal contacts rather
than mass media—an approach which is more successful in small,
conservative, sophisticated Switzerland.

When the "war criminals'" slander campaign was launched
it was called the "most carefully organized and intensive ever
put into operation" by the Kremlin's Cominform. In time it
penetrated even the neutrality of Switzerland. Meanwhile, agitation-propaganda rallies were staged in the captive nations of eastern Europe to protest against the "crimes" by the United States;
similar rallies were organized by Kremlin agents in the Middle
East. The "hate America" drives were kindled high in the USSR,
and Kremlin propaganda techniques of delusion were given full
rein in the United States. From Prague went an "appeal" to
our scientists to "denounce this crime" of germ warfare in Korea.
At the United Nations the Kremlin delegate, Malik, used every
meeting of the Disarmament Commission as an occasion to disseminate his false charges against our country. He requested the
commission to consider without delay the question of bacteriological warfare, to prevent its "further" use, and "to bring the
violators [of its prohibition] to account." Our delegate repeated
his request that an impartial investigator, the International Red
Cross, be asked to check the validity of the accusations.

The Swiss were skeptical but interested. The International
Committee of the Red Cross, composed entirely of Swiss citizens,
offered to send a team of experts to Korea to investigate the
charges and determine the cause of the epidemics which were said
to be spreading. When this group was turned down by the Red
Chinese and the North Koreans as "not independent enough"
their skepticism as to the validity of the charges turned to real
doubt.

However, when the Kremlin international "front," the World
Peace Council, subsequently selected six physicians and neurolo-
gists to make the trip, the Swiss picked up interest again. Assumption of professional integrity on the part of the scientists
and professors led them to place great importance on the findings;

the fact that the World Peace Council was a Kremlin communist propaganda "front" did not make a deep public impression, probably because it was not known to be one by the vast majority of the people.

At this juncture the local branch of the World Peace Council in Switzerland, the Swiss Peace Council, went into action. It circulated a report made by the president of the "national" Peace Council in France that the charges were true. The Frenchman, a journalist by trade, had paid an extended visit to Korea and copied down what he had been told by the scientists there, along with personal observations in the form of a diary. He made his report to the conference of the World Peace Council in Berlin in July of 1952.

The Swiss also had the word of Professor Joliot-Curie, the Nobel Prize-winning physicist and president of the World Peace Council, that our Air Force was dropping bombs containing germs over wide areas of Korea, and that epidemics were raging. There was no secret about Joliot-Curie's being a Kremlin communist, but his standing as a scientist did give weight to his words.

Official denials were reaching the Swiss press from the United States and from the other nations participating with us in the war in Korea, but I felt not enough was being done and wanted our office to enter the fray. I went to a German-Swiss editor, a good friend of mine, for advice. "Leave it to us to take care of the situation," was his reply. "It may take a long time but there is nothing the Swiss hate more than being pushed unless it is being played for suckers." Their dealing with the subject would be practical, thorough, definitive, he promised.

Some time later the six members of the World Peace Council's Investigating Committee completed their tour of Korea and China and published findings to the effect that the charges had been substantiated. Following their publication, the Swiss Peace Council held a public propaganda meeting in Zurich at which a leading neurologist and titular professor at the University of Zurich spoke. Dr. Rudolf Brun declared that he had consulted all the evidence and that as a scientist he pronounced the accusation valid. Be-

cause he was a professor and because he was Swiss, the propaganda
impact on the Swiss public was considerable.

However, although the USIS in Bern could not strike back,
a Swiss journalist did, and so justified the prediction of my friend.

A Dr. Robert Eibel inserted advertisements in several newspapers which stated it was "weird" for a person of Professor
Brun's standing to make such grave allegations. He observed that
this action could be explained only by a "fateful blinding which
turned Professor Brun into a tool of the Soviets."

The professor took exception, and in accordance with the Swiss
ritual prescribed for matters involving "honor," brought the journalist to court on charges of libel and vituperation in the press.
Dr. Brun testified under cross-examination that he had based his
conclusion and statement on the "careful and well-documented"
report of the president of the French Peace Council which "de-
served to be called downright scientific" and which bore witness
to the "extraordinarily objective and profoundly scientific character of the work" of investigation on the spot.

A lower court found Eibel guilty of "vituperation" on the basis
of the following two paragraphs from his advertisements:

> However, people like Professor Brun, who enjoy a re-
> spected position because of their scientific career, are
> much more dangerous (than notorious communists) when
> they consciously or unconsciously allow themselves to be
> misused by the Soviets. . . .
>
> In Switzerland, the university is not a propaganda in-
> strument. It therefore has no use for teachers who, in the
> communist way, consciously or unconsciously degrade
> science into an instrument of political combat.

The defendant took the case higher, to the Federal Court of
Appeal, and was acquitted on both counts of libel and vituperation in the press. The court gave this Kremlin machination the
kind of sober, penetrating analysis it requires to reveal its true
nature. The observations made in handing down the verdict are
a tribute to the experience and wisdom of the Swiss when con-

fronted by propaganda dissimulation. The step-by-step findings show the thoroughness of the Swiss mind and deserve to be studied by all serious persons interested in seeing how Kremlin subversion by propaganda works.

The court findings follow:

The opening premise was that in view of the gravity—from the points of view of morality and international law—of the charge that the American Air Force had spread bacteria in Korea in order to start epidemics among the population, it might be assumed that a Swiss scientist, who had established a reputation with his biological and entomological studies, would call such an accusation true only if he had unequivocal proof in his hands.

But he had relied on reports of a man who was president of the French "Peace Movement," which belonged to the World Peace Movement, an organization, the court noted, which was created and dominated by the communists. This man had received the "Stalin Peace Prize," was a communist himself, or at any rate a sympathizer. His ideological view by itself made it anything but certain that there would be impartial reporting on the highly political theme of germ warfare.

It followed that the report by the French source did not constitute a serious documentation. In these circumstances a Swiss scientist "had no cause responsibly to consider" this man's report as full proof of the charge that the Americans had resorted to germ warfare.

The court concluded that the professor had no cause, on the basis of the deficient data that were available, to declare germ warfare to be a proved fact. Since he did it anyway, the only explanation could be that "he had been uncritical to a degree that should not be expected from a ranking and reputable scientist, or that he consciously wanted to support the communist position."

In reversing the findings of the lower court on "vituperation" the Court of Appeal held that Professor Brun gave cause to people to suspect that he was "consciously" in the service of the Communists. Since he had been willing to act as scientific guarantor of the reports at hand, the professor had no right to complain

when his behavior was publicly criticized and when he was accused of consciously taking a partisan stand in favor of the communists.

Finally, the court concluded the reproach that Professor Brun,
by his stand at the "Peace Congress," had consciously or unconsciously allowed himself to be misused by the Soviets, was tenable
in every respect. The same applied to Dr. Eibel's second allegation, that the plaintiff had, in the communist way, consciously or
unconsciously degraded science into an instrument of political
combat.

Would that every slanderous charge against the United States
by the Kremlin were given this kind of analysis and exposure!

COLONIALIST OPPRESSORS

The transfer from Bern to Trieste in the early fall of 1952 not
only put me back into the active propaganda business but dropped
me into a political situation which was ready to boil over. Trieste
was one of the crisis spots in the Free World which the Kremlin
hoped to exacerbate for propaganda purposes. It was administered
by an Allied military government made up of British and American military and civilian personnel. The zone commander was a
British general, and my job was public information officer under
his direction.

The Kremlin propagandists took advantage of this joint effort
to try to convict the United States in the forum of world opinion
of being "oppressors" in guilt-by-association with the British.
The "colonialist" half of this slander was implied in Trieste and
developed further at the time of the Suez Crisis.

This campaign against us had begun at the end of World War
II when Great Britain abdicated her position of policeman of the
world and handed the badge to the United States. The Kremlin
tried at once to saddle us with the historic image of the British as
we undertook their responsibility to guarantee the peace.

Its propagandists found that the tag, "colonialist oppressors,"
for the British paid handsome propaganda dividends in Africa,

the Middle East, India, and Southeast Asia. So, if it worked so well in vilifying the British, why not try it on the Americans? In the minds of many people abroad the British and the Americans already had a lot in common: language, racial origins, physical characteristics, and past international political affiliation.

The particular situation in Trieste the Kremlin tried to exploit occurred in 1953, a few months after I arrived. The British and ourselves decided the time had come to withdraw from the military administration of Trieste and we announced jointly that we were going to hand over the reins of local government to the Italians.

Immediately there were screams of protests on all sides. The Yugoslavs who had expropriated the adjoining countryside after the war insisted that they should have more territory. The Italians were equally emotional about taking away from the Yugoslavs some of the farmland they had acquired. The flare-up was deeply imbedded in the bloody fight over the general area which occurred in World War I. Only the Triestini were calm; they wanted the allied forces to stay because the money we poured into the local coffers in one form or another gave them a higher standard of living than they could expect under any other administration.

Because the local population had not demonstrated on behalf of the Italian claims to land in the hands of the Yugoslavs, various political groups imported henchmen from other cities to stimulate some action. They arrived by the car- and bus-load. Among them we spotted several trained Kremlin communist agitators in their telltale short black leather trench coats. They were in their late thirties and forties, and they took their places at strategic points in the city to direct the gathering human mass in its parade through the streets.

As the march began these men mingled with the concentrated groups of youth and egged them on to shout and hurl paving stones at the zone policemen guarding the sidewalks. One of the imported demonstrators was seen flinging a hand grenade at the police who replied with revolver fire. From this fracas widespread rioting broke out, and the agitators saw that a church was desecrated. It lasted two days, and when it was brought to an end by the appearance of British and American troops, six demonstrators were dead and several demonstrators and policemen were wounded.

If demonstrators had not been imported it is doubtful that there would have been any rioting. And if the Kremlin communist agents had not been among them it is questionable whether there would have been any bloodshed. But the Kremlin would not have missed that opportunity to increase strife and thus embarrass the British and the Americans. It had no hope of taking over the territory in the name of the USSR or to impose political domination, but it had a perfect opportunity to acquire propaganda fodder for anti-Western slander which could be drawn upon for months to come.

On the first day of the rioting the Kremlin communist newspaper in Italy, *L'Unità,* ran the headline, "Anglo-Americans Have People in Trieste Fired Upon," with subheads: "Two dead and about a hundred injured" and "The Foreigner's Grapeshot."

The report read in part:

> ... on November 4 the citizens of Trieste were beaten up by a police force which obeys the orders given by a stranger who occupies Trieste ... on November 5 the streets of Trieste were bloodstained; the Anglo-Americans had the population fired on with the same cynical brutality with which they act in their colonies ... the Italian rulers had trusted the good intentions of Mr. Foster Dulles. These are the consequences. ...

Following the second day *L'Unità* wrote that Trieste was gathering the "bitter fruits" of foreign military occupation with all the violence, lack of liberty, fostering of hatred "which the Anglo-American occupiers" had sowed for years. Its summation was "Today 'Atlantic solidarity' is being celebrated in Trieste with the help of machine-gun bursts. ..."

A few days later it ran a commentary which, through the use

of tricky phraseology and juxtapositions, created the impression that the Anglo-Americans were guilty of starting the riots, killing the people, blaming it all on the Italians, approving the action of the "pitiless repression," and having slight sympathy for the Italian victims.

When the British and American troops were finally called out to make a show of strength toward the rioters they were posted in separate sections of the city. At the sight of British uniforms the crowd screamed "*basso*" and made insulting remarks. But as the American boys marched in the people applauded and shouted "*viva.*" The partiality was so obvious and insistent that it embarrassed us American members of the military government staff watching from the side lines next to our British colleagues.

The disparity in treatment was so great that the leader of the local Kremlin communist party was impelled to write an article for *L'Unità* in which he took the people of Trieste to task for their "jeers at the British soldiers" and their "cheers at the American soldiers." The "first responsible" were the governments of Washington and London, he declared, and added "there is no use in requesting that Winterton [the British zone commander] be replaced by another Winterton or by a Van Fleet or a MacArthur."

The same deliberate separation of the Americans from the British was displayed by the people a year later, after the Trieste question had at last been settled. On the day the military forces left, a crowd gathering early for the handing-over ceremony, brought out the town's supply of whistles to blow at the British and carried garlands of flowers to give to the Americans. But because of a threatening storm the British zone commander had his contingent put to sea early, which meant that the ceremony was cancelled. So no whistles were blown—but the flowers were given at dockside to American soldiers who sailed off at noon, when the weather had cleared.

Flowers also were tossed through the windows of the limousine of the American general as it inched its way through a smiling crowd. The people cheered the Stars and Stripes as it passed and called *"Viva America"* to the general and his lady, who waved in return from the back seat.

From Trieste I returned home to resign from the United States Information Agency, and joined the American Committee for Liberation from Bolshevism. It is a private organization, deals in propaganda to and about the USSR exclusively, and offers a broader scope for action than the government agency with its restrictions imposed by diplomatic considerations. Staff headquarters where I worked on policy and planning is in New York City, and there I had an opportunity not only to follow USSR propaganda on paper as part of my job but to witness it in action at the United Nations.

Here I watched a continuation of the Kremlin effort to convict the United States by associating us with the British and their historical "colonialism." Its propagandists went to work at the time of the Suez Crisis to divert attention from the USSR massacre of the Hungarian Revolution. They were rushed to build up an attack on us, and were confronted with a formidable task because the United States had enjoyed a noncolonial reputation for generations.

Our dealings with overseas territories have been liberal and generous, as demonstrated by the independence granted the Philippine Islands and statehood recently given to Hawaii. Puerto Rico—far from being exploited in the "colonialist" tradition—has been a continued welfare concern to our federal government. Besides, it was at least farfetched to accuse the United States of being "colonialist" through "guilt-by-association" with the very country from whose empire we once broke away for "colonial" reasons. These facts, plus our long-time isolationism, present a public record that had to be undermined by the Kremlin propagandists before they could begin to build the opposite image of us.

This "guilt-by-association" approach to their slander of us took me back to the days in Romania when we were called "Anglo-American imperialists" and "Anglo-American spies." I remembered two small seeds linking us with the British as "colonialists."

As early as 1947 TASS distributed a somewhat ironical dispatch, in view of subsequent developments: the United States government, it claimed, was ready to lend Egypt $25,000,000 for the defense of the Suez Canal. The comment added, "Well-informed Washington circles say that the Suez Canal will eventually pass under the direct control of the United States." The following year *Pravda* introduced a propaganda line which held that the United States was "taking over" Britain's "position toward colonies"; presumably it was just the "position" we were being "colonialist" about, not the territories themselves.

Then when Secretary Dulles withdrew our offer of aid to Egypt for building the Aswan Dam in 1956, Radio Moscow called our action "new evidence that America uses its notorious aid to underdeveloped countries as a means of making these countries subservient to its interests" . . . while "United States propagandists shout very loudly to convince the world" that America aids developing countries to consolidate their independence, United States politicians "openly tell the underdeveloped countries that, if they want to obtain foreign currency for their national needs, they must sell their sovereignty."

By the time Nasser took over Suez in July 1956 the Kremlin propagandists were using their entire reservoir of inverted semantics, half-truths, insidious insinuations, and outright lies to brand us "colonialists"—and "oppressors." The inconsistency of their propaganda in view of our opposing our good friends and allies and taking a positive anti-colonial stand did not deter them from the attack.

Three months later Radio Moscow, broadcasting in Arabic, accused Dulles of supporting a "colonialist" proposal, i.e., his Users' Association plan, "which runs counter to the interests of many peoples." It commented that American "colonial policy" appeared in the guise of "monopoly looting" of Arab oil resources. America's "aggressive policy" against Communist China—as manifested in the Formosa "occupation"—was another example of American colonialism, as were United States support for Portuguese colonialism in Goa and American control over Panama.

From this "evidence" Radio Moscow concluded that Dulles' "pretenses"—simply an attempt to conceal an "aggressive policy" against Asia and Africa—had been exposed as "hypocrisy" in the eyes of the world.

Izvestia then attacked the "provocative character" of the Anglo-French draft resolution on Suez submitted to the Security Council and said that Dulles' "hasty support" of the resolution revealed "the hypocrisy of American propaganda statements alleging that the United States occupies a position different from that of other colonial states in the Suez problem."

By the middle of November Radio Moscow broadcast in Arabic to the Near East that the United States was bound sooner or later to take "the same road as her partners in colonialism." "Wall Street," said the commentator, "would not permit the defeat of colonialism." Radio Moscow also asserted that the United States had been using the struggle over Suez, and Near East unrest in general, to replace British and French colonialism "with its own more subtle brand."

It charged that the United States' refusal to accept Bulgaria's proposal for joint action in Egypt was one of the main indications that the Americans "actually encourage aggression and encourage the colonialists to carry on with the work of international banditry and piracy."

At the end of November *Pravda* wrote there was a struggle going on within the "colonialist camp." It explained that certain differences among the American United Nations Delegation, as well as among representatives of the State Department, had become apparent, "a development openly discussed in the American press." The root of these differences was said to lie in the desire of the United States to help its allies and at the same time to pose as a supporter of the Asian-African desire for liberation from colonialism.

Radio Moscow continued with a broadcast which maintained that these days, when "naked colonialism" was no longer fashionable, the United States was following its monopolistic interest in the Near East "by pursuing a colonialist policy of its own." It "is guided by the idea of taking advantage of the loss of British prestige in that area to strengthen American positions."

Soviet Russia, Party organ of the Russian Soviet Republic, stated explicitly that whereas, on the surface, American Near East policy was designed to convince the Arabs that cooperation with the West was the only way out, the real basis of all the United States plans was "to compel, through force, the people who have embarked on the road to national independence to return to the colonial yoke."

In summing up the Suez controversy, the *New Times* wrote that the United States voted in favor of passing condemnation on its principal NATO partners at the same time it was making a bid for the "dividends" the Suez group was "hankering after." The article explained we voted for condemnation to curry favor with the Arabs as an opponent of aggression, and thus be able to deceive them more easily and "inveigle them into the toils of American servitude." It capped the campaign against us by ending with, "Incidentally, plans are being openly mooted in the United States to use the United Nations force as a means of establishing American influence in Egypt and the Middle East generally."

INCITERS TO REVOLUTION

The massacre ordered by Khrushchev in Budapest put the Kremlin propagandists in a difficult position. From Hungary came the word that the youth of the land indoctrinated by the followers of Pavlov in a closed society were the most fearless of the Freedom Fighters. Between October 23 and 27, 1956, it looked as if the force of world opinion might compel the Kremlin colonialists to retreat and their propagandists were helpless because the political wheels could not decide which way to turn. However, fortunately for them, the Suez Crisis reached a peak just in time and competed successfully for the world's attention. This deflection of interest gave the political administrators the opportunity to take a harsh position and the propagandists an issue to promote as a diversion from both the Hungarian uprising and later from its suppression by the USSR. The propagandists performed their difficult assignment adroitly and succeeded, up to a point, in confusing the thinking of the world public.

Their propaganda campaign had a twofold, immediate objective: inside the Iron Curtain, to discourage other captive nations or groups from rebelling; and outside, to keep the Free World from isolating the USSR as an inhuman force for terror and bloodshed.

Serving these two direct objectives was a third, an indirect one, that of calumniating the United States as "inciters to revolution." Thus the Kremlin propagandists tried to move from an unfavorable situation and to take the propaganda initiative. As usual they acted on the principle that an offensive is the best defense. By placing the blame on us for the Hungarian Revolution, they added another dimension to the diversionary tactic of exploiting the Suez Crisis and identifying us with the "colonialists." To keep the record straight, it must be noted here that they consistently used "counterrevolution" in the place of "revolution," and accused us of being its "organizers" as well as "inciters."

Until October 27, four days after the Revolution started, propaganda comment was left to radio stations of the captive nations. Radio Warsaw ridiculed Secretary Dulles for support of Polish freedom and discussed "imperialist" support of uprisings in Hungary in sharp tones similar to those used in its comment on the Poznań riots.

In their first frontal attack the Kremlin propagandists tied up our "concern" over Hungary with huge congressional appropriations, with election platforms of both parties, and with a "position" attributed to the American press as if it were a government-controlled monopoly like their own.

A *Pravda* article distributed abroad by TASS read:

"It is clear that the pre-election platforms of both major parties —Democratic and Republican—contain a clear indication of their intention to continue attempts to interfere in the internal affairs of the people's democracies and to restore the capitalist system in these countries."

At the same time Radio Moscow commentators were saying that "bourgeois propaganda" had enjoyed the blood bath "with unconcealed relish," that congressional appropriations were set aside for "this dirty business" of recruiting and training "sundry renegades" for the overthrow of the "people's regimes." They insinuated that American-financed radio stations with their "muddy torrents of bourgeois propaganda" had admitted that the "fascist *putsch*" was not spontaneous as "Hungary's false friends abroad insist."

The commentators added that Western "cloak-and-dagger" policy was the real cause of the Hungarian uprising and that American-instigated attempts to overthrow "people's democracies" misfired "because the people . . . will never return to the path of capitalism."

But SZABADNEP, the central Hungarian communist organ, took exception to this "interpretation." In an article addressed to the Kremlin, it refused to brand the "counterrevolutionaries" as fascist Western agents; it called Kremlin statements to this effect an insult to Hungarians. The fighting, said the newspaper, "was not instigated by some sort of undermining work. It was caused, alas, by your own faults and crimes."

Then, while USSR tanks were being turned on the Hungarians and the Revolution was being smothered in blood, Radio Moscow spoke of the "dark forces of world imperialism," which, hating socialism, "darken the bright sky of cooperation among nations and organize subversive activities." Adding that "American espionage services" had spent millions to aid the "counterrevolutionaries," it accused us of furnishing weapons and supplies to the "Hungarian fascists" and called President Eisenhower's offer of aid an open proposal to give money "to the reactionary circles in Hungary in order to strengthen their shaky position."

Kremlin official Mikhail Suslov in a speech in Moscow said the Hungarian "counterrevolution" was paid for by American dollars and supported by "lying radio propaganda and slanderous pamphlets and leaflets." Radio Moscow alleged that plans for the uprising were "agreed upon at the highest levels in the United

States," and provided for the dispatch of weapons and men from the West.

Under the heading "The Reason for the Commotion Around the Hungarian Question" *Pravda* ran an article which said that "the American press"—as if it functioned as one voice of the United States government—was waging a furious campaign against the USSR and the "people's democracies" to divert attention from the failure of the Anglo-French and Israeli aggression in Egypt and to encourage "defeated fascists" in Hungary with promises of United Nations support. It ended with:

"Irrefutable facts testify that it was indeed American reactionary circles who incited and activated the Horthyist underground which unleashed the bloody events in Hungary."

A Radio Moscow broadcast to North America held that "too much evidence to the contrary" undermined President Eisenhower's statement that the United States never had encouraged open revolts anywhere. As part of this "evidence" the broadcast cited the Kersten Amendment to the Mutual Security Act, Voice of America, and Radio Free Europe broadcasts allegedly calling for armed resistance in Hungary, American support for Hungarian émigrés, and United States "pressure" to get the Hungarian question before the United Nations.

Red Star, the Soviet Army paper, contrasted the "selfless" communist assistance extended to Hungary in the form of food and other supplies, with the stock piles of captured weapons—including many said to be American made—which had been "smuggled into Hungary from abroad" and then used by the "counter-revolutionaries" for their "dastardly crimes." The *Red Star* article asserted that the Hungarian people would never forget the moral and material instigators of these "bloody crimes," whose arms and ammunitions were used to murder defenseless women and children.

The Ukrainian radio followed up by broadcasting the text of a letter ostensibly written by three clergymen from the Transcarpathian Oblast, which borders on Hungary. It denied Western reports that mass deportations of Hungarians to the USSR were taking place, and concluded:

> We protest . . . against the slanderous broadcasts of the so-called free radio, Voice of America. This is the voice of Judas, the man who sold Christ for crucifixion: The Voice breathes death and does great harm to Christian life. We beg that such voices be stopped because the Voice of America broadcasts are poison for the people.

United Nations: Kremlin Forum

As they had done so often before, the Kremlin propagandists used the meetings of the United Nations as their forum, this time for slandering the United States as "inciters to revolution." They prepared for USSR delegates statements couched in sensational language, which could hardly fail to capture the attention of every reporter present. Because the sessions were covered by a huge press corps, guaranteeing a fast worldwide dissemination of the news and its "interpretations," these delegates read texts that "made news."

In the first meetings of the Security Council, on October 27 and 28, the Kremlin propagandists were cautious and relatively tame, and they tried to temporize. The best they could do was to have the USSR delegate Sobolov question the motives of the United States, Great Britain, and France in bringing a resolution before that body on the "internal situation" in Hungary. Sobolov asked for a postponement of discussion on the Revolution, but was turned down.

Not until after the Israeli forces had moved on Suez on October 30 were these propagandists given the go-ahead signal to mount a hard offensive. They had Sobolov declare that the "reactionary underground movement in Hungary had been organized with the assistance of the United States."

A few days later Sobolov declared in the Security Council that the reactionary elements which the United States had assisted were engaging in provocation, confusing and deceiving the Hungarian people by "propaganda containing nothing but lies." At this point in the so-called debates the moment had come to play the second Kremlin "line": the United States, Great Britain, and France were placing the Hungarian question before the Security Council to camouflage the action taken by Israel, Great Britain, and France against Egypt, according to Sobolov's declaration.

To this accusation he added the bold threat which frightened off several Western statesmen: "Interference by the United Nations and by Western countries in the Hungarian events might lead to complications."

When the USSR vetoed the resolution on Hungary in the Security Council, the issue was moved to the General Assembly. In this larger body the Kremlin pursued the same propaganda line. However, in both the emergency session and the subsequent regular session it focused its attack more and more completely on the United States. It even went so far as to draw a propaganda bead on a target within this target: the Free Europe Committee.

The reason for singling out this private, American-backed institution was that the Kremlin propagandists wanted to eliminate a small but effective opponent. The Free Europe Committee, with its Radio Free Europe speaking through former Hungarian citizens, had been active over the airwaves in keeping up the spirits of the Hungarian revolutionists—communist or otherwise —during their gallant but losing battle. The broadcasts gave the Kremlin some of its own propaganda medicine. The USSR retaliated through its official delegation to the United Nations, endeavoring to use diplomatic pressure to wipe out the Free Europe Committee.

With this in mind, but without naming it, the USSR delegate to the General Assembly Emergency Session meetings renewed the attack which he had just left off in the Security Council chambers. Sobolov "explained" that actions of the "reactionary forces" in Hungary were the result of long-standing preparation by the imperialist countries. With funds supplied by the imperialists, a slanderous campaign had been launched in which, according to him, balloons containing leaflets were set adrift over Hungary and incendiary broadcasts were made.

The USSR delegate then allowed the secondary delegates from the bloc to make rather perfunctory remarks about the United States' role as "inciter to revolution." The Free Europe Committee was not mentioned by name until the last day of the emergency session, November 9, when the bloc put on its customary final spurt. Kuznetzov, the USSR deputy foreign minister, substituting for Sobolov, accused the United States of responsibility for the broadcasts of the Voice of America and Radio Free Europe which allegedly appealed day and night for a counterrevolutionary coup in Hungary.

Ten days later, at the opening of the regular (eleventh) session of the General Assembly, Shepilov—then USSR minister of foreign affairs—charged United States interference in the internal affairs of Hungary through "systematic subversive broadcasts and mass distribution of slanderous leaflets." He also pointed an accusing finger at West Germany and Austria for permitting these "subversive organizations" to set up centers on their soil from which to dispatch "spies" and "saboteurs" into eastern European countries.

The Czech delegate branded Radio Free Europe a *"de facto* general staff" of the Hungarian Revolution; other "representatives" from the captive nations sang the same refrain. My old acquaintance from Romanian days, Preoteasa, was one of them. He was still furtive in manner, but seemed to be somewhat more self-assured since he had become foreign minister in place of his ousted mentor, Ana Pauker. He declared that activities of "ultra-revolutionary" groups connected with the Voice of America and Radio Free Europe in carrying on campaigns of provocation were "not new for Hungary and other people's democracies."

He appeared on one other occasion to speak against the United States but added nothing to what the production-line speeches had already offered. One of his subordinate colleagues, whom I remembered dimly, emerged on the podium a week later and emphasized the "sinister role played by the inflammatory propaganda of the American Radio Free Europe."

On December 3 Kuznetzov attacked "the activities of the United States organization which operates under the false name of 'Crusade for Freedom,'" and of its radio station "which bears the equally false name of Radio Free Europe." He claimed RFE became the center which directed "counterrevolutionary" activities in the days of the "fascist revolt" in Hungary.

By way of keeping the record straight, Chancellor Adenauer subsequently held a press conference after RFE taped broadcasts had been received. His statement was: "Promises of military aid and incitement to revolt were never broadcast by Radio Free Europe."

As the "debates" finished, Kuznetzov had this last word to say against the private American propaganda group. "The General Assembly has become the arena in a ruthless struggle between the forces of progress and the forces of international hatred and reaction headed by the United States of America. The USSR and the socialist countries are subjected to a constant flow of slander unleashed by those who held so much at heart the revolutionary *putsch* in Hungary and who are so alarmed by its failure."

Here was a prime example of the thief's calling another man "thief" to hide his own guilt.

WARMONGERS

The most durable and comprehensive slander slogan the Kremlin propagandists repeat against the United States is "warmongers." It was one of the first they used and is aimed not just at certain actions in our foreign policy but at the total image of the United States in the family of nations. "Warmonger" is the counterpart to "peace lover" which is what they actually call the Kremlin regime. Whenever they tell the world we are "warmongers" they mention themselves as "peace lovers," with the implication that we are warmongering if we simply say we oppose specific USSR actions or policies. The label also covers "imperialists," suggests "colonialists" and "oppressors," and is frequently connected with "spies," "war criminals," and "inciters to revolution."

Warmonger carried its most pungent propaganda flavor right after the end of the war, while we had a monopoly on the atom bomb. During that period its fears, the Kremlin felt, could be transmitted emotionally to others; but today, when the USSR possesses the secret to nuclear destruction, this anti-American slander label loses a bit of its former propaganda power. Consequently, the Kremlin propagandists are required to publicize the "peace lovers' " label for the USSR with increasing intensity.

A recent instance of slander against us as warmongers grew out of the U-2 incident and was built up into a concentrated worldwide anti-American attack. We were castigated, too, as "spies," but as the drive was handled for foreign consumption, "warmongering" was given the stronger play.

The Kremlin propagandists described the Powers mission as "provocative" because it violated the air space of the USSR and claimed the overflights constituted "aggression." Therefore we were considered "warmongering" in the most extreme sense of that term. But "provocative warmongering aggression" was too much of a mouthful to be manageable as a propaganda slogan.

By the time this attack of "warmongering" had leveled off and Khrushchev attended the United Nations General Assembly meeting in New York to bang his shoe on his desk, the Kremlin propagandists had redesigned the label. We became "provocation-mongers," which presumably is a rare breed of "warmongers."

In his two-hour speech Khrushchev said of us: "The provocation-mongers are seeking to create an atmosphere in which nations would live in constant fear." Leniency to "provocation-mongers" has been "shown by experience ultimately to lead to the outbreak of war," he warned.

However, it had been evident from the moment the dictator made the disclosure of the overflight to the Supreme Soviet that he had posed a serious dilemma for the Kremlin. This dilemma was a more significant consideration to the USSR than the mounting of a propaganda attack on the United States. She had a few questions to answer to the world. If the USSR had been unable to halt the overflights, how could she be the invincible power the Kremlin propagandists had made her out to be? If she was, indeed, so weak, what of the prestige the Kremlin had been avidly promoting among the peoples of the world? How could a would-be leader of the world, while boasting of its power, suddenly confess it had been unable for four years to prevent foreign reconnaissance planes from flying over its borders?

Consequently, the Kremlin had no alternative but to conduct a major campaign over the U-2 incident to restore the damaged military image for audiences both at home and abroad. First, it endeavored to frighten the listeners into respect by bellicose nuclear rocket rattling over a four-month period, and second, it tried to persuade them that their territory had not been successfully penetrated by "proving" at the trial that Powers, the pilot, was shot down from 68,000 feet. The slandering of us as "warmongers" provided an extra propaganda dividend, just as "colonialists" and "inciters to revolution" did during the Hungarian Revolution. The U-2 incident, of course, was only one of the numerous news pegs the Kremlin propagandists had used in their continuing campaign against us using the "warmonger" label.

The mix-up in Washington over "explaining" the U-2 overflight, and our failure to publicize the military weakness of the USSR quickly, gave the Kremlin propagandists an advantage which they did not hesitate to exploit. They used the U-2 "provocation" and "aggression" charges and the "warmongering" label to shake the world's confidence in the United States as a leader of the Free World. They also used the occasion to attempt to force the United States out of overseas military bases by rattling rockets at our allies on whose territory these bases were located. The occasion was an ideal one, in the absence of decisive American propaganda action, for the Kremlin propagandists to "prove" it was the United States which threatened the security of the world.

In this protracted attack the Kremlin propagandists set in motion all the media of communications available to them. The very organization of this operation, with its vast dissemination and coverage, gives an indication of the Kremlin's strength in subversion, perhaps even more vividly than the "message" carried to the target audiences.

Khrushchev provided the general line, but the "tough talk" was put in the mouth of the chief of their armed forces, Marshal Malinovsky, so that the current dictator would not be too deeply committed in future diplomatic negotiations with the West.

When he announced the "capture" of the plane, Khrushchev called us "aggressors" and characterized the U-2 flight as dangerous and not in the "spirit of international peaceful relations." He also took occasion to say to the countries with bases accommodating such flights that "we shall hit at such bases because we assess such actions as provocations against our country."

Marshal Malinovsky went further, declaring the overflight was of a "criminal character." He denounced the "imperialists" as "violent enemies of peace and of the sincerity of peoples," and declared it was evident that not even elementary order existed in the "lauded" country of the United States where, among its armed forces, were "raving militant generals and fanatics of atomic deaths without control."

Then he rattled the rockets:

"We reply to you firmly, gentlemen, American imperialists: no, you will not fly over our land! We are not Turkey, Pakistan, or South Korea. . . . We also warn the countries countenancing these evil doings, lending their territory and airfields for the flights of similar pirate planes over our country's borders—think before it is too late. We have the right to take any measures . . . against those bases and airfields . . . so that nothing remains of those bases and airfields. . . ."

This line was intensified considerably by the end of May, after the Kremlin decided to scuttle the Paris Conference. An illustration is taken from the USSR army paper, *Red Star,* which made a considerable point of the fact that Eisenhower, the President of the United States, confirmed that orders to collect intelligence data "by any possible means" were issued by him, that this was

the "transoceanic rulers' " official policy. The action was said to
be "impudent" as well as "provocative"; it indicated "how low"
we had fallen and had aroused "anger and indignation among all
decent people of the world."

This development of the line was given fast dissemination
abroad by TASS and Radio Moscow. It then underwent a theoretical treatment for basic guidance to agents abroad in an article
in the then-current issue of the *World Marxist Review: Problems
of Peace and Socialism,* which read:

> All peace supporters have deeply regretted the failure of
> the summit. It is, of course, bad for peace that the United
> States imperialists were able to torpedo the conference
> which, it was hoped, would normalize international rela-
> tions. But we should not overlook the other side of the
> matter; the aggressive forces did not succeed in deceiving
> the people by turning the long-awaited conference into
> an instrument for lulling public opinion. And this is
> very important, for the basic condition for maintaining
> and strengthening peace is a viligant public opinion
> capable of exposing in good time the intrigues of the
> warmongers, pillorying them and rendering them harm-
> less. This vigilance should in no way be relaxed, because
> the imperialists are not at all inclined to give up their
> evil aims; it is necessary to ensure there is no return to
> the past, when they decided the destinies of the people.

When reading the quotation care should be taken not to skim
through it in the spirit of an editorial, reacting only to the way
it sounds and to the way it was intended to sound to the uninitiated. It should be read as a specific set of instructions to
agents on how to present the propaganda line on the U-2 incident
with particular reference to labeling us "warmongers."

For instance, the first sentence means that all the agents should
strike a pose of "regret" at the failure of the summit conference,
take a "hurt" tone rather than a "belligerent" one, and say that
the USSR (the peace lover) regrets the failure—which the succeed·

ing sentences point out was the doing of the United States, not the USSR.

Through the *World Marxist Review* this general line was communicated to all agents worldwide, and they, in turn, were required to write an adaptation of it for consumption in the geographic areas for which they are responsible. The latter adaptation was then circulated through domestic communist party channels and covert "fronts" as propaganda-line directives.

To indict the United States as "warmonger," to blacken our image and whitewash their own, the Kremlin propagandists also tailored their product to the frame of reference of each individual country. In so doing they took into account the target audience's race, religion, and language, as well as national character and characteristics and aspirations; they exploited issues of political or social nature about which the audiences were sensitive. As usual, consistency was of no concern whatsoever to the followers of The System.

The tailored "messages" in turn were also published in the *World Marxist Review* and broadcast to agents and popular audiences over Radio Moscow. The news on the U-2 incident, on the collapse of the Summit Conference, and on the Powers' "trial" were used as pegs on which to hang the "warmonger" slander.

In Great Britain the guidance line to agents is typical of that included for countries where Kremlin communist parties exist:

> Pointing out that Britain is brought into grave danger by the adventurous actions of the United States militarists, the statement calls on the people to work for "an independent British foreign policy in support of peace, end subservience to the United States, finish with the NATO nuclear strategy, close down the United States bases in Britain, renounce the manufacture and use of nuclear weapons." (*World Marxist Review*)

So "the word" is to create dissension between the allies, the United States and Great Britain, by showing how the irresponsible acts of the United States endanger the safety of the people of the British Isles. It is also to trade upon Britain's pride and sensitivity following her loss of leadership in the Free World to the United States, to undermine NATO, agitate for the withdrawal of permission to the United States to use territory in the British Isles for bases, and step up the "peace offensive" and the "disarmament" campaign to curtail and deter the development of Britain's defense program.

This message over Radio Moscow contains the points to be communicated to countries where there are no Kremlin communist parties. It is aimed, too, at the general public and government officials:

> ... the people of those countries where United States war bases exist are becoming more conscious of the situation than when the United States warmongers began their aggressive activities from these bases against the Soviet Union and other peace-loving countries. Even representatives of these governments cannot hide the fear ... and they do not go along with the United States aggressive policy. But some of them are trying to escape their responsibilities by misleading the world public through trickery. Such is the case with the Pakistani government.
>
> In its siding with the United States warmongers' aggressive activities, the vacillating attitude of Pakistan cannot satisfy the Soviet Union and the other peace-loving countries. The Soviet government has strongly warned Pakistan that if any new provocative plane flights take off from Pakistani soil the Soviet Union will be forced to take necessary steps against the United States war bases in Pakistan.
>
> Premier Khrushchev said on May 28, 1960, that it is the Soviet government's wish that such events do not take place. It is his hope that the Pakistani government will take appropriate decisions in light of this warning.

The following breakdown distinguishes between those countries where American military bases are propagandized as the main issue and those where the slander of the U.S.A. or local politics is given priority treatment. It will be noted that a special frame of reference is carefully constructed by the Kremlin propagandists for each separate national target audience.

Addressing themselves to audiences where the issue is American bases, such as Norway, the Kremlin propagandists start with the statement, "The small Nordic countries cannot determine world politics," and proceed to suggest these countries could exert a beneficial influence by creating a zone of neutrality, which would "lessen international tensions." Norway is threatened over its American bases and reminded of the Nazi invasion in World War II by the line, "the Bundeswehr is already feeling too cramped," which means that the army of the German Federal Republic may move in their direction again.

In Germany the angle is that the U-2 incident prevented a Summit Conference and shattered the hopes of the Germans for a settlement of the "German problem"; the Kremlin propagandists do not mention reunification specifically but that is the implication. The United States "ruling circles," along with "aggressive forces of German imperialism," are responsible for the threat to West Germany's security.

An attack is leveled at De Gaulle for lining up with the dominating United States "imperialists" in supporting Adenauer and allowing United States and German bases on French soil. Mention of "revenge," "former Nazis," "the grandeur of France," seeks to use the World War II animosity between France and Germany as framework for agitation.

The long-range propaganda projection in Italy is similar to that used in France against relations with the United States "rulers." Here the slander against us has been pushed to an extreme: we are accused outright of preparing for a new war.

The approach in Spain is that Western powers advocating Western solidarity are endangering their security by entrusting leadership to the United States, whose foreign policy shows the American leaders do not sincerely desire peace.

Emphasis is laid on the presence of American generals at American bases on Turkish soil who are "absolute masters" and care not for the destinies of the peoples of small countries. An attempt is made by the propagandist to exacerbate relations between the American military forces and local populations.

Attention is called to the American bases in Saudi Arabia, Libya, and Morocco to suggest that they pose a threat to the peace of the entire area. United States militarists are mentioned in the same context as the invasion of Suez, the British and French "colonialists," and the enemy, Israel.

A similar orientation is used by the Kremlin propagandists toward Iran as toward Turkey, with a direct threat of nuclear destruction. The Shah is the center of attack for cooperating with the "warmongering" United States.

Another bald threat is made to Japan similar to that aimed at Turkey and Iran. The current government is held responsible for relations with the "provocative" Americans.

Those countries without United States air bases are treated with a lighter tone. There are no threats of nuclear destruction; the emphasis is laid upon the "irresponsibility" of the United States government, the "provocative and aggressive" actions of United States military circles, and "warmongering." The failure of the Summit Conference as a result of the U-2 incident is referred to in all these "tailored" subversive propaganda projections.

Yugoslavia presents a special problem to the Kremlin propagandists, since the government is composed of communists who are more loyal to Yugoslavia than to the USSR. While no threats are uttered, a particular point is made of the USSR military might, and there is the implication that association with the USSR is safe but association with the United States is dangerous.

Also, for the special consumption of the Yugoslav regime, considerable attention is given to the involvement of the Free Europe Committee, the "organization of reactionary refugees," as one of various American "channels" used to "prevent the Summit Conference." These "reactionary refugees" the USSR and Yugoslavia share as a common burden.

To Greece, where the Kremlin communist party was once legally active but is now outlawed, stress is laid on the connection between "the United States propaganda machine" slandering the "peaceful policy of the USSR" and the government in power in Athens. ". . . the Greek people are fed with the provocative noise made by the cold warmongers."

The long-range propaganda line in India is calm. No vituperation is used, because the propagandists wish to cater to the pacifist sensibilities of the Indian people. Routine appeals for "complete and general disarmament," for peace and for national independence for all peoples, take advantage of the audience's recent "colonial" past. Anti-American slander in a moralizing tone uses such terms in describing us as "cynicism," "international banditry," "gangsterism," which are "an insult to the people's conscience."

For Indonesia, the Kremlin propagandists compare Powers with a soldier of fortune of American nationality who was arrested for flying a plane for the rebel forces. They hold the United States government responsible for both actions. ". . . the new-type American colonialists, together with the British and Dutch colonialists, have inspired and sponsored the rebellion in Indonesia."

To the Australians and New Zealanders, similar to Americans in background, the attack has been centered on the decadence of our type of society. The same moralizing name-calling is used as in India. The U-2 flight is said to have been made for the purpose of nuclear weapons testing. "What do they [Americans] care about reputation, honor, and prestige?"

For South Africa that aspect of American foreign policy which favors the emerging black nations in the continent of Africa is given the center of propaganda attention. Herter is compared to Dulles in opposing relaxation of international tension. "Thus the infernal machine of warmongers was put into action which torpedoed the Paris meeting."

Anti-American sentiment is the point of departure for Argentina. "Militarists in Wall Street, the Pentagon, the White House" and the Frondizi government, which is anti-Kremlin, are coupled in the attack. The Organization of American States and the South Atlantic Pact are "imposed by U.S. Imperialism" which is "aiming at turning the cold war into a hot war."

Radio Moscow did not have a Cuban program at the time of the U-2 incident and its aftermath, but the Kremlin agents in Cuba were active over local radio and television stations which had been appropriated by Castro. They claimed that the United States was provoking a third World War, compared the U-2 incident with private American pilots flying nongovernment planes over Cuba, referred to "His Majesty Eisenhower I" and "Nikita," and said that the USSR could match with rockets on the borders of the United States the aggressive actions the United States was taking on USSR borders.

In one short-wave broadcast Radio Moscow tied up the U-2 incident with the United States "action" in Cuba.

> Everybody remembers the piratical invasion of Soviet airspace by the U-2, the torpedoing of the summit conferences by the United States, and the breaking up of the Geneva disarmament talks by the same people. United States policy has been exposed before the whole world as a policy of treachery, lawlessness, and the trampling underfoot of all the foundations of international law.
>
> The bold and resolute policy of the Soviet Union tore the repulsive, hypocritical mask from the face of Washington and showed the whole world its true gangster's countenance. . . .
>
> Washington is also active in Latin America, where it is making every effort to snuff out the popular liberation movement in Cuba to again put its noose around the necks of the freedom-loving people of Cuba. But the Cuban people are not alone in their struggle. They have the solidarity of all freedom-loving peoples, and the great Soviet power with them.

CHAPTER 2.

Subversion by Delusion

A foolish consistency is the hobgoblin of little minds, adored by little statesmen and philosophers and divines.

RALPH WALDO EMERSON, *Essays* (first series), "Self-Reliance"

People have always been and they always will be stupid victims of deceit and self-deception in politics, until they learn behind every kind of moral, religious, political, social phrase, declaration and promise to seek out the interests of this or that class or classes.

NIKOLAI LENIN, *The Three Sources and Three Constituent Parts of Marxism*

TARGET: UNITED STATES DEFENSE PROGRAM

IF THE Kremlin propagandists can maneuver us into reducing our military strength to a position below that of the USSR, they will have accomplished their most important assignment. United States military hardware is the one existing force that stands in the way of USSR aggression in both warfare and propaganda.

USSR officials fear its use in retaliation for their expansion by arms and also for their expansion by propaganda. They demonstrated their apprehension in 1956 by calling off their bluff to fly "volunteers" to Suez, by failing to provide substantial military as well as "technical" assistance to Lumumba in the Congo, and by withdrawing in confusion their rocket rattling at us over Castro in Cuba in 1960.

Consequently the prime target in the United States is our defense policy and program. To maneuver our government into modifying its policy and limiting its defense programs, the Kremlin propagandists conduct "disarmament" drives aimed at our public to bring pressure to bear on Congress and the administration to reduce our armaments, cut the size of our armed forces, and curtail or stall the development of our military potential. "Disarmament" is linked with "peace" and the USSR is referred to as a "peace lover," in that contrapuntal theme in which we are labeled "warmongers."

At the end of World War II the Kremlin propagandists, through their agents in this country, lent support to the campaign of American mothers to bring the boys home as part of their "peace" offensive, while the Kremlin militarists increased the USSR military build-up as rapidly as possible. Mutual trust, peace, and disarmament were for the other fellow. I can recall vividly—because then I was shocked—the wail of the United States Army colonel who was left in charge of the remains of our military establishment in Bucharest when the forces were withdrawn on September 15, 1947:

"It's a crime to pull even our token representation out of here . . . and demobilize! We're going to have to fight the Russians someday, so why not fight now, while we have the advantage. Mark my word—one of these days their German scientists will catch up with our German scientists, and then there'll be hell to pay!'"

The cynicism behind these superficially worthy "peace" enterprises is revealed in the bible of The System of the Kremlin, the proclamations by the Comintern. As early as 1928 the Kremlin Comintern held that the disarmament policy of the USSR must be utilized for purposes of agitation, to recruit sympathizers for the Russian Soviet Republic, to carry on propaganda among the masses, to expose "the imperialists," and to "eradicate all pacifist illusions" about them.

At the same time it was stated that not a single communist thought for a moment that "the imperialists" would accept the USSR disarmament proposals that grew out of this policy.

Not only are the persistence and duplicity of this propaganda line impressive, but so is the vastness of its implementation in the United States. Countless organizations, people, and media of communications virtually saturate our society with "peace," USSR "peaceful coexistence," and U.S.A. "disarmament." The Kremlin seeks to exploit, both directly and indirectly, the mechanism of representative government in our free society.

Whenever its propagandists find a statement by an influential American that fits into their line, they quote us against ourselves; whether the quotation is in context or not is a minor consideration. Dr. Linus Pauling, the Nobel Prize-winning physicist, is one of their more consistent and prolific references; his declarations are carried by nearly all Kremlin media.

The "disarmament" campaign (and others as well) is conducted by a number of organizations. They include Radio Moscow, the TASS News Agency and Kremlin publishing enterprises in Moscow and in the outside world, the propaganda units of the USSR Embassy in Washington and of the USSR mission to the United Nations in New York, the United States communist party, the Soviet-American Friendship Society, a dozen international "front" organizations, and countless national "front" groups set up as American outfits. These organizations have at their disposition short-wave broadcasting from Moscow, news services, a special magazine for our general public, press releases, and special bulletins, pamphlets, and periodicals—some well disguised—to reach different segments of our society. In these operations, coordination is established with the propaganda efforts of the governments of the captive nations of Eastern Europe and their diplomatic representatives in this country.

The Kremlin propagandists trade upon the desire of all human beings for peace and the vestiges of American national suspicion of foreign commitments that may entail military involvement. They promote feelings of pacifism, ideas of neutrality, and exploit guilt and shame for past military actions, including the bombings of Hiroshima and Nagasaki.

To each specific segment they angle the general line to the particular frame of reference of its members. Each group has its own vulnerability, and all members are approached as potential sympathizers, either active or passive, conscious or unwitting, direct or indirect.

General Public as Target Audience

The Kremlin reaches the general public of the United States directly through short-wave broadcasts from Radio Moscow and the magazine *USSR,* which is published especially for the American audience. Indirectly—but overtly—it operates through publications of the communist party of the U.S.A. and of the Soviet-American Friendship Society, which is one of the network of "friends" organizations established by the USSR in countries throughout the world. Indirectly and covertly it passes the propaganda line through activities and publications or the World Peace Council and national "front" organizations. The World Peace Council was mentioned in connection with the "germ-warfare" slander campaign against our armed forces fighting in Korea.

Output: The first stage in the propaganda process presents this line laid down by the Kremlin: The USSR is in favor of "general and complete" disarmament while the West, particularly the United States, is not; in fact, she is a "warmonger." Furthermore, within the United States it is the "military circles" that are to blame for the military build-up that is the threat to the world's security.

Impact: In this second stage, the first step is to arouse the American people, stirring up their desire for peace, their fear about physical and economic security, and any guilt they may feel for earlier atomic bombing. Tendencies toward pacifism or neutrality are exploited to turn the people against the "Pentagon," the "arms manufacturers," and "Wall Street." The second step, carried on simultaneously, is to confuse the issues in the minds of Americans, to obscure the facts that the USSR built up her military power at the end of the war while the United States reduced hers and that the USSR refuses to submit to adequate inspection behind its Iron Curtain. Finally, the Kremlin propagandists promote the idea that the USSR wants disarmament, that it favors ideological and economic competition rather than war, and that it has already cut down its armed forces. Items of topical news value and "human interest" stories are used as pegs for this idea.

Follow-up: The expectation of the Kremlin is that some of its target audience will somehow, by word or action or both, bring influence or pressure to bear on leaders and decision makers here to act in a way that will undermine the defense policy and program. Demonstrations, mass meetings, official visits of Kremlin emissaries—all demanding disarmament or stressing the danger of nuclear weapons—are designed to help trigger such action after the disorientation and directed impulses have been set in motion.

The first communication to the American people is by short-wave radio from Moscow. However, this medium is not relied upon heavily to influence public opinion because only a relatively few radio enthusiasts listen to short-wave broadcasting. The main purpose of the Radio Moscow programs is to keep the American agents of the Kremlin and their auxiliaries up to date on the shifts in line regarding disarmament as a live propaganda issue.

In a recent broadcast the complete line was packed in a very short paragraph: The people of the USSR are "unanimous" in their support of the USSR government's "peaceful" foreign policy, which, despite the "adventuristic" attempts of the United States' "aggressive quarters" to return the world to the worst period of the "cold war," adheres to the position of "peaceful coexistence" and works for "relaxation of international tensions" and for settlement of the problem of "general and complete disarmament."

Also aimed at the general public is *USSR*, a high-quality picture magazine patterned after *Life* and *Holiday*. It is published in Moscow in English exclusively for circulation in the United States. Fifty thousand copies are sent here and distributed by subscription and by sale at newsstands. By reciprocal agreement we send

50,000 copies of a picture magazine called *Amerika,* published in Russian, to the USSR.

When it started in 1956, *USSR* was sharply didactic in tone. As the American reaction to preaching was negative, the tone has been modified considerably since then. However, it still instructs its readers on how to live their lives.

This paternalistic, rather dictatorial approach is used to tell us what we should think about peace and disarmament. In the first half of 1960, when the disarmament drive was stepped up, each issue carried one or more pieces on the subject. Their titles include: "Toward a World Without Armies," "An Economist Looks at Disarmament," "Soviet People on the Armed Forces Reduction," "Abolish War Forever—Soviet People Speak of War and Peace," "A Family and the War," "Lenin Peace Prize Winners ... Cyrus Eaton ..."

A third direct communications medium, which is not acknowledged by the Kremlin as such, is *The Worker,* the weekly organ of the U.S. Kremlin communist party, which until June 15, 1958, had been a daily. It is published for the general public with a special angle toward unions and workers but is used primarily to maintain contact with agents and their sympathizers.

Impact: This stage features as public enemies the "lords of Big Business," the "high military brass," the bipartisan advocates of a firm foreign policy. The latter are called partisans of the "cold war" and the arms race who are "crippling democracy," undermining our republican form of government, and "corrupting the morality" of the country. The arms race and the "so-called" foreign-aid program have become one big monopoly "payola," with the people paying.

Follow-up: Its readers are told that "these elements" must not hold back the efforts of the American people to get their government to disarm. The first step is to ban further H-bomb tests that are "poisoning the atmosphere for our children and our children's children." Then the manufacture of nuclear weapons should be prohibited and atom-bomb stockpiles destroyed. Also, the move to give West Germany and other NATO countries nuclear weapons must be halted.

The "American people now have the chance to promote peace" with Khrushchev's proposal for "total disarmament," *The Worker* states, and urges its readers to write the President that they want serious consideration given to the disarmament proposal.

"Get your neighbors, church, club, and union to pass resolutions on this to send to the President and members of Congress."

The American chapter of the international network of USSR "friendship" societies has recently been playing down its connection with the Kremlin. Its name was changed to the "National Council of Soviet-American Friendship," and it is listed as an affiliate, not a full-fledged member.

Headquarters are in New York City, but the most active affiliate is in Chicago. The accent is on culture, and Rockwell Kent has been appointed its president. This group publishes and distributes pamphlets, booklets, and press releases on "peace" and "disarmament." Its monthly bulletin on slick paper, called *American-Soviet Facts,* is placed in thirty-two hundred public, college, and university libraries and is mailed to thousands of individuals; it carries one large permanent section with the heading "Negotiations—Peace—Disarmament."

In its international magazine, *Culture and Life,* "disarmament" propaganda is introduced under the guise of culture. There has been one article or more on disarmament in every issue over the past several months.

The quaintest piece on the subject is one written by the director of Oriental studies at the USSR Academy of Science. He quoted Montesquieu, the Indian statesman Asoka (of two thousand years ago), Erasmus, Immanuel Kant, Khrushchev, and Tu Fu, one of the oldest of Chinese poets, on the evils of war and echoed the Kremlin line on the benefits which mankind would derive from the adoption of USSR disarmament proposals.

Not so quaint was a press release put out last year by Kremlin propagandists in the name of the "National Council"; it represented direct agitation and interference in our internal political affairs. In the form of a general letter, it began "Dear Friend: We hope you will agree that we must make recovery from the Paris debacle as quickly as possible." It went on about the horrors of nuclear destruction, the desirability of peace, and the urgent need for the United States to disarm, and ended with five numbered exhortations:

1. Write President Eisenhower
2. Write directly to Ambassador James J. Wadsworth, United States representative on disarmament
3. Write directly to Frederick M. Eaton, chairman of the Disarmament Commission
4. Tell your present senators and congressmen what you think
5. Send letters to local newspapers.

It ended with "Join our efforts." "Organize citizen requests." If there is no "peace" movement, "start one."

For purposes of indirect subversion, the Kremlin has selected eleven segments within all societies of advanced development and has assigned an international "front" organization to deal with each one propagandistically. They are: trade unions, youth, students, women, teachers, lawyers, scientific workers, journalists, medical workers, radio and television workers, and recently international businessmen. For each group, propaganda is prepared on the basis of each segment's special interests, just as the propaganda addressed to each country is given a definite "national" character.

These international "front" organizations maintain direct contact with the Kremlin propagandists and operate all over the world. Each one issues publications in English, which are distributed in the United States, and promotes the "peace offensive" toward disarmament of the United States. In addition, there are many offshoots of these international "fronts" established here as national "fronts," working toward the same end but in a more covert manner.

Youth

The young are targets of two international "fronts"—youth and student organizations—no doubt because they are considered the most important and the most impressionable of all audiences. It is interesting that all segments of our society are approached in direct propaganda output, except youth. Perhaps the Kremlin considers that the young mind is too sensitive to absorb with equanimity the thought that it is being singled out for influencing.

An example is given of the indirect approach to youth on the subject of disarmament. The international "front" organizations, the World Federation of Democratic Youth and the International Union of Students, publish monthly magazines, respectively, *World Youth* and *World Student News*.

Impact: In the August 1960 issue of *World Youth* a typical article was inserted on the subject of disarmament. It took the form of a letter from Khrushchev to the secretary of the organization. It employed a confidential tone to suggest the dictator was meeting the young "man to man" and assured them that he had gone to the Paris Summit Conference with the desire "to liberate humanity and the young generation" from the threat of an atomic- and hydrogen-bomb war, "but President Eisenhower had other intentions."

Khrushchev is quoted as voicing the hope that the USSR plan for "general and total disarmament" to bring a "better future for the young generation of today" would win the approval of the youth organization.

Follow-up: Khrushchev went this far in urging action: "I think, my dear young friends, that the noble role of being the most active and audacious combatants in strengthening peace falls upon you. . . ."

Journalists

Daily mimeographed releases are distributed to the press all over the United States. The most important distribution point is the USSR embassy in Washington. The releases consist of Kremlin official pronouncements, press articles published in Moscow, and special items prepared for the American public. What the embassy agents hope for is that one of our press services will pick up the release and give it country-wide distribution; and that, perhaps, some of its materials will be printed by a newspaper which has no correspondent stationed in Moscow.

Impact: A supply of good, clearly written messages which require little or no thought or editing saves labor in preparing copy; all newspapermen are overworked, some are also lazy. If the item is controversial enough it might make news, and then an important columnist may give it circulation.

Follow-up: Write, mold public opinion to favor peace in the world and disarmament at home. Also, pass on the image of the USSR as a "peace lover."

An article written by a leading USSR economist titled "Will Disarmament Lead to Economic Crisis?" was released by the USSR embassy and received the best play of any piece in recent months. Two syndicated columnists, among others, gave it a big play. One article was published in the *Congressional Record.*

The line taken by the USSR economist was that disarmament for us would actually help our economy. One columnist quoted the economist at length and chided the USSR for changing its propaganda line which had long been that disarmament is impossible for the United States because it must lead to economic crisis for us. The columnist's article was published in a Washington, D. C., newspaper among others, and the USSR embassy got additional publicity by having the economist write a letter to the editor. On the day the letter was published, this newspaper went so far as to refute some of the economist's arguments on the editorial page.

The *follow-up* was successful. The American press was put to use to spread USSR propaganda.

Businessmen

First Deputy Premier Anastas I. Mikoyan was sent as trade commissar to the United States. His avowed purpose was to meet with business leaders and arrange for an increase in trade between the two countries; he held that disarmament and concentration of investment in "peaceful" enterprises would be profitable for them.

Impact: "Trade can strengthen peace; peace can make a proper atmosphere for trade," he declared.

To an industrialist in Detroit he explained that the USSR wished the end of the arms race so as to speed up the process of producing a car for every worker in the USSR, just as we were doing in Detroit.

To Henry Ford II he said, "... your grandfather decided to recognize us. He helped build our industry. He was smarter than your government."

He added that as a result of his visit he could see "now" that American businessmen would not want a new war because their plants would be destroyed.

When he returned to New York the deputy premier told 1,100 American businessmen at a testimonial dinner: "There was a time when you knew what you could sell to us, but during the Cold War you have apparently forgotten ... while you ponder, we are placing our orders in other countries." He suggested that American businessmen should put pressure on their government for free trade now. He added that the American business people want peace, but the constructive proposals which the USSR advances for peace "meet from you a nyet, nyet, nyet."

Follow-up: Induce American businessmen for the sake of profits to pressure the government to cut down the use of American business production for arms in favor of trade with the USSR.

Labor Unions

Through the *New Times* the Kremlin reaches labor unions. This weekly magazine is also aimed at socialists and is similar in format to the American periodical the *New Leader*. Articles which recently appeared include "Victor Perlo on the American Economy," "The Armaments Business" (featuring Du Pont and General Dynamics), "Hiroshima—a Symbol."

The *New Times,* as well as other Kremlin publications, uses an

American economist named Victor Perlo, who evidently has taken up permanent residence in the USSR. He is described as "a well-known specialist in statistics and economics," a former "young government expert," author of *American Imperialism, The Empire of High Finance,* and coauthor of *The Dollars and Sense of Disarmament.*

Impact: In a recent feature article Mr. Perlo both asked the questions and answered them on the economics of disarmament in the United States for the benefit of the "working class." He asked if there have been any serious studies in the "business press" or by "bourgeois economists" of what effect disarmament or arms reduction is likely to have on American industry "and individual branches thereof."

And he answered "yes," and added that they all had concluded improved economic conditions were likely to accompany disarmament or could be guaranteed by appropriate policies. He claimed the failure of the "working class" to take the lead in fighting for both disarmament and a "pro-labor program" to accompany it, made it possible for the "most belligerent circles" to carry through their drive for a renewed policy of "provocation and war preparation" which would be detrimental to the interests of the "working class."

Follow-up: The element of agitation is found in the accusation against American labor unions in the above passage. They should fight for disarmament and a "pro-labor" program. The unions don't have to be told *how* to "fight"; they know the efficacy of public appeals, pressure on Congress, etc.

Women

Direct contact is established by Moscow with women's groups in this country through the monthly magazine *Soviet Woman.* It is said to be devoted to social and political problems, literature, and art. Articles include such titles as "Hands Off Cuba and the Congo" and again "Hiroshima . . . a Reminder" plus another piece by Victor Perlo.

Impact: In the June 1960 issue the first page proclaimed June 11 as International Children's Day, and the back cover carried a photograph of a child with doves. The title was, "May the skies above him always be peaceful." The lead article was titled, "Not Words, but Deeds," with subtitle, "American Women in the Fight for World Peace," by Anna Darkwood, who was identified as an American. She quoted from an article in the Negro weekly, the *Los Angeles Tribune,* in which it was stated that propagandists were trying to "refreeze" the "cold war" after Khrushchev's visit, and that if we were to win the peace the little people in America must do it. The quotation continued to say that there was no doubt that the "prowar" forces in the United States were trying to "brain-wash" the American people, but the desire "to end the manufacture of all war materials" was gaining momentum.

Follow-up: Another article by an American woman agitated for action, stating it was the "sacred duty" of American women, especially mothers, to demand that "our soldiers" be called home from all foreign bases. (This is reminiscent of the Kremlin action after the end of World War II.) She suggested they raise their voices in churches and parent-teacher associations to demand the end of nuclear tests, the banning of the bomb, and total disarmament. She ended by saying 31,000,000 American women were eligible to vote in the November 1960 presidential elections and thus urged them to use their influence through their ballots.

Religious Groups

The Kremlin propagandists have even put the Russian Orthodox Church to work to carry out their disarmament campaign in the United States. They had an appeal spread by a press release from the USSR embassy in Washington which quoted from *Izvestia.*

Impact: The press release read in part:

> To us Orthodox Christians of the Soviet Union this proposal of our government represents an expression of the sincere desire to deliver mankind from the threat of a new world war. We see in this plan a true way for a real

improvement of international relations which are continually darkened by the fatal competition in armaments.

Reading the plan for disarmament, we Christians cannot help recalling the Old Testament prophecy of Isaiah about the time when the peoples "will beat swords into ploughshares and spears into sickles."

The fact that the Soviet proposal for general and complete disarmament is in harmony with Christian faith offers encouraging hope that the Western Powers will carry it out in the spirit of Christian trust.

It then called the proposal the outstanding event of our time, praised Khrushchev, appealed to the Western Powers, prayed to the Lord for peace, quoted from Isaiah 2:4:

Nation shall not lift up sword against nation, neither shall they learn war any longer.

and from Matthew 5:9:

Blessed are the peacemakers for they shall be called the children of God.

Follow-up: In the body of the appeal there were two paragraphs which suggested that the word of the Orthodox churches should be used, first, to remind the Christian world that destruction of human beings is incompatible with the Christian religion, and, second, to influence the will of the people for general disarmament so they can "find support in heavenly love."

The Kremlin atheists will even quote the Scriptures if it suits their propaganda purposes.

TARGET: UNITED STATES FOREIGN POLICY

The policy of peaceful coexistence in its social essence is a form of vigorous economic, political, and ideological struggle of the proletariat against the aggressive forces of imperialism in the international arena.

KHRUSHCHEV, speech before Party organization of highest party school, Academy of Social Sciences, and the Institute of Marxism–Leninism. (*Kommunist* No. 1, 1961)

The second most important target in this country for Kremlin propaganda is our foreign policy. The objective is to paralyze any action of the United States in the political field abroad which would compete with the USSR for world power or would deter her from world domination. The Kremlin propagandists' techniques of confusion and delusion are aimed directly at our general public, as in the case of the disarmament campaign, but also indirectly, at our foreign policy advisors, formulators, and implementers, both in and outside the federal government.

Their outstanding successes are to be found in 1955 at Geneva, when our experts succumbed to the "Spirit of Geneva"; in 1956, when fear of "provoking the Russians" to nuclear irresponsibility not only prevented adoption of proposals for military intervention in Hungary but also muted our propaganda attacks; in 1959, when the "Spirit of Geneva" was revived at Camp David, and Khrushchev was accepted for a time by the public as a demi-American; in 1960, when Castro was allowed to enter the fatal embrace of the current dictator; in early 1961, when we were maneuvered into backing neutralism in Laos and turning a cold shoulder to pro-Western elements in the Congo.

The campaign which the Kremlin propagandists have used to attempt to delude our statesmen, politicians, working diplomats, analysts of international affairs, commentators, and general public is summed up in the slogan "peaceful coexistence." This line has been hardy enough to survive mass murder in Hungary, threats over the U-2 incident of nuclear destruction to our allies who permit our military bases on their territory, sabotage of the Summit Conference, subversive political backing of Lumumba, and threats to the United States over both the U-2 and Cuba.

The slogan "peaceful coexistence" is accepted as a loose concept by the noncommunist world and is therefore a handy instrument for Kremlin propagandists; it is subject to many interpretations depending, generally, on which particular aspect a noncommunist is induced to emphasize. Because we are fatigued by World War II and horrified at the prospect of World War III, many of us Americans are inclined to accept at face value the suggestions of the Kremlin propagandists that it is a "live-and-let-live" plank in the USSR foreign-policy platform.

This delusion is not dispelled when we are faced squarely with the slogan clearly defined by the Kremlin out of the other side of its collective mouth. To the world of communism the current regime says "peaceful coexistence" stands for "intensification of the ideological struggle." Those initiated into the jargon understand by this that all methods of propaganda or political activation are to be stepped up—agitation, infiltration, bribery, forgery, murder, subversion, revolution, civil war, to name a few—any activity which stops short of starting World War III. The "ideological struggle" aspect is no debating-society exercise, as many of us are learning, while "peaceful coexistence" with the United States means merely the absence of our firing shots—or bombs—directly at each other.

Actually, "peaceful coexistence" was taken by Khrushchev from historical Comintern and Lenin proclamations and cultivated assiduously until it grew from an idea to a slogan, then to the semblance of a policy position and, finally, to a dynamic, aggressive weapon in propaganda.

Khrushchev also uses it as a trade mark to place the badge of "responsible world citizen" on himself and to whitewash the black image of the USSR left to the world by Stalin. Using this image of "Khrushchev the Responsible Statesman," Kremlin propagandists try to take in our foreign policy specialists by the subtle—and hope-inspiring—suggestions of the Kremlin's desire for relaxation of tensions. Actually, Khrushchev's image and the "peaceful coexistence" slogan are integral parts of the Kremlin's propaganda strategy.

The argument the propagandists advance is that the alternatives to Khrushchev, such as another Stalin, or some member of the "anti-party" group such as Molotov, or Mao Tse-tung are far

less attractive. They suggest that Khrushchev is less likely to
trigger nuclear destruction than any probable replacement; they
present him as a restraining influence in the world of communism.
They state that "peaceful coexistence" is preferable to its contrapuntal Leninist theme—"war is inevitable" with capitalist
countries. They draw upon our specialists' memories of the Stalin
era and hold that the present "coexistence" is the most peaceful
one we can expect from the USSR.

The fact is that the complementary, competing slogan—"war is
inevitable" with capitalist countries—is far more honest than
"peaceful coexistence" in its implications to the Free World.
The West, and particularly the United States, can grasp the concept of "war" as an area of conflict and competition, but not so
the concept of "peace."

The combination of deliberate delusion on the part of the
Kremlin propagandists and of habitual, optimistic wishful thinking on the part of our general public, makes "peaceful coexistence"
seem almost friendly, when in fact the Kremlin has signed our
death warrant just as irrevocably as if it had promised us nuclear
destruction. "We will bury you," said Khrushchev, and the graves
he had in mind are just as ominous for us whether they are dug in
the ground or in our own minds. Therefore, we are more vulnerable today under the threat of "peaceful coexistence" as the
Kremlin weapon of subversion than we were when the dictator
in the USSR was Stalin, or would be if China should gain the
ascendancy with its slogan "war is inevitable."

To understand the true intentions behind the "peaceful coexistence" line it is necessary to go back to the historical statements which constitute the bible of The System. As pointed out
above, they are binding on this reactionary Kremlin dictatorship.

As early as 1918 the prophet Lenin stated that "international
imperialism" (meaning: Western democracy) could not, under any
circumstances, on any condition, live side by side with the Soviet
Republic. A year later he said the existence of the Soviet Republic side by side with "imperialist states" for a long time was
unthinkable. To settle all doubts, he added that "as soon as we

are strong enough to defeat capitalism as a whole, we shall immediately take it by the scruff of the neck." His coexistence was
hardly peaceful.

Stalin in 1927 went a bit further. He suggested peaceful relations for an ulterior purpose and acknowledged coexistence, but
he did not put them together. The maintenance of peaceful relations with capitalist countries—and the postponing of war
("which is inevitable")—"is an obligatory task for us, until we
become strong enough," and here he quoted Lenin. The basis of
his country's relations with capitalist countries consisted in "admitting the coexistence of the opposed systems." The following
year the Comintern read this "policy" into the record and added
that it was merely another, and under prevailing conditions a
more advantageous, way of fighting capitalism.

Without abandoning these fundamental beliefs, Stalin presented an "interpretation" in 1936 for purposes of deluding our
foreign policy specialists into considering the transitional "coexistence" period as a continuing condition. He said that "American democracy and the Soviet system can exist peacefully side by
side and compete with each other. But the one cannot evolve into
American democracy and vice versa."

His actions hardly sustained this line, as we all know, and he
did not see fit to build up "peaceful coexistence" as an important
propaganda tool or slogan. Perhaps in the days when the USSR
was not a military threat to the world's security reassurance to
the world as to its peaceful intentions was not considered propagandistically necessary.

It was this "interpretation" for which Khrushchev reached back
nearly twenty years later to develop into the slogan "peaceful
coexistence." His chore was a difficult one because the two different meanings he projected of "live and let live" and "intensification of the ideological struggle" were contradictory and mutually
exclusive. However, he found inspiration in Pavlov's discoveries
to create the necessary "frame of reference" to apply successfully
"peaceful coexistence" to both the noncommunist world and the
world of communism at the same time. On the international scene

the current dictator varied the "carrot" with the "stick"—the positive with the negative signals—thus trying to condition the reflexes of the world.

He stage-managed the "Spirit of Geneva" and then attacked us for allegedly inciting the Hungarian Revolution; promoted the Camp David Spirit and threatened us with rockets over the U-2 incident; torpedoed the Paris Summit Conference and sought a new one with President Kennedy. The result is that a few of us to a great degree, and many of us to a limited degree, rely upon his "interpretation" of his "policy" rather than upon our own logic to analyze and judge it. Because we tend to be confused and to depend upon him, we respond spontaneously to his most recent statement regardless of whether it contradicts an earlier one, and we do not always discount either statement because of its inconsistency. Thus, we are susceptible to his direction of our behavior.

Added to this method of propaganda application is the force of Khrushchev's personality propaganda in which he seeks to induce us to explain away his warlike threats as his personal irritability of the moment and to give serious consideration to professions of "peaceful coexistence" as statements of USSR policy.

The propagandists have written their copy on "peaceful co-existence" primarily for Khrushchev to mouth. Thanks to their gradual build-up he is associated in the minds of the world with this "policy." Also he carries the most impressive titles, and is his own best public relations man. A retrospective look at some of his statements will show the cleverness of the techniques of delusion by implications, suggestions, deliberately and falsely shaded nuances of meanings. It will also reveal that the dictates of the bible of The System have not, in fact, been abandoned.

In 1955 he saw that "The Spirit" at Geneva was spread abroad as part of his "policy" of "peaceful coexistence." Then lest any of the Kremlin agents get the impression that he had stopped or slowed down the attack by subversion on free societies, he added a balancing statement to be translated from the jargon. "We will never renounce the ... struggle for victory of communism" he pontificated, and added that people who thought the USSR had done so, misunderstood the "Geneva Spirit." He elaborated further that his country was not violating this "spirit" by refusing to "disarm ideologically."

On August 1, 1956, he claimed he was doing "everything necessary" for the "peaceful coexistence" of the two systems and of eliminating the possibility of an outbreak of war.

There was no need to balance off this "carrot" by "stick." Three months later the crushing of the Hungarian Revolution reassured the agents that the "struggle" was being intensified at the top of the Kremlin hierarchy. "Peaceful coexistence" was invoked for consumption by the noncommunist world as a warning to us to keep out—it was stated to be "the noninterference in the internal affairs of other countries." It was also clarified that "peaceful coexistence" did not apply to relations between the Kremlin and the captive states inside its empire.

In 1958 the Kremlin propagandists put together one simple sentence which is a gem because it packs within its few words the "stick" of war, the "carrot" of peace, the delusion of "ideas" competition, and agitation directives for the initiated. "It is not an army, but peace that is required to propagate communist ideas, disseminate them, and establish them in the minds of men."

During the same year Khrushchev made a statement for the consumption of noncommunists which implied that the USSR was dropping the "ideological struggle." He said that every government which correctly realizes its responsibility for the future of peace must put itself above ideological differences. But then perhaps he meant every *other* government, since in *Foreign Affairs* as an advance build-up to his visit to this country the next year, the Kremlin propagandists wrote an article for his signature which said that the "main thing is to keep to the positions of ideological struggle, without resorting to arms to prove that one is right." An added observation looked like a direct quotation from Stalin in 1927: "It is high time to understand that ... two diametrically opposed social and economic systems exist in the world today side by side. ..."

Immediately after the "good-will" tour of this country and the Camp David "peaceful coexistence" demonstration, Khrushchev sought to clear the atmosphere for the Kremlin agents and affiliates by addressing the Supreme Soviet. He explained solemnly that mutual concessions in the interest of "peaceful coexistence" must not be confused with concessions of principle or ideology: in this there could be neither concessions nor adaptation.

In early 1960 the current dictator proclaimed blandly that all must see to it that "peaceful coexistence" (his "policy") shall be transferred from a mere absence of war into active cooperation among all states "in our sphere of" economics, culture, and science.

But the "stick" came in a message primarily for Kremlin communist party members in the theoretical journal *Kommunist* signed by V. Moskovsky. "Peaceful coexistence," he explained, was not the tranquil parallel development of socialism (communism) and capitalism. It was a most acute economic and ideological struggle between them, a struggle not only for supremacy in the development of productive forces, but also for the winning over of the millions of the minds and hearts of the toilers of the whole world.

With the U-2 incident, the torpedoing of the Paris Summit Conference, and the current dictator's shoe-banging sideshow at the United Nations General Assembly, "peaceful coexistence" was explained and re-explained, just as it had been done in the previous five years. In the final reckoning it came to signify the nature of things as the Kremlin propagandists and their principal actor want the world to think they are, in any situation at any time.

Of all the specific issues in our foreign policy at which the Kremlin has aimed the propaganda slogan "peaceful coexistence" and utilized the "carrot-and-stick" method of delusion, Cuba currently is the most enlightening. The reasons are that it is closest to home, has disproven the theory that conquest by Kremlin propaganda requires military intervention, and has succeeded in fooling some of our top foreign policy analysts.

It will be recalled that the USSR severed diplomatic relations with Cuba in 1952 when Havana customs officials refused entry to two USSR couriers who would not reveal the contents of their luggage. In 1956 Premier Bulganin announced the USSR willingness to reopen diplomatic and trade relations with countries of Latin America. This was an effort to persuade the Cuban people that coexistence was not impossible. In November of that year even Herbert L. Matthews, *New York Times* expert, called the Castro movement socialistic, nationalistic, anti-Yankee, "radical, democratic, therefore anticommunist."

In 1958 a leading Kremlin official set 1959 as the year for serious penetration of Latin America and from January 1959 until April 1960 sixteen articles of "guidance" to agents in Latin America were published in the *World Marxist Review*. Following the 21st CPSU Congress in Moscow, January–February 1959, communist delegates from nineteen Latin American countries met with Soviet representatives to work out in detail a campaign for promoting communism in Latin America.

The principal line of strategy and tactics developed at the Moscow meeting included the decisions: (1) to merge communist propaganda and activities with nationalistic and neutralist movements wherever that could be done; (2) to set up a common political "front" with these movements, where feasible; (3) to stress communist "front" activities, especially where the communist party is banned; and (4) to concentrate on winning control of student, youth, women's, and labor organizations.

It was also agreed at the Moscow meeting that Latin American communists for the most part should remain in the background in areas where there is friction to give the impression that such outbreaks were spontaneous expressions of nationalism. At the same time, the communists were instructed to promote and exploit "anti-colonial" and "anti-imperialist" demonstrations against the United States.

Further, Latin American communist "front" organizations were to emphasize the "popular" and "democratic" aspects of communist regimes and picture them as the true exponents of "peace in the world." This propaganda line was designed to counter the adverse effects on Latin American public opinion resulting from Soviet intervention in Hungary; and, later, Communist China's aggressive policies in Tibet, on the Indian frontier, and in Southeast Asia.

In 1959, two months after he became premier, Castro declared, "I have said very clearly that we are not communists," denied that Cuba would be neutral in a conflict between the West and the USSR, and implied that she would support the West.

This same soft, misleading line was proclaimed by Khrushchev in January 9, 1960: "We consider that it is impossible to impose on other peoples something they object to, something they do not want. The communists are convinced that no ideology, communist ideology included, can be introduced forcibly, by war, by bayonets. But there is yet another side to the matter, which the ideologists of imperialism are also endeavoring to conceal. No state frontiers can stem the spread of communist ideology, the teaching of Marxism-Leninism." Then he went on to list Latin American countries among the underdeveloped, semi-colonial countries of the world, exploited by imperialists and colonialists, and to say that the USSR in its policy of "peaceful coexistence" would champion the interests of these downtrodden peoples.

A joint communiqué was issued in Havana by Castro and Mikoyan the next month following a sugar contract which said in part: "... there was expressly set forth the interest of both governments in actively collaborating, in the United Nations Organization, in favor of coexistence, cooperation, and friendship of all the peoples of the earth. The two parties considered that the consolidation of world peace depends, in notable measure, on the development of the most ample and effective international collaboration, on the basis of complete mutual respect, and the inalienable right of every nation freely to decide its own political, economic, and social structure."

By May of that year the USSR and Cuba resumed diplomatic relations and Castro's government announced that active anti-communism was "divisive" and "counterrevolutionary." At this point the "stick," the harder line, was applied, and after the Summit Conference fiasco Khrushchev said, ". . . and we are happy to hear the pulse of Latin America's struggle for independence against American imperialism . . . I can but welcome events in Cuba . . . I am convinced that the other Latin American countries will also rise up in the struggle for their independence."

To strengthen the backbone of his agents in Cuba, Khrushchev followed up three months later with his strongest backing to Castro and his strongest threat against the United States. He said the peoples of the USSR should help their brothers, the Cubans, against American imperialists and monopolists, that the USSR would "do everything to support Cuba," and "no one will succeed in enslaving the Cuban people." Then he added that the United States was not at "an unreachable distance from the USSR" and Soviet artillerymen . . . "can with their rocket power support the Cuban people . . . that is, if you like, a warning. . . ."

At this point another American foreign policy expert, Walter Lippmann, felt impelled to observe that the Latin American states feared our intervention more than Russia's, "which as yet is only talk . . . we shall have to live with the Cuban revolution, just as Britain has had to live with the revolution in Egypt and Iraq."

By August, when the regime in Cuba was well entrenched and the United States had declared that she would "take definite action" if Cuba should fall under the control of international communism, the tactic by the Kremlin was changed to the "carrot" line.

Khrushchev declared that the USSR policy was aimed at supporting "everything honest and sacred that fights for independence and the happiness of the peoples." The USSR embassy in Washington added in its press release:

> These words of the head of the Soviet government reveal the lofty purpose of Soviet policy toward Cuba. The Soviet people admire the courageous struggle waged by the Cuban people who are upholding the independence of their country and the gains of the Revolution.

It goes without saying that no concoctions concerning Soviet-Cuban relations can change the friendly nature of these relations. They will continue to grow and strengthen in the interests of the peoples of both countries, in the interests of world peace.

Mikoyan then denied that the USSR was interfering in Cuban affairs and in October Khrushchev "clarified" his previous rocket-rattling threats against the United States by calling them "symbolic." The next month the Kremlin retreated even further. According to the *New York Times,* Castro was told to stop rattling USSR rockets at the United States and was warned that USSR relations with the new administration of President-elect Kennedy counted for more than the Cuban problem.

When the United States broke off diplomatic relations with Cuba in January, TASS denounced the move as "far beyond the limits of diplomatic maneuvering" and assured the Cubans that the USSR was their sincere and unselfish friend and would not leave them "in the lurch."

This retreat and disassociation from identification with dominating Cuba through Castro were spelled out in *Pravda* in February 1961. Under the title "The Only Sensible Way to Coexistence," it commented on President Kennedy's State of the Union report and set forth the complete Kremlin line: "... and how strange it is to read, after all that, in the address that 'communist agents' are allegedly setting up bases in Cuba.... In his address Kennedy repeats fabrications about some nonexistent agents in Latin America. Why revive these dead myths? A repetition of these fabrications is not a sensible course."

On the same day *Izvestia* in an article, "Search for Means of Easing International Tensions," observed:

"... No one is threatening to attack the U.S.A. There is no threat anywhere to the national interests of the United States Government."

However, it took the *Baltimore Sun* to place this political-propaganda situation in really correct perspective. It observed that the attitude of the Kremlin leaders appeared to be that party and government affairs are distinct and different. "While they hope for better state-to-state relations, they believe the United States should overlook those party vows which pledge the destruction of capitalism and therefore the United States."

TARGET: UNITED STATES GOVERNMENT ORGANIZATION

"It is not for nothing that the proverb says 'an obliging bear is more dangerous than an enemy' . . ."

STALIN

Every four years the democracy of the United States is vulnerable. The citizens pause to appraise the two major parties which are trying to place their candidates in the White House. During the months leading up to the primaries, the conventions and then the campaigns, a long, penetrating gaze is directed at the party of the administration, at its record since the previous election, and, consequently, at the organization of the federal government itself. Unlike other countries where politics is a year-round preoccupation, the United States pays serious notice only periodically, but when it does, minds are extraordinarily inquisitive and sensitive to impression.

The Kremlin propagandists, well aware of our quadrennial vulnerability, launched in 1959–60 a major propaganda campaign which lasted until November 7, the cutoff date. Their objective was to shake the faith of the electorate, of the American population at large, in the capacity of the government organization in Washington to cope with today's critical problems in world affairs.

This campaign was a sort of gamble. It represented the most daring attack ever launched on this country and suggested that there are no limits to the Kremlin's subversive designs. The approach was to denigrate the present incumbent and to undermine the office of the presidency, then to cast doubt on his successor, whoever he might be.

A two-phased "carrot-and-stick" propaganda operation was set in motion; the first half, all "carrot," was aimed at taking in the American people emotionally and the second, all "stick," at frightening them into compliance. To begin with, Kremlin propagandists built up Khrushchev in a personality propaganda drive so that all our leaders would appear to suffer by comparison. Then they mixed rocket rattling with an attempt to assassinate the character of President Eisenhower and later to portray Kennedy and Nixon as unworthy of the trust of the great American people.

When the propaganda campaign was concluded, the Kremlin propagandists had suggested or stated outright that the office of the presidency of the United States was too equivocal to lead the world, whereas the combination of three positions held by the current dictator was unswerving and made for more secure world leadership; Eisenhower had failed as the "man of peace," whereas Khrushchev had succeeded because of superior personal qualities; and neither Kennedy nor Nixon could be expected to match the mature judgment, the wisdom in world leadership, of the current dictator.

The first step the Kremlin propagandists needed to take was to get Khrushchev an invitation to visit the United States. Some of our foreign policy experts felt that, on balance, a visit to this country by Khrushchev would be a bargain price to pay for a visit by President Eisenhower to the USSR. And it might well have been, if the Kremlin invitation for a return visit had been sincere.

In 1959 President Eisenhower was at the peak of his symbolic position as "man of peace," and he was most sincere in his desire to explore all possibilities for re-establishing the kind of peace we knew prior to World War II. It was in keeping with his desire for peace that he should want to take what he considered an ultimate step toward this end. So, he not only invited the USSR dictator to visit this country, but received him warmly, and thus furnished him at the outset with a status-raising endorsement as a world figure.

Meanwhile, the USSR embassy in Washington was busily at work to be certain the red carpet laid out for their dictator spread as far as possible across our land. Embassy personnel advised the Kremlin propagandists on articles for inclusion in the magazine *USSR*. On the cover of the issue dedicated to the visit his smoothed-out, touched-up portrait in color appeared under the legend: "N. S. Khrushchev: We Go to the U.S.A. with an Open Heart." His photograph was printed on the reverse side of the cover with Vice President Nixon, then alone in the lead story "Outstanding International Event," and forty times in the next twenty pages. There is no question, judging by these picture stories, that he was presented as all things to all people.

The USSR embassy also produced a thirty-two page pamphlet of sycophantic eulogy which was distributed across the nation in untold numbers of copies. In it this deluding statement is attributed to Khrushchev:

> We proceed from the fact that reciprocal visits by states-men and public leaders . . . make an atmosphere which warms body and soul, and creates an opportunity to live without fear for the future, to exclude war and establish peaceful coexistence.

Aiding the USSR embassy in Washington were their United Nations mission press and cultural attachés in New York, members of the local communist party, leaders and auxiliaries in the front organizations, infiltrators in our mass media communications in-dustry—and, unwittingly, our noncommunist free press. Among them they built up a campaign for Khrushchev along lines re-sembling in many ways those to be followed shortly by the senator and the vice president. Although that of the current dictator lasted only twelve days against about three months for the pres-idential candidates, he managed to dwarf them on several propa-ganda counts: Of course, he was running for an office higher than they were—that of president-maker.

The plan for this particular maneuver centered on having Khrushchev make a deep enough impression on the electorate to stand out as a political issue. The first step was to project his image deeply into our national affairs and let him "sell" himself through his personal public relations efforts. Once he managed to figure prominently in our public awareness as a world leader, he would pressure the voters into basing their choice of candidate on an estimate of the candidate's ability to "get along with Khrushchev" or to "stand up to Khrushchev." In either case, both Kennedy and Nixon would have to campaign on the issue of Khrushchev, and the aggregate effect would be greater influence for the USSR and lowered comparative respect for the government organization in Washington. Had this been accomplished it would have been a simple matter for the Kremlin propagandists to use Khrushchev as a continuing mouthpiece for propaganda subversion of our system of government.

But their task was not easy. The man whom the Kremlin propagandists were building up had been a Stalinist in his own right and a mass liquidator of human beings in both the Ukraine and Hungary. They did their best to play down his past and concentrate on his present role.

As a means of paving his way to serious consideration they pointed to his rank, to his accumulated titles of chief of state, secretary (and head) of the Kremlin Communist party, and chairman of the Council of Ministers—and they succeeded. The American public was impressed. They were also impressed by the fact that a chief of state from the USSR was paying them a visit for the first time.

As Khrushchev took off from the USSR to the United States, the first Lunik took off to the moon. He said the timing was a coincidence, but the Kremlin propagandists had carefully planned for the dramatization of the dictator's visit. Not only was he going to get the headlines, but so was the might of the USSR. Scientific progress, advance in education, and the military future of the USSR were daily stressed in the columns of the American press alongside every detail of Khrushchev's movements. The timing is an excellent example of the tricks of the Kremlin propaganda trade.

When Khrushchev arrived in this country, he lost no time putting his personality to work to create the illusion that he possessed the stature of a world leader. He sought to display himself as the strong, amicable, flexible, powerful, down-to-earth, benevolent, president type who came from peasant stock. He used those demagogic antics which have proven effective for both ward heelers in the United States and dictators in the USSR. He wanted to show himself as partly American, and in this he was given a major assist by President Eisenhower. On his arrival in Washington, Khrushchev was able to have his photograph taken with the President in amicable good fellowship of the heart-warming American variety. This association, acceptance, and image of cooperation between the United States and the USSR helped him to establish himself most favorably in the hearts and minds of the people of America—and the world at large. It also permitted him to carry with him on his tour of our country some of the aura of the beguiling Eisenhower charm to the President's idolizing electorate.

His success in deluding our people about himself can be surmised from the following composite remark put together from comments I heard when Khrushchev took his departure:

"Why can't we have a colorful, vital, interesting candidate like Khrushchev? He is so like us; if he were only an American!"

Just as beguiling and deluding as his personality was the line Khrushchev spun out along the countryside. On arriving at New York he said he would like to voice the "profound respect" he had for the American people and to predict good times of "warm, friendly relations" between the governments of the USSR and the United States.

To the solons of the United States Senate he said he would be the first to raise his hand in favor of capitalism, if history should show that this type of society "proves more able" than the communist system. The city officials of San Francisco heard him quote Christ and imply that he, too, was a Christian in his audience's understanding of that term. He said his country wanted to build a society "under" which every man will be a brother to his neighbor . . . as . . . was preached by Christ. For the occasion, Khru-shchev chose to disregard the strong atheistic stand of the Krem-lin regime.

Then at the same dinner meeting he added the most appealing line of his entire trip. He said that the peoples of the USSR and the United States had many qualities in common and listed love of peace; industriousness; quest for the new, for knowledge and technical progress; and finally such good human traits as frank-ness, sense of humor, good will, and love of country.

After identifying himself as a leader, a legislator, a Christian, and one of the people, he became a corporation big businessman at the Economic Club of New York. He said he represented a communist corporation, as did his audience a capitalist corpora-tion, and urged that the two compete honestly and peacefully as corporations "might" do in the United States.

Khrushchev held up his most direct attempt to shake the public faith in the office of the presidency until just before he left for the USSR. On a nationwide television hookup he began by saying that he had no doubt that the President desired an im-provement in the relations between the two countries. Then he delivered his punch line: "It seems to me that the President of the United States is, however, in a more difficult position than I am. Evidently those forces in the United States which hinder the improvement of relations between our two countries and an inter-national détente are still influential, and this cannot fail to be taken into account."

This was the impression he wanted to leave with the American public—that his office and he were of the caliber necessary to international understanding, peace, and leadership, while our office of the presidency and incidentally the present incumbent were not.

The USSR dictator followed up his attack on the quality and qualifications of the United States government when he decided to scrap the Summit Conference. It was at this point that the Kremlin had to shift from its soft line of beguiling the American public to one of threatening it, while it stepped up the attempt to undermine our leadership.

The confusion in Washington in explaining the U-2 overflights gave the people of the United States and the world at large some real doubts about the adequacy of the federal government to its tasks in foreign affairs.

The Kremlin propagandists let the confusion speak for itself and concentrated on the line that our government apparatus was incompetent because the U-2 flights were allowed in the first place. Of course, they copiously quoted our own critics of the administration, who attacked the government machinery which handled foreign relations. Khrushchev denounced Secretary of State Herter for saying the USSR was to blame for the flights because of its secrecy of arms build-up, which was a threat to world security. He used these words to ridicule the State Department:

> I believe Herter, by his statement, raised the coverings of reality, wiped off the make-up, and showed the true fangs of the imperialists. But now no one is afraid of the imperialists' fangs. They only give rise to ridicule and laughter.

He added later that Herter's statement was another move to "lead American public opinion" away from criticism of the American government.

Having dealt with the secretary of state as a "warmonger" and therefore unworthy of his position, the dictator turned his attack upon the capability of our President. In June, again at a press conference, he charged our Chief of State with incompetence, lack of will power, and indifference. He added that he would give the President, when he retired, a job of orphanage director if he chose to work in the USSR, and said parenthetically, "I am sure he will not hurt the children."

Turning from ridicule to charges of inadequacy of the individual, with implications directed at the office itself, Khrushchev stated it was "dangerous for a man like that to run a state, for he might cause so much trouble that it would be hard to get out of it."

A month later Khrushchev suggested that our government organization was irresponsible. Speaking at a Kremlin news conference covering the RB-47 plane incident, he prefaced his remarks with the statement that the American people, as well as people throughout the rest of the world, must know the truth. After this introduction he made a flat charge of recklessness: "... the government of the United States of America is gambling dangerously with the destiny of the world, with the destinies of the people."

The Kremlin propagandists carried their campaign to paint a false picture of our government organization in world affairs right into the heat of the conventions and the campaigns. They attacked the competence of the Republicans, questioned whether the Democrats would or could be any better. They wrote a letter over Khrushchev's signature in reply to one which had been sent to him by four leaders of the Democratic party protesting his cancellation of the Paris Summit Conference. It was timed to break upon the American public just six weeks before the opening of the Democratic convention.

Not only did they thus interfere in the domestic affairs of our country, but they sought to play on the partisan spirit of the convention to condemn the then-present government administration. The letter said that the USSR "peaceful coexistence" policy met the interests "of the whole of mankind" but that everything did not depend on the USSR government. Much depended, too, on the government of the United States of America, but the present government had shown that what it sought was "not to improve relations between our two countries but to reduce to nothing the positive results achieved over the past year," especially during Khrushchev's visit to the United States. It added that "broad sections" of the American public and "many prominent political figures in the United States" showed serious concern over the foreign policy of the Administration.

The letter was broadcast to the world and published all over the United States. The "message" was simply that the USSR held the solutions to the problems of the world, but the United States government was standing in the way of peace and world security. Again there was the implicit question of whether our government organization is equal to its responsibilities.

Later, in June, Khrushchev extended this line when he bid the United States "vote wisely" in its elections because the USSR was interested in the election of "such a president" and the formation of "such a government" as would remedy the mistakes made by the present government.

July 11, the day the Democratic National Convention opened, the Kremlin propagandists dramatized the "irresponsibility" of the Republican administration. They announced that the missing American RB-47 plane had been shot down by a Soviet fighter plane somewhere along the northern coast of the USSR, and that the surviving crew members would be brought to trial.

Next, Khrushchev shifted from downgrading the Republican administration to questioning the potential competence of each of the candidates. He said, "If the President is Nixon, he will be no better than Eisenhower," and observed that Eisenhower and Nixon had the same policy and that it collapsed. Then he asked, "And if the President be Kennedy? Will it be better or worse?" His answer was that Kennedy and Nixon were like a pair of boots, "which is better . . . is difficult to judge." In this way he tied up the prospects of both candidates with the charges he had made to denigrate the office of the presidency and Eisenhower personally.

The USSR dictator ended his "treatment" of our elections with a statement which reveals the temerity of the Kremlin propagandists in pursuing their goals.

Khrushchev said: "I would prefer as the President of the United States, of course, the most progressive person, a communist. Communists have a correct understanding of the development of society. At present, however, conditions are not yet matured for this. But tomorrow they will mature. When this tomorrow arrives . . . in how many years it will arrive, is another question: but it will come despite all, for the future is with communism."

The success of their propagandists in shaking our faith in the adequacy of our government organization in Washington could conceivably lead to this dénouement.

CHAPTER 3.

Defense by Control

Where the single Party member is spoken of, he is rendered
psychologically asceptic by having his individuality removed;
he becomes a *comrade* or a *cadre*.

HARRY and BONARO OVERSTREET, *What We Must Know
about Communism*, 1958

A STRONG element in the Russian national character is the
traditional, accepted authoritarian relationship between the ruler
and the ruled. Both the tsars and the subsequent dictators have
talked down to their subjects and the people have looked up to
them.

Accordingly, the prime requirement today for the dictator and
his ruling few is absolute control over the population. Control is
necessary to satisfy the traditional demands of the national character; it is also needed by the regime to reach the end goals of
The System. Stalin had himself called "Father" and tried to com-
bine an ikon-like status with the image of a year-round Santa
Claus, like a few of the longer-remembered tsars.

Because the Kremlin regime is imposed by a very small minority
on the peoples of the USSR, it is potentially vulnerable to overthrow from within, possibly by a new "revolutionary" heir to
Lenin.

The current Kremlin dictatorship fears, too, the subsurface
dissatisfaction and potentially explosive reaction of the different
nationalities and races which have been incorporated, and in
varying degrees absorbed, into the empire built around the so-
called "Russian Republic." The Ukraine, Byelorussia, Georgia,

Armenia, Kazakhstan, Uzbekistan, Tadzhikistan, Azerbaijan are all prospective allies of another "revolutionary" movement, although their captivity predates the "dictatorship of the proletariat." The Baltic states—Lithuania, Latvia, and Estonia—having known independence between the two world wars, are next on the list. And the captive European nations are tinderboxes. Taken over as colonies, they may not wait for revolt within the USSR to start their own uprisings as already witnessed in Hungary and suggested in Poland.

Of all the threats to the entrenched Kremlin dictatorship today, the most menacing is perhaps that of Red China. That country could bring about the destruction of the current regime in the USSR. Because the Chinese have a similar form of government, they easily see through the hocus-pocus of the Kremlin façade of "communism"; and they see the true Russia behind the Potemkin villages, the dual approaches, the duplicity, the delusive maneuvers which so frequently confuse us in the West.

By comparison the apprehension felt by the Kremlin regime about the United States is not that our country will or can offer a challenge from the outside but that our influence may prove corrupting inside the USSR. Our concept of the intrinsic value of the individual as a human being and of the human being as an individual—which in and by itself grants him the inalienable right to determine the way in which his society is to be governed—is disturbing to the dictatorial regime in the Kremlin. This concept, if held by its subjects, would constitute treason to The System. The danger is all the more real because the people of the USSR have identified themselves closely with the people of the United States in the material progress they have made in the past four decades.

I can remember the stories told me during my assignment in Berlin in 1931 and 1932 by American engineers who came out of the USSR after spending long periods there setting up factories and training programs. Their trainees all wanted to be like Americans, at least like the engineers they watched and admired.

The chances are that we could exert considerable influence on the peoples of the USSR if we were ever given the opportunity. In a very small way we are doing so every time the Kremlin allows its subjects to come in contact with us. The regime appreciates this fact, and therefore carefully weighs the question in each instance of whether it stands to gain more than it might lose in terms of its ultimate objectives.

DEFACED AMERICAN IMAGE

The Kremlin uses the image of Uncle Sam concurrently as a bogeyman and as an ideal. On the same day Khrushchev may denounce the United States as a threat to the people's security and Mikoyan may uphold her as an example of material progress. Our economic growth and industrial production are singled out by the regime as the goal toward which the subjects must strive in their never-ending series of five- and seven-year plans. Simultaneously our society is talked about as "decadent," the symbol of retrogression and reaction, in contrast to that in the USSR which constitutes forward-looking progress, the hope of the future.

As usual, the obvious inconsistency does not bother the Kremlin propagandists. They proceed on the theory that the public is neither consistent nor logical, and that its memory is short.

The image of Uncle Sam as "the ogre from abroad" is made more lurid for the subjects inside the USSR—and elsewhere behind the Iron Curtain—than for the noncommunists in the Free World. The subject peoples have been propagandized so intensively over the years that they have become partially immune to normal dosage. They have to be given very strong propaganda shots in order to produce a reaction at all. People with a modicum of intelligence have become adept at "reading between the lines," discounting the exaggerations, adjusting the misrepresentations, the half-truths, the shaded influences, and the false emphases.

The vilifications of the ogre from abroad are constant in their projection, but they are also subject to periodic intensifications; then they become virtual "Hate-America Campaigns." There was a highly dramatized drive in motion at the end of Stalin's life;

a recent one was staged for the Powers' trial. Long-time Greek residents of the USSR, lately repatriated, report that the U-2 propaganda did succeed in arousing a surge of chauvinism among the Russians. Apparently a majority believed that the United States was planning aggression against the USSR; even people who formerly protested against the low living standards voiced support for their government, in the face of the "external menace." Added to these campaigns as shots in the public arm were "spy" scares, which had the additional objective of cutting down fraternization with visiting Americans, particularly tourists who are not under the same rigid, controlled travel "guidance" as are the "official" groups.

No statement could be more complimentary than that about the United States made by Khrushchev to the Supreme Soviet on May 5, 1960, when he revealed the U-2 overflight. He said that "we," the social planners, were setting up a goal after implementation of the current seven-year plan "to catch up with and then outstrip the United States in consumer commodities, including textiles and footwear. . . ." Then he predicted that in consumer goods the USSR would in the immediate future reach the production and consumption level of "the United States, that wealthiest country of the capitalist world."

He had declared earlier that our meat production would be equaled in ten years and our raw materials as well as machine tools could also be matched. Later, an *Izvestia* article added refrigerators, television sets, and furniture to the list. To the initiated, the question of time is the key point here—the public is always prodded to look ahead, the "plans" are gigantic work norms, not programs which upon their completion will produce benefits realizable in the personal lives of the workers.

The American ideal held out to the people is materialistic, yet in another context our society is attacked for being "materialistic." In a recent issue of *Pravda* reference is made about our "capitalist ideology which boils down to one thing—profit. All the rest—religion, philosophy, slogans about 'freedom of the indi-

vidual'—serve only to fool the masses." The reference ends with
the statement that the capitalist structure is condemned by history to swift and final destruction and "is now incapable of in-
spiring ideological enthusiasm," which means it is no "wave of
the future" like Kremlin communism.

The Kremlin's *New Times* recently published a special supple-
ment for the express purpose of tearing us down and at the same
time spurring the USSR workers on. It was entitled "The Slums
of New York: Facts about the American Way of Life." In it, the
Kremlin propagandists quoted our own writers against our society
—out of context, of course, and sharply reslanted.

The lead article says that living conditions described by the
New York Times reporter Harrison Salisbury in "Shook-up Generation" "will come as an eyeopener to those who are inclined
to believe the legend that America's free enterprise system benefits
the common man." It observes that the difference between poor
living conditions in Moscow and the slums of New York is that
the Moscow citizen "does not feel an outcast. He knows what
efforts the country is making to solve the housing problem in
the shortest possible time. . . ."

The Kremlin propagandists have used the "trial" of pilot
Powers to denigrate to the youth of the land the kind of society
that produced this "spy." *Komsomolskaya Pravda*, the organ of
the government youth organization, printed a question asking of
whom "this physically strong but morally wasted" young man
reminded one. The answer given was the young men twenty years
before who "fed on Hitler bread . . . destroyed cities, and bestially
murdered millions . . ." who were "unthinking monsters of
cruelty" to whom fascism gave birth. Summing up, it said that
Powers was "through and through a representative of the American way of life."

The Kremlin must walk a tight rope in stimulating its subjects
to greater efforts to reach the goals we have long ago attained,
and, at the same time, keep out of their minds the realization that
our total achievements can be accounted for only by free private
enterprise.

CONTROL BY CENSORSHIP AND PROPAGANDA

To filter out alien ideas, the Kremlin employs a massive staff under the Section of Agitation and Propaganda, Agitprop, which acts as propagandist as well as censor. Its field staff is said to number four hundred thousand full-time agitators, organizers, and lecturers. They are assigned to the organized groups into which the totalitarian society is subdivided and in which membership is obligatory. This section not only directs all writings for the propaganda media but also the words of the oral propagandists, the agitators.

Consequently, nothing unfavorable to the Kremlin government dictatorship or the Kremlin communist party ever appears in the press or is heard over the radio. In speech and writing all actions taken by the regime or the Kremlin communist party are presented in terms of "irrefutable rightness," and all official claims and pronouncements are assumed—and said—to be matters of "undeniable fact."

Under this principle of controlled ignorance the great mass of Kremlin subjects have no means of understanding or judging events that take place outside the Iron Curtain, or even within the USSR itself. Many of them resent the treatment enough to risk reprisals by using whatever opportunity they can find to break through the dictatorially-imposed isolationism. They listen surreptitiously to short-wave broadcasts from the West and from their former fellow citizens now affiliated with Americans. They pay exorbitant prices for copies of the magazine *Amerika,* which the United States Information Agency publishes exclusively for the Russian-speaking population of the empire, in exchange for the Kremlin's opportunity to distribute its magazine *USSR* in the United States.

Yet resentment is limited because even the intelligent ones who automatically discount regime propaganda conclude that control of thought is essential to their society—essential because *somebody else* might get out of line.

Besides censorship and thought control, propaganda to build

up the current dictator is carried on at home, as it is abroad, for USSR prestige. By this means Stalin constructed what was called a "cult of personality," which is the Kremlin euphemism for "absolute dictator." Ever since Khrushchev took over all the top offices, he, too, has been fostering a fairly active cult of himself. He has advanced from being a member of the "collective leadership" to "first among equals" to a position of eminence reflected by the eulogy given him by a follower in the Supreme Soviet in January 1960.

> In the image of Nikita Sergeyevitch Khrushchev we see a rare combination of the talent of a theoretician with a profound knowledge of life. The seething energy, the indefatigability of an organizer, the flaming ardor of a propagandist, the firm consistency and flexibility in policy, the Leninist resolution and sagacity, the tremendous love for the people, his simplicity and approachability— all these are the noble qualities which our dearest Nikita Sergeyevitch Khrushchev has.

Thus the cruelty and unpredictable ruthlessness of the Georgian tyrant has been traded for the shrewdness of the Ukrainian peasant and a quite predictable ruthlessness.

As late as January 10 of last year the regime called upon the entire mechanism of its domestic communist party to tighten up on "propaganda in present-day conditions." One of the reasons was undoubtedly that the regime felt the infiltration of foreign ideas had reached a point where it needed slowing down. They spoke of "raising the level of awareness of the working people" and explained "persuasion and education of the masses are becoming to an ever greater extent the chief method of regulating the activity of USSR society." This work must reach the "heart and intellect" of every person in the USSR. The goal: ". . . the molding of a new man with communist traits, habits, and ethics, and the eliminating of survivals of capitalism in the minds of the people are at present among the main practical tasks."

The long arm of the Pavlovian psychologists was seen here

again, and the warning against smuggling in treasonable ideas
from capitalist societies was sounded to make certain that the talk
of "peaceful coexistence" with "states of different social systems"
did not suggest that the propaganda of Kremlin communism had
slackened off. The agents at home, like those abroad, were assured
that the "implacable struggle for [Kremlin] communist ideology"
would continue.

Additional recognition of the influence of alien ideas came
later in the same month. Because its propaganda blanket did not
prove effective enough, the Kremlin introduced a weekly magazine of thirty-two pages called *Za Rubezhom (Abroad)*, which presented selected current foreign ideas in the context thought desirable for local consumption. One trick used by the editors was to
choose quotes from statements made by our leaders—such as Adlai
Stevenson and Governor Rockefeller—to undermine some of the
"unacceptable" contentions of the platforms of the two political
parties.

Perhaps some of the "readers between the lines" are also being
served. The last known circulation of one hundred thousand
fell far short of the demand.

MUTUAL (?) EXCHANGES

The Kremlin operates on the principle that political negotiation can lead to agreement only if the deal promises to promote
the interests of The System, i.e., if it will facilitate Kremlin world
conquest. The same principle applies to the reciprocal agreements
on exchanges of people and cultural and scientific offerings between the governments of the USSR and the United States. Of
course no USSR subjects are permitted to escape the Iron Curtain
except for a specified purpose and then under strict control; there
are no visits to the United States by ordinary USSR tourists,
because there are no ordinary USSR tourists. To qualify as a
traveler, all subjects must prove that their visits abroad are in
the interests of the regime.

The exchanges are used by the regime as part of the dual

approach to the United States as the prototype to emulate in material progress and to avoid in social depravity. They are also used to promote a favorable image of the USSR among the people of the United States.

Exchanges of persons and cultural and scientific products cannot be reciprocal in effect, because the USSR government controls and restricts their circulation and consequently their impact on the public. Our free society does not grant the federal government such dictatorial control powers. So the net result of the exchanges would appear to benefit the USSR more than us. However, the Kremlin does accept a calculated risk in allowing any exchanges of persons, no matter how controlled and restricted. Even its "reliable," regimented, indoctrinated subjects occasionally cannot endure the thought of continued residence in a cage. Once let out of the cage, they may want to stay out, to choose freedom. That is why defections have occurred and will occur, despite the well-publicized threats of retaliation against the families the defectors leave behind.

Diplomats

In the exchanges of people, the only continuous, enduring deal between the two governments is in official representatives at the respective embassies in Moscow and Washington. At least the deal has been continuous since 1933, when diplomatic relations were resumed after a break of sixteen years. The Kremlin found a way to profit on this exchange by flagrantly restricting the travel of our representatives and using the *persona non grata* declaration to get rid of diplomats where personal relations with the people were so close that ideas of freedom seeped into the community. In recent years we have countered with travel restrictions and recall requests for USSR representatives in our country. To this extent we have learned to deal in the spirit of the Old Testament's an eye-for-an-eye, tooth-for-a-tooth trading which is the only kind the USSR understands.

What we have not yet learned is how to counteract slander and vilification of certain American foreign representatives who are

knowledgeable of USSR ulterior purposes and not deluded by
Kremlin propaganda. In the late 1940's a clerk in the American
embassy in Moscow defected for love and appeared as author of
a book accusing officers and staff members of shortcomings from
inefficiency to illegal dealings on the black market to sex devia-
tion. The intensity of the attack on an individual rose along with
the Kremlin's estimate of the degree of his opposition to its
attempts at world conquest.

This book was published in a number of languages and circulated abroad where the American officers named were transferred
on post. Loy W. Henderson, one of those most strongly attacked,
saw a copy of the book on the bookshelf of Nehru when he paid
his formal call on arrival in New Delhi as American ambassador.
Other American chiefs of mission, as well as subordinate officers
named in it, are followed by this book even today to their various
posts abroad.

Eisenhower Invitation to Visit

When agreement was reached on a mutual exchange of visits
of the chiefs of state of the United States and the USSR, the only
problem the Kremlin had was to find a pretext in sufficient time
to withdraw its invitation to President Eisenhower. There was no
question but that on balance the regime would lose in permitting
his visit to take place. On the other hand, the Kremlin saw a great
prospective propaganda gain in Khrushchev's visit to the United
States. The solution was simple: arrange things in such a way
that the one visit would take place and the other would not. Thus
the interests of The System would be served in both instances.
If the U-2 incident had not furnished the pretext, another one
would have been found.

Isolated and uninformed as the USSR subjects were kept, they
still were looking forward with keen anticipation to the visit of
a man who to them combined perhaps the most interesting personal qualities with the most impressive position in the world.
It had been part of the Kremlin propagandists' formula to flatter
Eisenhower while seeking the invitation for Khrushchev and

while the dictator toured our country. These personal eulogies were unmistakable and could not be given the double interpretation—one for the Kremlin communists and one for noncommunists—which the Kremlin reserves for propaganda slogans.

So a campaign had to be undertaken to blacken the reputation of our President—and our presidency—in order to persuade the subjects that the reason for withdrawing the invitation was legitimate and that they were not really missing very much. The slander fitted in well with the concurrent drives to stick the "warmonger" label on the United States, to re-establish domestic prestige of the current regime after the U-2 penetration, to foster a spirit of USSR chauvinism, to divert attention from broken promises of more consumer goods and housing.

The "big smear" campaign against President Eisenhower was even more virulent inside the USSR than it was abroad. Khrushchev's barnyard attack on the President in Paris was the signal for a "hate-America campaign" reminiscent of Stalin's days. The "human" touch that Nixon used in Warsaw with so much spontaneous success may well have helped to warn the Kremlin off. The question they would have had to answer—and couldn't—was "If the President of the United States can treat us this way, why can't our beloved Nikita?"

Above all, the substance of the things Eisenhower would have said in talking to the people would not soon have died in the memories of subjects of the Kremlin. The outright opponents of the dictatorial regime, the persons with reservations about any kind of dictatorship would have taken heart. Thinkers and artists, thirsting for creative freedom, would have been inspired. The curious—clandestine listeners to foreign radio programs, secret readers of forbidden literature, students in quest of academic freedom—all would have been stirred and encouraged to seek greater independence of thought. It would have been impossible for the Kremlin, in view of the freedom of speech and unrestricted dissemination accorded Khrushchev on his visit here, to censor President Eisenhower's talk in the manner they censor other alien ideas. As it was, the Kremlin censors had to redouble their efforts to keep out the comments made abroad about Khrushchev's "uncultured" behavior in attacking President Eisenhower in Paris.

When he was seeking something from the United States, Khrushchev referred to Eisenhower as a "big man" who understood "big politics," who had courage and a strong will, withstood pressures from nearsighted politicians and supporters of the "cold war" around him. He said the President was ready to bring about agreement between the peoples of the two countries and to solve urgent issues in the interests of the consolidation of peace. When he decided to turn on Eisenhower, he devoted two press conferences to reviling him. At one he recalled his 1955 meeting in Geneva with the President who, he said, was taking orders from Dulles, and he wondered who was running "the vast, great, and powerful nation," after all. "For such a President can take God knows what kind of decisions. . . . One shuddered at the thought of a great force in such hands." The inconsistency of having praised him in 1955, evidently, did not make any difference to the current dictator. His attacks were designed also to shake the confidence of the world at large in the qualifications of the United States for world leadership.

At a second press conference a month later, in July 1960, primarily for local consumption, Khrushchev said that the Russian people always received guests hospitably, then asked, "How do peoples everywhere receive a brigand? With a cudgel?"

The Kremlin propagandists were also working through media such as Radio Volga to reach special audiences whose minds needed "reorientation" after the visit had been canceled. A broadcast addressed to the USSR forces abroad was designed to undermine Eisenhower's image as a leading general. After castigating him for the U-2 overflight and quoting him against himself from his writings about military matters, the commentator called him "a warmonger and faithful servant of the American monopolies: an important capitalist." Stock he was supposed to own was listed with the comment "he is not ashamed of having shares in a company . . . which produces lipstick." Then the commentator quoted the *Daily Mirror* to accuse the President of evading income tax amounting to half a million dollars.

Through *Pravda* and *Izvestia* the Kremlin propagandists told their captive audiences that, toward the end of his second presidential term, "the prestige of the head of the strongest capitalistic state was shattered; it seems that he was unable to surpass the intellectual level and morality of a rank-and-file staff general of a capitalistic country." In another attack they referred to him as "growing old and concerned most of all with going down in history as a peacemaker," and now he was feeble and had accomplished very little.

To members of labor unions of the world the *New Times* said in a piece entitled, "The Revelations of Saint Dwight": "In proposing to create all mankind in the image of the United States, Eisenhower is obviously parodying the word of the Lord God who created man in his own image." And in another place, "Eisenhower would have liked to have departed from the historical scene with ... the majesty of a godhead. ... But he is leaving it like an actor booed off the stage. ... He believed in himself as a god. But he is departing into the desert. ..."

Radio Moscow broadcast a program to the general public which made fun of President Eisenhower by imagining the kind of advice he might offer his successor:

> Mr. Eisenhower is passing his last months in the presidential chair in the White House. What advice could he offer to his successor? The radio journal has studied the nature and actions of this man and found that his will might read thus:
>
> I, the undersigned, Dwight Eisenhower, enjoying perfect mental health, deem it necessary to leave this advice to my successor, whoever he might be: Every United States president must be goodhearted and pure minded. This is what I was during my presidency. Ben Gurion, Batista, Syngman Rhee, Menderes, Chiang Kai-shek, and Kishi came to me. I did not [refuse] any of them, but

helped them all as much as I could. None of them could accuse me of being a miser, for I gave them absolutely all I had in the way of rockets, aircraft, and guns, and I built in their countries atom and rocket bases only for their own good. True, in case of war many of them might be struck in retaliation, but only God knows the future.

The president must be a ... busybody. This is most important. He must know all that is going on in the world. Not a single airport, factory, or training ground, in the Near East, Asia, Africa, or Europe—should remain secret and unknown to the United States President. It might happen that a spy aircraft falls in the hands of the enemy. Let him lie and deny; such lying is a means of saving oneself.

The President must also be healthy and merry. He must play golf to strengthen his body and raise his spirit. I have practiced this game all my life, and on all my trips, no matter how short, I took with me all the necessary equipment. I advise my successor to do the same. If he follows my advice, he will gain glory in the same way I have. Here ends my will.

What do you think, gentlemen? Do you think that the new United States President will heed this advice? History will tell.

Correspondents

The exchange of newspaper correspondents would be reciprocal if those from the USSR were not government employees. As it is, they all work for the same employer. There is no competition, no professional news gathering for the sake of writing a competent, informative story. The Kremlin propagandists already have all the "story lines"; they have been worked out under The System. What they need is an event or news peg to capture reader or auditor or viewer interest, plus enough local color and significant detail to make the resulting "report" sound convincing.

The enthusiasm shown by American correspondents behind the Iron Curtain for digging out solid facts and seeking out "the truth" has frequently earned them violent abuse on the part of the regime. Max Frankel of the *New York Times*, with three years in Moscow, explained the situation this way: "It is when you are innocently taken in, or when you fight back, stupidly demanding 'the truth,' that you are contemptible and loathsome in Russian eyes. But once you've learned this game and it is still the truth that you want, it is time to leave."

Another correspondent of the *New York Times*, A. M. Rosenthal, who won a Pulitzer prize for his reporting from behind the Iron Curtain, quite eloquently describes the pressures brought to bear on a correspondent stationed in a satellite capital:

> The realization comes slowly to a Western newspaperman working in a communist satellite that he is not only writing about the people of eastern Europe but for them. It is not a particularly happy or comfortable thought, but there is no getting around it. It is part of the changing role of the foreign correspondent, even though he didn't ask for it. There is no great political mystery involved, and no political motivation on the reporter's part. It all happens quite simply, and quite inevitably. . . .
>
> There is no censorship for foreign correspondents in any communist satellite. Naturally, there are plenty of hidden censorships: The call to the Foreign Office for a dressing-down, the frightening away of friends, the closing up of sources, the threat of ouster, the withholding of visas, and, finally, the bounce. . . .
>
> The communist governments allow the foreign correspondent to be censorship free because this is part of the pleasant image of liberalization; and also because they know they can quite often influence or control him without the fuss and nastiness of imposing censorship. The communist governments detest most foreign correspondents, but they want them around anyway—most of the

time. They feel a corps of foreign correspondents adds a certain importance to a capital. They know that times come when the communists themselves will want their stories . . . printed abroad.

These governments pay a price for having foreign correspondents around—and sometimes they decide the price is just too high. The correspondent may be getting a little too inquisitive, a little too unheeding of pressure.

And sometimes there is a domestic crisis. The whole nation knows about the crisis in general terms but their papers give no real information. The foreign correspondent gets hold of a good deal more of the story. He writes it, and within hours the whole domestic censorship apparatus is destroyed by the broadcasts coming back. Somebody in the party picks up the phone, the Foreign Office gets its instructions, the correspondent is asked to drop around, right away, and the Official Spokesman tells him: "A pleasant morning, but I'm afraid I have some unpleasant news for you."

Cultural Exchanges of Persons

Under negotiated agreements between the USSR and the United States special categories of persons are agreed upon for exchange. The USSR favors entertainers and artists, athletes and specialized technical workers to impress the American public and to pick up helpful information for developing at home those fields in which they think we excel. We are proud to impress the public of the USSR with our ballet because we admire theirs, with our sportsmen because we think we can beat them, but we are not looking for scientific information. We would like to have our liberal arts students learn about the way of life in the USSR, and we would like some of the freedom-for-the-individual dust to rub off on the contacts of our citizens there.

Both sides, for their own reasons, like to send professors on visits but neither side wants the other's professors to teach at its universities.

The Kremlin propagandists' "line" runs something like this:

> Much of the existing international tension could be reduced by an increase of East-West contacts in the political, economic, and cultural fields. Lack of contact is the result of Western intransigence, in particular the unwillingness of the United States to talk over outstanding political problems with the USSR. In the broad cultural field, this unwillingness amounts to an "iron curtain." Aware of the danger inherent in continued mutual misunderstanding, the peoples of the world desire and expect the two camps to sit down together.

But the "good will" demanded by these propagandists does not seem forthcoming. Khrushchev during his visit here accused the State Department of desiring to reduce our cultural relations with the USSR. A "spokesman" replied that the dictator simply wanted to pressure the Department into agreeing to anything he wanted, regardless of United States reciprocal interests.

George V. Allen, head of the United States Information Agency during the latter part of the Eisenhower administration, said on the exchange of libraries: "All they want is for us to supply the Soviet government with the works they want. They will run the place. There will be no magazines, no newspapers, no American librarian to decide how the volumes should be displayed."

Chief Cultural Relations Commissar Zhukov accused the United States of using the exchanges "as a 'Trojan horse' whose stomach could be filled with anti-Soviet material." Zhukov defined this kind of material as including Western newspapers, "corrupted" films, and art. His government would censor all imports: "We shall not accept spoiled goods."

A report from Moscow summed up the problem neatly by recounting what a "neutral" Asian diplomat told an American and a Russian colleague on their cultural exchange program:

"What," he asked the Russian, "are you exchanging? All you really want in this world is to be as prosperous as the Americans, to take their power in the world and comforts of home, without losing control in your own country."

"And what are you exchanging?" he asked the American. "You don't like these people's system, but what have you to tell them that would make any sense? Do you want to start a revolution here or just teach them better manners? Are you offering the two-party system? Or do you want the steel mills returned to private owners?"

Kremlin Crackdowns

The coercive measures the Kremlin has devised to crack down on "offenders" are varied and comprehensive. In diplomacy, it has used the device of declaring our official representatives *persona non grata* simply to get rid of them. Generally the victim is accused of being a spy, but when the truth is known, more often than not he is too "friendly" with the subjects and too warmly received by them and has become too knowledgeable of The System.

Undesirable newspaper correspondents are unceremoniously told to get out. They, too, may be found to be exerting too much influence locally or, as pointed out above, may be too persistent in their search for "truth."

American tourists, particularly the youth, have been the target of Kremlin wrath recently. During the "hate-America" campaign of August 1960 several were ordered to leave the country in rapid succession; USSR youth finds common ground too easily with American youth to suit the regime.

In an effort to create a "spy" hysteria against Americans, the USSR police arrested tourists for snapping photographs of the countryside, giving presents to friends, and carrying on orderly discussions on international affairs with USSR subjects. One young American woman who had demonstrated refrigerators at the

United States Exhibition in Moscow the previous summer was accused of asking two USSR youths to obtain information about the location of scientific institutes, the system of registration of reserve-service officers, and economic data on collective farms in Tula Province, Russian Republic. In return she was said to have offered them chewing gum and "rock 'n roll" records.

The young lady, a Radcliffe girl and graduate student in political science, declared she did nothing she was accused of, but did give away some outdated copies of *Life* magazine; she added shamefacedly she didn't even know where the Tula region was.

Not only are the contamination cases quarantined, but there is considerable preventive medicine, administered especially to the youth traveling to the United States as entertainers, who may be more interested in their art than in the Marxist-Leninist line. Secret service "chaperons" accompany all of the artistic groups to keep them from defecting and to censor not only what they do but also what and whom they see.

Five young women, ballet dancers between the ages of nineteen and twenty-two, managed to elude their "chaperon" on a few occasions while performing in New York City. A young Harvard graduate who is fluent in Russian met them and wanted to show them around town. He speculated on what might interest them and decided it would be the new fashions which were just then being displayed. But they wanted to visit only three places— all of them forbidden by the USSR: the New York Stock Exchange, St. Patrick's Cathedral on Fifth Avenue, and the Museum of Modern Art. One of the dancers took all the snapshots she had film for of objects of modern art, particularly of Jackson Pollock paintings. Our decadence? The internal anti-American propaganda certainly was "counterproductive" in these cases.

Another artist from the USSR, Igor Moiseyev, who brought his talented ballet troupes on a visit to this country, created quite a problem for the Kremlin. He liked what he saw! That by itself was bad enough. But after he returned to Moscow he talked about it among his friends and had the audacity to voice his enthusiasm in public; that was even worse.

He found the tempo in New York infectious; it possessed a quality he had never experienced before. He was impressed with the restaurants of nearly every nationality; the variety of goods at reasonable prices; the number of items that could be bought in drugstores besides medicine; the highway system, which was even more marvelous than West Germany's. Moiseyev ended by denying allegations that the United States had nothing much to offer in contemporary drama. "That is completely wrong," he stated; "New York and other cities offer a wide variety ... that is dynamic and contemporary."

The artist was called on the carpet by the commissar of culture and reprimanded. His exposition "lacked balance," he was told; he was advised "to weigh his words in the future and to consider the larger implications of excessively favorable commentaries about capitalistic and specifically American society."

To others who were allowed to travel abroad it was found necessary to give a warning. Under the title "Be Vigilant," *Sovetskaya Rossiya* declared that foreign intelligence services abroad were trying to provoke and recruit USSR travelers. To do this, they had opened small shops stocked with goods at reduced prices chosen just to suit the tastes of tourists from the USSR. Although these citizens were loyal, when abroad they lacked the "necessary self-control" and were both garrulous and gullible, and this would sometimes lead to the "most deplorable consequences."

Exchanges of Products

It is far easier for the Kremlin censors and counterpropagandists to control the infiltration of ideas of freedom through products than through people. Products are traded under the official cultural exchanges program endorsed by the two governments.

Amerika, the Russian-language monthly now in its fifth year, is sent to the USSR in exchange for *USSR,* each in 50,000 copies. The agreement is for them to be sold at newsstands and by subscription in each country. The difference is that in the USSR all distribution agencies are operated by the government. Therefore the Kremlin can determine which people and institutions will have access to the magazine. There has been frequent evidence that its distribution has been curtailed sharply. Our government has no reciprocal control, since the distribution agencies here are private, and the sale depends on the demand. The American embassy in Moscow sends out two thousand complimentary copies of *Amerika,* and the number of *USSR* magazines mailed from the USSR embassy in Washington is believed to be many times that figure.

Because of the control of *Amerika,* a lively black-market trade has developed in its back numbers as well as current issues. Old copies have been resold for as much as six times the normal sales price.

Other American magazines, books, and newspapers are under strict government censorship; only a few are allowed in, mostly for official use only. When questioned on this by an American newsman, Khrushchev said they "want to know the truth, have good spiritual fare which helps them better to arrange their lives and understand world events more clearly." Your papers "print a lot of untruths and misinformation. Why should we force that on our readers?"

American motion pictures, which are equally as popular as *Amerika* in the USSR, are also covered by an exchange agreement. Out of 102 movie houses operating in Moscow at the end of June last year, 45 were showing American films. The Kremlin censors select the films very carefully in regard to subject and treatment. They see to it that the "decadence" of American society is portrayed in all its Hollywood tinsel. However, material progress and an impression of the advantages of life in a free society get through to the movie-goer. Eventually he must wonder whether such advantages would be available to him under a different form of government.

Sometimes the censor misjudges. A case in point is the showing of *The Grapes of Wrath.* After it had been viewed extensively by the public, censors discovered that the audience was commenting audibly on the high standard of living in the United States—even the "wetbacks" had automobiles! The USSR audience discounted the fact that the wetbacks' cars were old and battered jalopies. An automobile was an automobile, and for one of the "underprivileged" to be able to own one was impressive. This film was ultimately withdrawn from circulation.

The program of counteracting the influence of American and Western movies includes periodic diatribes against them and exhortations to the public not to be unduly impressed.

Izvestia ran a series of three articles in August 1960 on the subject of films from the West. In commenting on the Cannes Film Festival it wrote that the majority of Western films shown at the festival did not rise above the level of solutions to sexual problems at times amounting to frank pornography. Only one film cited by critics and judges of the festival "in its bitter assertion of the fundamental moral degradation among the leading strata of the Western society" rose to an acceptable level. This *Izvestia* series ended with: "Having become the teacher of life, the cinema has lost its right to petty plots, approximations, and lies. There are too many students in the world who thirst to hear the truth from us. We are obliged to offer them this truth."

However, of all the influences on the young with which the cultural arbiters have difficulty, American jazz takes first place. They cannot pinpoint the idea which they want to brand subversive, and they have to depend on the power of association with decadence. American jazz is popular all over the empire, and its great impetus came in the first instance from a Voice of America program called "Music, USA."

Young people received the jazz programs on short-wave radio sets and took them down on tape or disks. The clamor was so great that Radio Moscow was forced to put on a jazz program of its own, using our recordings but without identification of origin.

American jazz records are smuggled into the country and sold on the black market, as are the clandestinely recorded radio programs. *Sovetskaya Kultura* decided to take a position against "this sort of thing" in its August issue. The "wages of sin is death" was the theme of two articles written for a major in the militia to sign. It told how students of "higher educational institutions, couples, twitched and made ridiculous movements of the feet . . . embracing and clinging to one another . . . like the ceremonial rite of some savage tribe. . . ."

Then two of the students went into business together selling "outrageous trash 'on the ribs' " (transcribed) in thousands of copies. "There was a demand, there were many customers, and assistants were not hard to find." "The shame of it . . . nobody was disturbed. . . ." But they were caught by the militia, according to the article. The ringleader, "a brusque fellow in tight-fitting trousers," who after a furtive glance around him would quietly say, "we have some rock and boogie, sweetheart," was given two years in jail and his cohorts "lesser terms."

JAMMING OUT TREASON

If it were not for foreign radio broadcasts the Kremlin would have almost complete control over its subjects' access to outside sources of information and ideas. The Kremlin does what it can to shut out the disturbing voices from abroad without adding foreign-broadcast listening to the list of punishable offenses controlled by the secret police. As the situation stands today, listening has to be done surreptitiously because it is looked upon with disfavor by the present regime. People are no longer sent to jail for bootleg listening as they were in Stalin's time, but they know it is entered as a black mark on their ever-growing personal dossier in police headquarters.

The Kremlin has set up a massive radio jamming operation which in large cities manages to drown out the incoming foreign broadcasts most of the hours of the day and night. However, huge as the regime's effort is, it cannot be 100 per cent effective. Modern broadcasting techniques have become too refined and programs get through in all rural areas and as close to Moscow as the *dacha* or country-house suburb which is twenty-five miles outside of town. And then the word-of-mouth transmission of news, which has been practiced so adroitly under the oppression of both the tsars and the Kremlin dictators, assures that the news from abroad is circulated through the countryside.

Evidence that the broadcasting signal from abroad gets through the jamming is provided by monitors stationed on the periphery of the USSR, by foreign government personnel, and tourists traveling in the country with their short-wave sets, by defectors, by repatriates, particularly to Greece and Spain, and by letters to mail drops outside the Iron Curtain addressed to fictitious names mentioned by the broadcasters in their programs.

This jamming operation is aimed at two American short-wave broadcasting networks, one official and one private. Our official radio, the Voice of America, beams programs in Russian, Ukrainian, Armenian, and Georgian to the USSR. It also broadcasts in the native languages of the Baltic countries, annexed by the Kremlin after World War II. The privately sponsored Radio Liberty broadcasts its programs exclusively to the USSR, twenty-four hours a day, seven days a week. Its transmitters are kept on a schedule of "saturation broadcasting." At the latest count, seventeen different languages, all actually spoken in the USSR, are used in RL's programs.

It has been estimated that the Kremlin spends more money every year on jamming than the United States Information Agency does on all its operations. Informed radio engineers estimate that jammers on the air throughout the USSR, Red China, and the "satellite" countries number between 2,000 and 2,500. They claim that in 1959 the Polish government decided to put an end to its jamming operations in order to save some $30,000,000 a year, and that the Kremlin promptly made up the difference. But, according to these sources, if every available radio station in the USSR were used for jamming purposes, they would not be able to drown out all foreign broadcasts.

This situation puts a strain on the broadcasting resources of the USSR. Squabbles among "jamming" and "broadcasting" bureaucrats over allocation of transmitters and frequencies are bound to develop, since jamming foreign short-wave broadcasts interferes also with the short-wave programs of regime radio stations beamed across the far reaches of the empire. The disagreement is so acute that it broke out in the open a few months ago at Geneva. At a United Nations conference on allocation of frequencies, one USSR faction turned on the other USSR faction in full committee meeting.

The Kremlin has always regarded broadcasting, including the jamming of foreign programs, as a vital element in propaganda warfare. Characteristically, the monthly magazine *Radio* was called *The Radio Front* in its early years, from 1930 to 1941. Also, the Ministry for the Radio Industry has throughout its existence, right up to this day, been able to maintain an independent status within the "apparat."

Broadcasts from Spain were the first to be jammed in 1946. Two years later the VOA broadcasts to the USSR were included. When Washington protested, the Kremlin at first blandly denied the action then called jamming justified as a measure "to eliminate interference" with the operation of the stations. In 1949 André Vishinsky, in an exchange with the British delegate to the United Nations, admitted that the USSR government practiced jamming. The "explanation" he gave was that the USSR government was afraid its people would react so violently against what they heard that cooperation between the two countries would suffer.

The USSR and its bloc subsequently abstained from voting on United Nations resolutions condemning jamming as incompatible with human rights. The USSR delegate claimed expressly the Kremlin had the "right and duty . . . to paralyze the aggressor in this radio war" and to protect the people of the USSR from "false and libelous" communications from abroad.

In justification to its subjects, the Kremlin propagandists have repeatedly attacked "reactionary circles" in the United States for "meddling" in USSR affairs, as well as interfering with the normal operations of domestic radio stations; this creation of "not unimportant obstacles" to the "defense of peace" should be resolutely opposed, the people are told. Incongruously, such expressions of serious preoccupation with American broadcasts are occasionally followed by derisive and belittling references to VOA as inept and ineffective.

At moments of crisis, looking backward, the Kremlin propagandists have been most anxious to maintain their monopoly of information and interpretation for their subjects. In 1956, throughout the Hungarian massacre and the Suez invasion, every available jammer was put to work to keep up a constant barrage not only against VOA, BBC, Radio Free Europe, and Radio Liberty, but even with maximum intensity against smaller stations located in Tel Aviv, Ankara, Athens, Rome, the Vatican, Luxembourg, Madrid, and Canada. Apart from programs in Russian and the languages of the national minorities of the USSR, VOA programs in Serbo-Croatian were also blanketed. So were BBC programs in Finnish, Hebrew, Persian, and German; and Tel Aviv programs in Hebrew and Yiddish.

Again, during the 1958 Lebanese crisis, jamming was stepped up so much that VOA broadcasts of the United Nations General Assembly debates, as recorded by the United Nations technical services, were blanketed.

On the eve of Khrushchev's visit to the United States, the Kremlin strategists made a new move: on September 15, 1959, for the first time in eleven years, a VOA broadcast beamed to the USSR was left unmolested. BBC and Radio Liberty transmissions continued to be blanketed, as before. Three days later, while Washington officials were still congratulating themselves on their "victory" in the propaganda contest, the Kremlin shifted again. It started the practice of "selective jamming." Whereas VOA programs carrying texts of statements made by Khrushchev while in this country were allowed to come through, the transmission of the text of Secretary of State Herter's speech before the United Nations General Assembly was jammed. This set the pattern for the following days: news items on Khrushchev's tour of the United States were left alone, comments which the regime considered objectionable were jammed. When questioned about the resumption of the jamming of the official United States radio, Khrushchev candidly stated, "As head of the working class, I will protect workers from capitalist propaganda," but quickly added, "We want to avoid our people's getting the wrong view of the American people." The second statement was more in keeping with earlier remarks of his to the effect that the Voice of America was not the voice of the American people.

Several weeks after the Kremlin's adoption of the "selective jamming" technique, a spokesman for the Department of State felt it necessary to deny allegations that the VOA had been instructed to avoid using terms such as "Free World," which the government of the USSR might find objectionable.

Some Western propaganda experts had alleged that by alternating vague promises of completely abandoning jamming with careful selective jamming, the Kremlin propaganda strategists had indeed managed to induce the VOA to eliminate certain types of information and of programming approach which they knew from experience would be jammed. Others maintained that, even if this were true, the broadcasts remained valuable because the listeners in the USSR would still get some items of information not carried by the Kremlin information monopoly. However this may be, the Kremlin propaganda strategists will surely not be satisfied until foreign broadcasting has been reduced to the level of political harmlessness achieved for cultural exchanges, as typified by the Van Cliburn concerts and *My Fair Lady* performances in Moscow and other cities of the USSR.

Following the signing of a cultural agreement between the USSR and Great Britain, the Kremlin early in February 1960 ordered all jamming of the BBC to be stopped—a move which prompted the then director of the United States Information Agency, George V. Allen, to comment hopefully, ". . . I believe they have now come to realize the counterproductive nature of jamming." But by March 10 of the same year BBC was being jammed selectively again. The BBC had been found guilty of indulging in "crude anti-Soviet falsifications," Radio Moscow reported. Apparently, the charge referred to BBC's broadcasting commentaries from the British press which voiced some skepticism as to the success of Khrushchev's Asian trip. And in May, at the time of the Paris Summit fiasco, VOA programs were heavily jammed; even Gromyko's speech before the United Nations Security Council, carried by VOA, suffered the same fate. BBC fared somewhat better; it is estimated that roughly only one quarter of its programs beamed to the USSR were blanketed.

The series of crises in United States-USSR relations manufactured by the Kremlin from the U-2 incident apparently induced many listeners in the USSR to try to see the "whole picture" by supplementing the information supplied by Soviet mass media with items from foreign radio programs. This is indicated by the Kremlin's decision during July to publish in *Sovietskaya Rossiya* a particularly vituperative attack on the Voice of America and Radio Free Europe.

Being aware of the fact that Radio Free Europe does not beam programs to the USSR or broadcast in languages of that country, the Kremlin propagandists no doubt deliberately used the wrong name; in reality they were talking about Radio Liberty. By hiding the true identity of the station, they "protected" some possibly curious owners of short-wave radio sets from the temptation of listening to these dangerous tools of the "spreaders of lies," "warmongers," and "imperialists."

Why do the Kremlin propaganda strategists evince particular concern about the possible influence of Radio Liberty on audiences in the USSR? Why have they waged their most relentless jamming war on this station ever since it went on the air in 1953? Why have they tried to hide its name from their subjects and, at the same time, to hurl their most virulent abuse at the people working for the privately sponsored station? There can be only one reason: they are genuinely afraid of Radio Liberty and even more so of the people for whom it speaks.

GENUINE KREMLIN FEAR

The American Committee for Liberation is made up of a group of Americans dedicated to fostering an active partnership between Americans and exiles from the USSR in their struggle against the Kremlin dictatorship. There are about two million such exiles living in the Free World. These are the people of whom the men in the Kremlin are afraid. The very existence of a sizable emigration constitutes a threat, as well as a reproach, to the Bolshevik regime. The regime has always had an almost pathological fear of the emigration, evidently believing in the possibility that one day the emigration may produce a new revolutionary leader to emulate Lenin and overturn The System. This fear may seem unrealistic to the Western observer, but the men in the Kremlin know how "unrealistic" Lenin's chances looked in 1917.

Moreover, the Kremlin propagandists are constantly embarrassed by exile witnesses whose testimony exposes Kremlin propaganda claims as false and hypocritical. By telling what they know from personal experience, by describing what the Kremlin regime did to them, to their parents, brothers, and sisters, to their friends, to their national groups, they can do more to stop the Kremlin's drive to win over the uncommitted peoples of the world than any amount of anti-Kremlin pronouncements on the part of Western governments. Because of their experience, insights, alertness, and intuitive understanding of the people and their problems in their former homelands, these exiles are also eminently qualified to analyze and interpret Kremlin actions. They unquestionably deserve a greater measure of consideration and respect from the political leaders of the noncommunist world than they have been accorded so far.

Fortunately for the United States, and the Free World in general, at least one major effort to utilize émigré talents in the struggle against Kremlin communism has been under way for some time. A group of American experts on Russian and Soviet affairs succeeded in 1951 in establishing a public committee providing the organizational framework within which Americans and exiles could cooperate in their common cause. Out of this the American Committee for Liberation came to life. In the ten years that have elapsed since then, the Committee has been quietly expanded into a substantial organization, with headquarters in New York and a large operational unit in Munich, Germany. Besides Radio Liberty broadcasting to the USSR, it supports the "Institute for the Study of the USSR" in Munich, Germany.

People, both inside the USSR and in the Free World, are listening to what the emigration has to say. Actually, proof is supplied by the Kremlin regime itself. Its cries of outrage are eloquent as to its estimate of the effectiveness of this opposition.

On February 24, 1957, a Party spokesman said in a speech broadcast by Radio Riga:

> The reactionary elements of the world are losing their mental balance, they become wild. Recently they have launched a reckless anti-Soviet, anticommunist campaign. Tens of radio stations, thousands of newspapers and journals in the capitalist countries pour forth, day and night, as from a cornucopia and in all languages, a torrent of vile gossip and lies about the Soviet Union and socialism, and spread all kinds of rumors and malicious falsehoods. . . . It would seem that Goebbels has been resuscitated. Significantly, the principal and largest lie and gossip factories employed by these world reactionaries are American radio stations: Voice of America, Free Europe, Radio Liberation, and the like. Hundreds of other organizations engage in anti-Soviet propaganda, espionage, and sabotage against the socialist countries. These [radio stations] are located in West Germany, the birthplace of German fascism. . . . The Voices of America, which are to be heard from Adenauer's fatherland are the voices of the blackest of all reactions, they are voices of fascism and war. Some people who particularly like to listen to the Voices of America now and then will have to consider this point.

At the time, Radio Liberty was known as "Radio Liberation." The same reaction is found to the committee's work in the Free World. The following testimonial to the émigré scholars associ-

ated with the Institute for the Study of the USSR appeared in
Istoriya SSSR (Organ of the Institute of History, USSR Academy
of Sciences) of January 1960:

> The "Institute for the Study of the USSR" was founded
> in 1950. It plays the role of the central organization of
> Russian white-guardists and traitors to the Soviet mother-
> land in all countries of the world. The collaborators of
> the Institute pass themselves off as "free scholars."

Since the Kremlin counterpropaganda experts are unable to
silence their accusers, they resort to slander and vilification.
Every exile who speaks up is a traitor and a "tool of the imperialist
warmongers," the people in the USSR are told, and anyone who
listens to them is almost as bad. But too many in the USSR know
that all exiles are not traitors to the best interests of their people
so they continue listening.

Even if no one within the USSR would listen, the émigrés
would still be a threat to The System as long as they kept warning
others about the menace of Kremlin communism. For the Kremlin there is only one real solution to the problem: the silencing
of the emigration. To accomplish this, it has spared no effort.
There have been unsolved murders of particularly able émigré
anti-Kremlin propagandists; there have been kidnapings; there
has been blackmail of exiles, with the use of relatives in the USSR
as hostages. Silencing exiles is desirable, making them return
"home" is even more so, from the Kremlin's point of view. Once
the émigré has been induced, through either threats or blandish-
ment, to accept the hospitality of the motherland, he no longer
constitutes a problem. He is persuaded to serve the Kremlin's
propaganda interests from then on, or he disappears.

In 1955 a "Committee for the Return to the Homeland" set
up shop in East Berlin. It had considerable funds at its disposal.
Its radio station broadcast appeals for "missing relatives" to return
home and sang the glories of life in the USSR from morning till
night. Its newspaper soon began to appear in exile mailboxes all
over the world. By some coincidence, several offices of refugee

organizations in Germany had been ransacked by burglars a few months before; all reported their mailing lists as missing.

Massive letter-writing campaigns were started. Particular targets were exiles living in straitened circumstances who found it difficult to adapt to life in Western society, as well as elderly people who had emigrated during the Bolshevik revolution and did not know much about actual conditions in the USSR. The campaign was conducted energetically and imaginatively. One trick was to have a relative, in, say, Kiev, telephone the exile and appeal to his sense of filial duty. Or an agent, sometimes a staff member of the nearest consulate of the USSR, would magically appear on the doorstep and offer "moral" and material support to the compatriot in a strange land. If the exile accepted the support, the moment would invariably come when the kindly friend would undertake to persuade him to "go home."

The brutal crushing of the Hungarian uprising had an adverse effect on the repatriation campaign. Many exiles were reminded in time of the Kremlin's unchanging belief in the effectiveness of ruthless terror. A few thousand hapless exiles, listening to the "Homeland Committee" siren songs, had allowed themselves to be railroaded into oblivion. But the vast majority of knowing exiles had remained firm. They knew, and no power on earth could move them to go back voluntarily.

The Kremlin has also tried to maneuver Free World governments into silencing exiles under their jurisdiction. Here, again, it has achieved scant success. In the official pronouncements of the Kremlin, all émigré activities in the territories of countries which maintain diplomatic relations with the USSR are "incompatible with the recognized norms of international law and . . . normal relations between governments." This is the way *Sovetskaya Rossiya* summed up the Kremlin arguments shortly after the collapse of the Paris Summit meeting.

In their anxiety to obtain results, the Kremlin propaganda strategists have gone even further: they have tried to mobilize Free World public opinion against exile activities. At the twenty-first Party Congress, the highest-ranking woman in the apparatus,

Furtseva, charged that the radio operation of the American Committee was "in the service of the organizers of the cold war" who, unable to face the "bright and pure communist ideals," were resorting to slander. Taking its cue from Furtseva, *Return to the Homeland* charged that Radio Liberty was an "abominable nest of provocateurs and slanderers."

The idea behind the drive is that the governments concerned might be forced to give in to "popular demands" and shut up the troublesome exiles.

PART III

MORE DIFFICULT THAN WAR

Just as the Soviet Union aims at making all the world communist, so we should aim at making all the world free—men as well as nations. We cannot expect to win the cold war while we fail to proclaim to the world as our cold-war aim that which is the core of our civilization and culture. For while we so fail, our side will be bewildered and confused, divided and open to the infiltration of the more determined strategy and the more skilful tactics of communism.

The key fact of our time is the growth of the power and importance of world public opinion.

SALVADOR DE MADARIAGA
The Blowing Up of the Parthenon
1960

CHAPTER 1.

United States Media: The Unwitting Carriers

IN its propaganda drives to slander and delude us, the Kremlin enjoys the ready assistance of our own communications media. This is not because our communicators have turned Kremlin communist agents but because they are businessmen operating in the field of news in a free society.

The nature of communications in the United States enables the USSR to exploit our media and effectively enter the frames of interest and reference of audiences in the Free World in order to assure the spread of her propaganda output. In an open society anyone and everyone has access to our communications outlets, regardless of whether he is a Kremlin agent or his objectives are political and even subversive. Any bit of information which qualifies as news may be spread throughout the United States and disseminated abroad. The major criterion is whether it will "sell."

The Kremlin propagandists' awareness of this profitable situation, their trading upon it, and our almost eager cooperation have been aptly described by the French journalist, Mme. Suzanne Labin:

> Strange as it may seem, a ... motive force behind Soviet propaganda—and not the least—is the eagerness of the Free World's press to respond to it without charge. The real power of the Kremlin's propaganda substantially surpasses the formidable magnitude we have evaluated, because it is voluntarily taken up and orchestrated by all democratic organs. With their love of sensation, their search for exciting news, their need to see, their naïveté

about Soviet tricks and lies, they repeat a number of these tricks and lies of their own free will, without even having to be induced to do so by the auxiliaries who infiltrate them. Thus the Soviets dispose of many more mirrors than their own for catching their larks.

In my experience the most dramatic example of how the free press works to the advantage of the Kremlin is the following story. It is not generally known and occurred without the instigation of Kremlin propagandists, but they managed to manipulate it to their great advantage in world opinion.

One of our leading diplomats, assigned at the time to a country in the USSR bloc, held a press conference while he was vacationing outside in the Free World. The conference was limited to American correspondents and it was understood all around that what the diplomat said was "off the record" and therefore not for quotation in the press. By way of incidental comparison—not a main point in the discourse—the diplomat likened the atmosphere of the capital in which he was posted to that of a totalitarian capital he had experienced just prior to World War II.

One American correspondent, in his zealousness to score a "beat," to profit for his employers, reported on the conference and featured this minor, inconsequential comparison. The Kremlin propagandists and their stooges seized on the story after it appeared in American newspapers, to charge the diplomat with offensive, undiplomatic behavior. They attacked him personally and professionally and used the occasion to sling mud at the entire American foreign representation. Finally the government to which he was accredited declared him *persona non grata* and asked for his recall.

The correspondent—who told me of this incident himself— explained that, as a professional journalist, he could not suppress a story of this nature. Had he been a member of TASS, he would probably have been arrested for treason.

Another American correspondent—who shall also be nameless

—deliberately and consciously furthered the cause of Kremlin propaganda. Again, professional and not ideological considerations determined his actions. He had once been assigned to Moscow and reported the truth as he saw it so faithfully that he was denied a visa to return after he went home on vacation.

Considerable time passed and still no visa was forthcoming. Then a highly placed Kremlin operator made a visit to the United States. This correspondent's employers had him cover the trip of the official through the United States. The copy he wrote sounded to some readers more like public relations releases than objective news reporting. The Kremlin must have been pleased, for within a short while this correspondent found himself the happy recipient of a visa to the USSR.

The problem for our publishers, news agencies, and networks is simple. If their correspondent writes anything which is critical enough to be considered damaging to USSR propaganda, he is out; if not, he is in. Since "news" from the USSR sells at a high rate in the press of the United States, it is profitable to have a special representative reporting out of Moscow. So, for many the policy is to "play ball" up to the delicate point of maintaining professional integrity. They cannot ask our government to give reciprocal or equivalent treatment to USSR correspondents in the United States in order to balance and restrict this coercive practice of the Kremlin: in peacetime our government cannot impose censorship, either direct or indirect, on news despatches from this country which are considered detrimental to our national interests or prestige.

In 1959, when Khrushchev was invited to visit the United States, vast preparations by the USSR embassy in Washington were made to take advantage of the American press and its buying public on two major counts. These were the native interest and curiosity about a chief of state—particularly of the mysterious and mighty Russia—and the vast concern to learn about the personal, the human side of the boss of the Kremlin.

Everything Khrushchev said or did "made news," and everything written about him on his trip would be read; the build-up in advance was worthy of P. T. Barnum. And so many reporters—three hundred in all—went along on the trip and overran the Garst farm in Iowa that the host kicked the nearest correspondent in the shins. He turned out to be the Pulitzer Prize–winning journalist, Harrison Salisbury, of the *New York Times*. So avid were the members of the Fourth Estate to report every detail down to Khrushchev's breakfast menus that James Reston was moved to write: "They [the reporters] are not the obscure witnesses of history but the principal characters in the drama, whose very presence is so ubiquitous that most of the time Mr. Khrushchev is addressing them or addressing others with them in mind." The propagandists back in the Kremlin must have been pleased; they planned the tour that way.

In their competitive efforts to produce copy that would sell, the various reporters, photographers, feature writers, women's magazine specialists posed and directed Khrushchev, the actor, so that his image would produce the maximum reader and viewer appeal. Leading questions were asked him and "human-interest" shots were made of him from all angles. Television cameramen urged him on to perform like any grassroots American political aspirant. He slapped backs, gave his bear hug generously to all his "friends," and excelled in kissing babies.

Khrushchev was portrayed as folksy, human, down to earth. One of the most telling shots of him was taken by a *Life* photographer, and it appeared on the cover of the October 5, 1959, issue of the magazine. The dictator was smiling the beguiling smile of a peasant and holding a magnificent ear of yellow corn which he presumably had picked from the fields of Mr. Garst. If one picture is worth a thousand words, this one was worth at least five thousand. No untutored American could imagine as he looked at this picture that here was Stalin's liquidator of the Ukraine, the Kremlin dictator who had ordered the massacre in Hungary.

But the American press did not let Khrushchev off scot free, although their probing was contained within sharply defined limits. It took place at the outset of his visit, at the National Press Club in Washington. Here members of the press asked him embarrassing questions about his past and present activities as boss of the world-wide conspiracy of Kremlin communism, about his involvement in the "crimes" of Stalin.

To this old professional demagogue the embarrassment was momentary and superficial. He answered those questions he felt would make good propaganda and only parts of other questions which contained elements of bad publicity for him. Since all questions had to be submitted in writing in advance, he took no real risk of losing the initiative in front of the microphone. The list of questions he did not answer has been circulated privately by the National Press Club. It makes interesting reading and could be used in large part even today; the fraud and discrepancies in Kremlin propaganda and its No. 1 "front" man are continuing and constant.

At this meeting the Kremlin employed a rather ingenious trick. It assigned as interpreter Oleg A. Troyanovsky, the son of a former Russian ambassador to Washington, who had received his early schooling in this country. He showed himself sensitive to the nuances in our American language and to the reactions of our people, and also politically astute and nimble-witted. In translating the questions put to Khrushchev and answers the dictator gave he managed to rephrase both with remarkable speed and to recast the meaning for maximum propaganda impact on the American target audience. For our consumption he softened some of the more outspoken, unpalatable replies uttered by his leader.

For example, when he was asked about USSR intervention in Hungary, Khrushchev was quoted by Troyanovsky as having replied: "If there is a desire that our discussion here take that turn, of course we, for our part, could think of quite a few questions of a similar character."

What Khrushchev actually said was, "If you want to steer the conversation in this direction, I can toss more than one cat your way, even fresher, you know, than the question about Hungary." An interesting comparison has been made of the Troyanovsky interpretations, the actual equivalent in English, and what was printed in *Pravda*. All are different. The version for Russian readers has been "edited" just as Troyanovsky "edited" Khrushchev. The actuality has no significance to the Kremlin; what counts is the effect on the particular type of reader.

The Kremlin also takes advantage of free, uncontrolled dissemination of information in the United States as has been described in connection with its "peace offensive" and campaign for "complete and general disarmament." When the USSR embassy in Washington made its contribution to the propaganda drive over the U-2 incident, it traded upon this facility on two counts: first, that its press releases would go through the mails unhindered; and second, that the recipients, the most articulate residents of the United States, the writers, would be able to publish their opinions without fear of retaliation.

Thus it was able to distribute freely a release signed by a dozen outstanding USSR writers all of whom had recently visited the United States and had played hosts to American writers visiting their country.

It started with the appeal:

"We feel sure that the vast majority of the writers and people of the United States want peace just as ardently as the Soviet people and writers."

Then it laid down the political line: "We were deeply shocked by the flight of an American spy plane over Soviet territory. It was a provocative act hardly paralleled in all of history."

Four paragraphs followed indicting the United States for "aggression" and then the propagandists used their favorite double-barreled trick:

"When a thief is caught, he too tries to evade responsibility and cast doubt on the honesty of his intended victim. That is exactly how Mr. Herter has acted in accusing the Soviet Union of entertaining aggressive aims, without possessing any facts. We all know that trick!"

The press release ended with this pitch:

"Writers are a great force in any society. By their books they foster noble or base feeling, plant seeds from which wheat or weeds will grow, serve the cause of good or evil. No honest writer can be silent when the fate of his own people and whole nations is at stake and danger threatens all the treasures mankind has created in the course of centuries of hard and conscientious work.

"We want to hear what our colleagues in the United States have to say about this development.

"Much depends on us writers!"

Presented in this way, the open letter may appear obtuse. However, in its entirety, it was "selling" copy.

The Kremlin propagandists put out a continuing stream of news releases on the young aviator they captured up until the day his trial started. They used Western and American press services and newspaper correspondents in Moscow to build up anticipation and concern for his fate. Through these professionals and their own outlets in the United States the Kremlin propagandists painted a heart-warming picture of a nice, clean young man who was politically naïve and a tool and victim of American "military circles," but who finally saw that he had done the United States an ill service. This presentation was tailored particularly for the American press because it would sell. A totally different picture of Powers was presented to the USSR public. Powers, the individual, was not given much play in Kremlin propaganda to third countries.

By the time the trial began the Kremlin had oiled the machinery in Moscow to get the story out fast. The consideration accorded the various members of the Powers family who attended was extraordinary and completely out of character with the lack of concern for individuals normally shown by the Kremlin. So, in a way, was the manner in which Powers was handled in the dock. When it was over the Kremlin propagandists made a big claim of being "fair" and "just," and even went so far as to pretend to humanitarianism.

During the trial the Moscow censors cleared immediately all "sob-sister" copy and intimate photographs of the aviator and his loved ones. The Kremlin propagandists practically wrote a daily soap opera to be orchestrated and disseminated by American correspondents and American newspapers and radio.

A New York tabloid ran a story on the trial every day from August 8 until August 26 complete with photographs. The titles included "Powers' Dad: Expect Worst," "They'll Try to Find the Heart of the Kremlin" (with photo of Mr. and Mrs. Powers weeping), "Mrs. Powers: He Did Right in Guilty Plea." "Powers Is Branded Pawn in Four-hour Show," "Red Press Plays up Theme: United States on Trial with Powers," "Lawyer Aims at Light Penalty" and "Dips Her Pen in Tears, Writes K" (with photo of Mrs. Powers).

The story was the thing. There had to be a story every day and it spoke for itself, layer after layer. There was no "depth" reporting, no interpretation, and every correspondent in Moscow was scrambling for a "beat" or an "exclusive." The editors back here would pay anything because in the profession it was news, even if they recognized it as manufactured by the Kremlin, in fact, a series of propaganda gimmicks. And comparison of the treatment given the Powers' trial in this tabloid with that in the outstanding American newspaper for foreign coverage shows scant difference in terms of the realization of Kremlin objectives.

Then on October 9, 1960, after Khrushchev had insulted both our President and the presidency, the Kremlin agents were able to make an arrangement to have him appear on a nationwide television hookup. The dictator was given a propaganda rostrum free, and he made the most of it. His interviewer tried to bait Khrushchev, to reveal him in something of his true colors, but the experienced Kremlin operator treated him like his son.

He took the opportunity to say to his nationwide audience:

> Recall that last year I was in this country as a guest
> of your government. . . . I wanted to establish good per-
> sonal relations with the President. . . . Because, after all,
> if such good relations exist between the United States
> and the USSR, that means that there will be no war
> between our two countries, or in the whole world. . . .
> What did your government do? . . . The United States
> government sent a U-2 plane into the USSR. And we
> held a conclusion that the United States government was
> not sincere. . . . Such a policy or plan in the long run can
> ultimately lead to the outbreak of war. . . . That is what
> I want to reply to you. . . . To you and to all who are
> listening tonight. We want to let the public be the judge.
> We are certainly honest, and we keep our word when we
> give our word. We are always true to what we say. But
> you send your planes.

The sponsor of the program was aware of the prospective
propaganda impact, so he began by giving up his commercials
in favor of plugs for Radio Free Europe and its drive for public
contributions, and ended by canceling his sponsorship because
he disapproved so intensely of this promotion job for the Kremlin.

The public was, indeed, taken in. The mail response to the
program was considerable, and most respondents took exception
to the insertion of the RFE plugs as unworthy of the American
tradition of fair play and as undignified treatment of a chief
of state. Even today there is no general comprehension that the
descriptions of the broadcasting to the captive nations of eastern
Europe constituted a relatively small gesture to neutralize the
effects of the propaganda of a man who uses the prerogatives
of his high office to subvert our politically unsophisticated people.

Khrushchev, for one, appreciated this opportunity to infiltrate
millions of American homes. In the propaganda book following
his 1959 visit, which was distributed all over the United States,
he is quoted as stating:

They say an American home is more likely to have no windows than no television set. It is not too great an exaggeration. There are over 50 million television sets in the United States. Radio and cable tieups enable cities to exchange TV programs on a broad scale. In its power to influence public opinion, American television has long since outdistanced press, radio, and cinema.

TASS reported that despite the "dirty methods" employed by the American television company, Khrushchev succeeded in impressing his audience with the USSR's peaceful policy. All USSR media took particular exception to the interviewer's "unfriendly and provocative" questions, to the "distortions" of the dictator's statements by the discussion panel following the interview, and to the "anti-Soviet" films shown during intermissions in the program.

The Kremlin news agency maintained that efforts to dissuade "patriotic" Americans from tuning in to the program were in vain and that they heard an "unusually lively, frank talk, fascinating in form and profound in meaning." And it added that when Khrushchev called for peace and friendship, it seemed that "all upright, thoughtful, peace-loving Americans stretched out a hand to the envoy of the Soviet people and, sincere and convinced, told him: We agree with you, Premier Khrushchev!"

The exploitation of our free press is illustrated further by the launching of the weekly magazine *Za Rubezhom* (*Abroad*) which was mentioned above. In this sheet critics of conditions in the United States—President Kennedy himself, Admiral Burke, leading newspapers and magazines—are quoted to show how unfavorable our living conditions are and how unwise our foreign policy is.

Finally, the Kremlin is known to plant its agents in the offices of opinion molders, columnists, and foreign affairs experts writing or speaking for our media. One example is found in the experiences of the late Dorothy Thompson who wrote an article on how her office had been "infiltrated" during the years after the end of World War II.

Miss Thompson wrote that she did not like to admit she had been a dupe, but felt that her experience should be read as a warning to others. She told of how she hired a researcher, an émigré, to collect newspapers and magazines on world developments and make précis for her of what he read. After years of using his summaries she discovered they were slanted. "Editorials and comments were almost exclusively collected from left-wing newspapers tooting the slogan 'Trust the Russians,'" she wrote.

When she ultimately fired the researcher, she wrote, "And yet I was still not *sure* this man was a communist...." Later she was given proof that he was.

However, it was Miss Thompson's final observations which give one particular pause; it will be remembered that she was at one time one of our leading columnists.

> I ask myself why, apart from finding cozy berths, should communists go out of the way to place themselves in confidential positions with such unofficial persons. Could they influence us? Reviewing the four war years, I find I was never influenced toward communism, but was perhaps somewhat influenced by the "trust" lullaby.

This columnist found that her experience was not unique, that four of her friends, all well-known journalists, had had communists planted on them. Miss Thompson ended her article with, "... if the American Age of Innocence does not emerge into adult realizations, innocence no less than malice can prove our undoing."

. . . .

C H A P T E R 2.

Problems for the American Propagandists

THE basic difficulty of the American propagandist when he competes with the Kremlin propagandist is that American propaganda is geared to respond to the propaganda initiative of other states, while the USSR variety is designed to take this initiative and keep it. We propagate words to endear and persuade, and leave the action pretty much up to the audience; they project stimuli toward thought and feeling that induce both fear and respect, and then follow these up with agitation which will promote specific action. Ours is a channel of communication used in a public relations manner toward a general political objective of national prestige; theirs is a purposeful approach designed to achieve specific political objectives in their drive toward world conquest.

We leave out the element of agitation, the indispensable counterpart of propaganda in the Kremlin approach. As will be recalled from the USSR definitions, *agitation* comes closer to what its propagandists actually undertake than does *propaganda*.

We act as we do because foreign propaganda has always been largely a government function determined by members of our career diplomatic service. To them, agitation in a country means meddling in the internal affairs of that country, and such action is forbidden by principles of diplomacy. The exception is the gathering of military intelligence, which has long been considered acceptable by all nations, if kept under cover.

These Foreign Service and State Department officials, and members of the executive branch as well, tend to hold that political contact among states should be restricted to negotiations—to treaties and agreements arrived at by diplomats and foreign offices. The Kremlin sees the opportunity to influence its political relationships with states through propaganda and agitation by going over the heads of the officials directly to the people. When American propagandists attempt to do this and consequently disturb negotiations with foreign government representatives at the conference table, the American diplomats clamp down.

The need for traditional state-to-state relations was reiterated, for instance, by President Kennedy and Secretary of State Rusk before the Cuban fiasco caused the President to take a hard look at our entire approach to Kremlin communist subversion. What our traditionalist diplomats have overlooked is that "correct" state-to-state relations depend upon the cooperation of other states. They must respect treaties, abide by agreements, and abandon agitation propaganda as a means of securing political ends. The USSR has refused to cooperate in this way ever since the Bolsheviks took over the government.

It is a fact that highly placed officials in our government have had—and perhaps still have—serious doubts about the political effectiveness of propaganda as psychological warfare in peacetime. They see it as action which can make a bad political situation better—or worse—and a good political situation worse—or better. They do not realize that propaganda can actually create a political situation, or that the foreign policy of a country can profitably be determined in a specific instance primarily for purposes of influencing world public opinion. The Kremlin understands this principle full well as it has demonstrated, for example, in its handling of the U-2 overflight incident.

Besides disapproving of propaganda as a serious instrument of foreign policy, these experts are also repelled to a certain extent by the underhandedness which, like the general public, they associate with anything called propaganda. They have yet to grasp the fact that propaganda need not be lies; that truth projected politically for purposes of influencing opinion and swaying action will win out in the long run if we invest as much in it as does the Kremlin in delusion.

The result of this estimate at the highest government levels is that there is no propaganda planning as such. Also, until the new administration took over, scant provision for world psychological reaction and possible consequent action was made at the planning stage of foreign policy. Of course, no foreign policy moves have been made simply for propaganda purposes.

Left to their own resources as communicators, the American propagandists both in government agencies and in private organizations have had to make their own policy. In government this has meant a mild form of information tailored so it will not offend the other states from a diplomatic point of view. In private organizations, the more venturesome of the agitators have been severely criticized, as was the case with Radio Free Europe for its alleged activities in the Hungarian Revolution.

Today there is very little aggressive propaganda by either group. The tendency is to project Americana, to describe the advantages of life in the Free World, and to hope that all listeners will prefer freedom in a democratic form of government. Our propagandists live from crisis to crisis and endeavor to counteract the false accusations made against us whenever these are considered virulent and serious enough. We explain ourselves rather than expose our detractors.

Without political-propaganda guidance, without having decided for them first what political results should be obtained from their output, American propagandists look beyond the government foreign affairs specialists for help. They look to the political scientists for some basic formulae and again they are disappointed. This group of academics tends to drag its feet, because many feel they would be compromised in the academic profession if some of their suggestions should produce unfortunate results in our dealings with other countries.

Then, because they not only need guidance but must have documented backing for their propaganda projections, the American propagandists turn to the sociologists and the social psychologists. These specialists make surveys of audience responses and estimate the trend of popular reactions to American propaganda and to the prestige of the United States in the family of nations.

From such studies the propagandists can see whether their target audiences are being reached. They cannot get Hooper ratings behind the Iron Curtain but they can discover whether their programs find favor in the reactions of a few refugees, travelers, and audacious letter writers. If the measurements and statistics reveal that the people have liked the product, then the product is analyzed for clues as to how future propaganda policy should be formulated. Also, and frequently of greater importance, if the popular reaction has been judged favorable, the propagandists are provided with concrete backing to present to congressional or other skeptics in regard to the efficacy of propaganda in general.

This working backward from the result is hardly an adequate substitute for determining the substance of the propaganda in advance and projecting it. The Kremlin does not go in for widespread polls. It does not even concern itself whether the popular reaction has been favorable or unfavorable. Its assumption is that its "message," repeated often enough, will have an effect even if the first popular reaction to it is reserved, unbelieving, or distasteful—which is hardly new to Madison Avenue.

Since agitation and political propaganda are virtually ruled out for American propagandists, their attention becomes focused more strongly on the tools of their communications trade. They seek higher appropriation grants for more concentrated dissemination of materials and wider coverage of audiences. They look for technological improvements to increase the power of their projections. And as communications specialists in one medium or another, they endeavor to guide their efforts and to judge their potential effectiveness by the technical quality of specific programs or materials.

While this approach has its merits up to a point, it is not a reliable yardstick. The small samples of listener reactions to Voice of America broadcasts in Romania taken in 1947–50 showed that listener interest was based on neither strength of signal nor professional quality of program. The program, of course, had to be received, but even if it was picked up by only a few sets, it was spread by word of mouth throughout the country if it contained facts or points of view of specific interest to the audiences. The BBC rated higher in quality of programs than VOA, but the people preferred to listen to VOA. The reason was that the United States had taken the place of Great Britain as their white hope for liberation from the Russians.

The American propagandists have their problems not only with what they say but with the timing of their output for maximum impact. Once the policy line and objectives are decided upon there is the timing. The projecting of the message must be arranged so that it will get top attention in the world press. What is required is a news peg and synchronization of announcements from the West and the United States so news pegs do not compete with other Western propaganda pitches. Also needed is a full-scale dissemination from the maximum number of media using the same basic line in a cooperative effort not only for breadth of coverage but for intensity of impression made. This cooperation until now has been lacking. The disadvantages to the American propagandists are obvious. Without central control and direction to back them up they can hardly be expected to mount unified massive campaigns which are successful. The Kremlin, of course, has no such problem in implementing and timing its propaganda dictates.

The USSR is our propaganda target number one, just as we are the prime target of Kremlin propaganda. Yet we, in 1961, are challenging the Kremlin far less directly than we did in Stalin's day despite the fact that the Kremlin has greatly intensified, during the intervening years, its anti-American drive throughout the world. The regard for diplomatic niceties evidenced by our federal government until the Cuban fiasco, has kept our propagandists from directing their fire at the USSR or any of its official representatives. What they *have* been allowed to do is to denounce "world communism" on appropriate occasions. But vigorous attacks on the inhuman, despotic system holding sway within the expanding confines of the Kremlin empire and singling out the USSR as the aggressor are apparently ruled out for American propaganda disseminated to audiences both inside and outside the USSR.

Nor have we fully mined the propaganda bonanza found in the presence of anti-Kremlin émigrés outside the Iron Curtain. These hundreds of thousands of self-exiled refugees from the USSR and the captive nations are the living proof of the failure of the Kremlin System in terms of human values. They furnish a greater indictment, as well as exposure, of the fraud of USSR claims than any amount of argument advanced by foreigners. Many of them are eager to dedicate the remainder of their lives to the struggle against the oppressors of their countrymen and to warning others about what would be in store for them if the Kremlin should take over. In American propaganda addressed to the USSR and eastern Europe, these exiles are used up to a point. But when we speak to other countries outside the Kremlin empire we make very little use of the contribution they could make either as propagandists or as political analysts.

It is obvious that in propaganda to the USSR and its captive nations the émigrés can be very effective. They know their own people better than any foreigner can ever hope to, and many of them are familiar with the workings of The System. Also, because of their personal stake in the liberation of their relatives and friends left behind, they may be counted upon to make a militant, sustained propaganda effort.

Working harmoniously with the exiles is not easy: they have a strong tendency to form splinter groups, to become engrossed in divisive quarrels and personal feuds. There is, for instance, a seemingly irreconcilable cleavage between the Great Russian and the so-called nationality groups, i.e., between those whose native language is Russian and those who represent groups (roughly half the population of the USSR) whose native language is not Russian, but Ukrainian, Armenian, Georgian, etc. They appear to be more concerned with squabbling over how the country will be ruled once the present regime is liquidated than in cooperating to overthrow it.

Nevertheless, it should be possible for American propagandists to avoid becoming embroiled in internal squabbles of the exiles while availing themselves of the talent the exiles have to offer by way of advice and guidance on how to communicate with audiences behind the Iron Curtain, and how to expose The System to third countries.

Again, there is a conflict of views among the specialists, or Sovietologists, both exiles and Americans. Some believe that only revolution can change the type of government in power; others believe this can be accomplished by supplying people with information which will eventually induce them to press for a more democratic form of government.

A further complicating factor is found in the actions of the socialists, both exiles and native Americans, some of whom were formerly Mensheviks. They pull their propaganda punches because they will not attack The System of the government, the Marxist and collectivist framework of the present rulers.

The result of these counterbalancing influences is that, in our propaganda to audiences in both the USSR and third countries, we tend to pit the idea of our way of life against the idea of what the Kremlin says its communist way of life is. We dwell upon "Americana," stressing the benefits of national independence for countries, of liberty and a high standard of living for individuals. This is what some people call the "positive" approach. The "negative approach," according to the same people, consists of trying to expose the true intentions of the Kremlin and of documenting the misery of life as it is really lived in the Kremlin empire. Where the "positive" approach falls down is that it is based on the mistaken assumption that public opinion in states with totalitarian regimes can erode or modify the form of government, and that leaders in states in the early stages of political and economic development can afford high-priced consumer benefits. What good will it do us, if some people in such audiences become convinced that, theoretically, the American way of life is attractive? The so-called "negative" approach would be more effective because it could induce the people behind the Iron Curtain to think about the overthrow of totalitarianism. Also, it could stimulate people and their leaders in emerging countries to think twice before irrevocably binding themselves to the Kremlin.

If there is a desire on our part to do so, we can draw upon a wealth of materials to expose the Kremlin's claims and pretensions as fraudulent and misleading. Stalin was the molder of the USSR; it was Stalin who fashioned the present system of government in the USSR. The current ruler of the USSR has frequently acknowledged this fact. At the same time, Khrushchev has branded Stalin as a bloodthirsty tyrant, who committed countless crimes against his defenseless subjects. Khrushchev himself also has a background "rich" in inhumanity and terror. It includes wholesale "liquidations" when he was Stalin's henchman in the Ukraine, and the treacherous, bloody suppression of the Hungarian Revolution. Any number of self-exiled émigrés from the USSR would be happy to write the script for a documentary on Khrushchev the man, Khrushchev the chief of state, Khrushchev the chairman of the Council of Ministers, and Khrushchev, the secretary of the CPSU showing the efficient ruthlessness with which he reached the top. But we have not only failed to dwell on the murderous characteristics of the leaders of the Kremlin, we have also shrunk from exposing fully the essential role which dictatorship plays in the Kremlin communist form of government. After more than forty years of Kremlin rule, it has become obvious that The System depends on the presence of a ruthless dictator, on the suppression of human freedoms, on an iron curtain around the country. Events in the captive European countries as well as Cuba have furnished dramatic evidence of this.

The problem of the American propagandists is to find all the approaches they can from any political position in order to expose the Kremlin for what it is and to undermine its power to expand its empire. They cannot afford to base their efforts on the expectation that they can determine in advance the character and degree of change in the USSR, either revolutionary or evolutionary. The best they can do is to work for change itself and to realize that once real change begins only the people inside the USSR will have the deciding role in determining the direction it will take.

CHAPTER 3.

Needed: A Political Blueprint

JUST solving the propaganda problems posed by the Kremlin is not enough. The result would amount to little more than neutralizing the efforts of the USSR if our counteraction were successful. What is required is an affirmative, aggressive propaganda action against the power expansion by the country which calls us The Enemy. As a first step in organizing and implementing such action it is essential to identify the political targets against which American propaganda must be directed.

The American propagandists need a political blueprint which will spell out the vulnerabilities of the USSR both outside its own borders and inside them. These vulnerabilities must be chosen for their potential sensitiveness to our propaganda attacks: they cannot be simply someone's estimate of the shortcomings of The System. They must block USSR expansion and roll her back to her own borders; inside the USSR, they must undermine and disrupt the current regime as a mechanism of aggression abroad.

The three outstanding political vulnerabilities of the USSR are totalitarian rule, Kremlin communism, and USSR behavior in the family of nations. Of these, only communism has been singled out by our officials as a propaganda target, at least until President Kennedy spoke out against Kremlin-directed subversion in reviewing the situation in Cuba on April 20, 1961.

Propaganda capital can be made of the fact that the USSR uses dictatorship as her form of government. It is a total, an absolute dictatorship, in many respects like Hitler's or like the despotism of some tsars. The Kremlin has deliberately tried to deprive its masses of their character. They are allowed nothing for themselves. There is no bulwark, no security left for a person in the USSR except inside the party or inside state institutions, which are practically synonymous. The people are not allowed to cherish loyalties which may compete with the required total allegiance to the regime. Religious faith is undermined by the atheistic state, family ties are loosened to the breaking point, and sentiment, love, and compassion are discouraged. The dictatorship is all-powerful, speaks to its subjects in one voice, and seeks to control their minds and hearts.

Since dictatorship does not square with the theory of Marxism in its ultimate "perfection," the Kremlin attempts to explain away the contradiction by claiming that dictatorship is a temporary stage which will eventually be replaced by one in which the achievement of pure communism is complete. No limit has been set upon the time needed for this process and nearly forty-five years have already passed without showing the slightest hint of relinquishment of control at the top.

The totalitarian nature of Kremlin dictatorship is the main reason why many communists have defected from the USSR and the captive nations of eastern Europe. Without an opportunity to benefit personally from their own productive efforts, without a chance to develop normal human relationships, without freedom of inquiry, they have ended by abandoning their country. But in many instances this has not meant they have abandoned the objectives or the ideals of a planned society as well.

The word and concept of dictatorship have been politically embarrassing to the Bolshevik hierarchy as far back as 1919. In that year the communist party of Russia brought together in Moscow a number of left-wing socialists. At their meeting a leading Marxist theoretician, Karl Kautsky, took exception to the term "dictatorship" in the then newly conceived slogan "dictatorship of the proletariat." He held that "literally the word [dictatorship] means elimination of democracy. But if we use a literal interpretation, it also means the sole rule of one individual, who is not bound by any law." Lenin subsequently arranged for Kautsky's silence.

Fraudulent concepts and arguments of this sort run all through the Kremlin brand of communism and provide the American propagandists with countless opportunities of exploitation. As pointed out in the foregoing chapters, the main fraud lies in the pretense that Kremlin communism is a world movement in which foreigners can participate freely and voluntarily.

It has been seen from Comintern proclamations that foreign party members are required in time of war to pay allegience first to the Russian Soviet Republic, thus becoming agents of the Kremlin who can be used against the interests of their own countries.

The employment by the USSR of social doctrine as a come-on to recruit agents, and to build up the image of the USSR lends itself also to continued attack.

Professor Gerhart Niemeyer, a political scientist, who has made the study of totalitarianism his specialty, points out that present-day communist ideology has held on with particular tenacity to the irrational element of Marx's theory, namely, to the claim that the "immutable laws of history" enable man to predict "scientifically" the future development of society. Niemeyer sees the main attraction of communism in the fact that it claims to be infallible, that it offers its adherents a total view of the world, an explanation of everything that has happened, is happening, and will happen in human society. To the devout communist, it simply is not possible to hold an alternative view.

Apparently, dedicated communist believers are not unduly bothered by the obvious contradiction inherent in a theory which, on the one hand, propounds the functioning of immutable historical laws which cannot be vitiated by human action, and, on the other hand, advocates human action, including the use of terror and violence, to impose the communist system on unwilling majorities.

To quote Professor Niemeyer:

> The objective of the communists is the intensification
> of their party's power, not with the idea that this will do

any immediate good to anyone but only with the expectation that history will somehow produce from the totalitarian power of the communist party a society of complete freedom.

This is so irrational a belief that it borders on the ridiculous, but nevertheless it is the sole justification the communists give for their quest for more and total power. On the basis of this "knowledge" they arrogate to themselves the right to determine who is "progressive" and who "reactionary," and they mean by these terms not the intentions of people but people themselves in terms of their existence. So they, like the Nazis, divide people into those who deserve to exist and others who don't.

It is a fact—a highly unpalatable fact to the Kremlin—that in today's world there are many communisms which speak with different voices, have different objectives, and acknowledge neither the exclusive dictatorship of the Kremlin nor the monolithic quality of a world movement. This phenomenon dates back to 1948, when Tito broke away from the growing USSR empire.

This defection underscored the basic differences between the communism of the Kremlin and that of Yugoslavia. The one important difference to us was that the USSR type had the aspirations and means for world conquest and the other did not. The American propagandists can profitably draw upon these differences in addressing audiences both inside and outside the USSR. We may not approve of the form of government which Tito heads but we don't disapprove sufficiently to refuse him military and economic aid. Since we have already made political investment in his deterrent value against the USSR, we can do the same in propaganda; the expectations of returns are equal on each score.

The very existence of many communisms, and of competition between the USSR and Yugoslavia, the USSR and Red China, and even occasionally between the USSR and Poland, is injurious to the propaganda face put on by the Kremlin. It is a constant situation and presents a continuing source of materials upon which American propagandists can draw.

The problem we have in relation to the world's security and this country's security is not whether a third country has a form of government which some call communist but whether that government belongs to a network, is under the domination of a strong power which is dedicated to world conquest. From a propaganda standpoint, the USSR is vulnerable because, once she has taken over a country, she imposes totalitarian rule and exploits the country to her political and economic advantage. If our propagandists were free to show that American concern for the interests of a third country is more sincere, profound, and long-lasting than that of the USSR, regardless of the type of government that country has, it could go far toward eliminating the menace of Kremlin communism and consequently of the USSR as a belligerent state.

The third propaganda vulnerability—the behavior, or rather misbehavior, of the USSR in the family of nations—in a sense includes the other two, since the totalitarian nature of her dictatorship and the duplicity of her communist appeal offer both planning and operational frameworks for her aggression. Her flaunting of all norms of civilized diplomatic practices, hammered out painfully by compromise over past generations, reveals her irresponsibility as a member of the world community of states.

A long series of past unilateral abrogation of treaties, of negotiation simply for the purpose of gaining time and scope for propaganda aggression, and of attempts at undermining the United Nations, are an eloquent indictment of the Kremlin. For American propagandists the assignment should be clear: to look up the records and draw upon them relentlessly and consistently. Continuing behavior of this sort on the part of the USSR certainly provides us with opportunities to give an historical run-down of past performances which will, in the aggregate, convict the Kremlin before the court of world public opinion. We would do well to remember the ancient Russian saying that "repetition is the mother of learning."

In some of the foregoing chapters attention has been called to
the propaganda techniques of revolutionary parliamentarianism
and to the use of the United Nations as a propaganda forum by
the Kremlin. This practice is in direct opposition to, and defiance
of, the purposes for which the United Nations was formed. That
the USSR has never had any intention of participating in this
body to discuss differences between states or to try to iron them
out is demonstrated by the Kremlin's own words. Directives by
the Second Congress of the Communist International, held at
Moscow in 1920, said in part:

> Consequently, communism repudiates parliamentar-
> ianism . . . its aim is to destroy parliamentarianism.
> Therefore, it is only possible to speak of utilizing the
> bourgeois State organizations with the object of destroy-
> ing them.
>
> The communist party enters such institutions not for
> the purpose of organization work, but in order to blow
> up the whole bourgeois machinery and the parliament
> itself from within.
>
> This work within the parliaments . . . consists chiefly
> in making revolutionary propaganda from the parlia-
> mentary platform.

Viewed against this background, Khrushchev's interpretations
and table-pounding at the United Nations General Assembly in
the fall of 1960 should surprise no one. The dictates put out under
the regime of Lenin are being faithfully applied by the current
dictator. It will be noted that Kremlin communists are not content merely to gain control of parliaments. Their objective is to
destroy parliaments and not leave even a minority voice to the
opposition. This holds true, of course, not only for the United
Nations but for national parliaments into which Kremlin agents
manage to infiltrate.

Again the American propagandists need do no more than con-
sult their reference material to expose and convict the USSR by

her own stated intentions, objectives, and current instructions to mouthpieces and agents.

Finally, of all the vulnerabilities of the USSR which are valuable for propaganda exploitation, the one that has the greatest "agitation" value is her treatment of subject peoples. The patent formulae of character assassination of individuals who oppose her aggression, of infiltration, delusion, subversion of target audiences, and of absorption of subject peoples in a totalitarian dictatorship, have been demonstrated again and again. They have been applied in the USSR itself, in the Baltic States, in the captive nations of eastern Europe, and now in Cuba.

The siphoning off of resources and the retooling of all subject government machineries to mesh with the Kremlin machinery have also been employed as steps in the process of exploitation, regimentation, and colonization. To this has been added the deliberate destruction of the cultural characteristics and identity of groups of peoples through mass shipments of individuals to remote areas such as Siberia, and conversely through importation of Russians and trusted agents from other nationality groups in the USSR to take their places. This denationalization has been practiced on a large scale in the Ukraine and Armenia, and among the Caucasian and Moslem cultural and religious entities which were added to the Russian empire before the Bolsheviks took over the regime. The Baltic States and the captive nations of eastern Europe have suffered the same fate.

In the Kremlin record of forced Russification and even genocide American propagandists would find rich material for communication to natives of third countries bound to these oppressed groups in the USSR empire by ethnic, cultural, or religious bonds. And although the oppressed peoples of the USSR themselves are not likely now to respond in the same way the Hungarians responded to oppression in their country, the subsurface discontent is such that judicious propaganda prodding would go far to undermine and cause serious administrative difficulties to the present Bolshevik regime.

This last vulnerability—in the opinions of leading Sovietologists

—must be dealt with carefully, on a long-term, well-planned basis. Agitation, once started among the temperamentally explosive minority peoples of the USSR, cannot be easily stopped—and certainly not from outside the country. So it is in the area of propaganda addressed to audiences inside the USSR proper that American propagandists require the most precise and statesmanlike guidance from makers of United States foreign policy.

CHAPTER 4.

Prescription for the Interested Citizen

THE investment the Kremlin makes in propaganda and its head start on the United States in this area of international relations are impressive. The question arises of what can be done by this country to deal with it effectively. I would like to try to answer this question in two parts: first, for the interested American citizen, and second, in the following chapter, for the professional American propagandist.

The interested citizen should study Kremlin propaganda until he can recognize and understand it. Thus he will not be so easily confused, deluded, or subverted. Having seen USSR propaganda described, and operating in a number of situations, it is time to subject its methods and techniques to a close critical analysis.

Campaigns and Slogans

In carrying out their propaganda campaigns the Kremlin propagandists create themes or slogans much as Madison Avenue advertisers do to sell products on television. In 1917 the favorite slogan was "Peace, land, bread!" Later "Independence!" was added but was used only outside the USSR bloc. These slogans put the accent on positive, political action and suggested attendant sacrifices.

More recent slogans and themes, put to work in the cold-war era, include:

"USSR policy stands for peace."

"The USSR desires 'complete and general disarmament.'"

"The states representing the two systems, socialist and capitalist, can coexist peacefully."

"The ideological struggle ... between the two systems ... will continue unabated."

"The imperialists, especially 'military circles' in the United States, pursue a policy of aggression directed mainly against the USSR, but also against all other countries, with world domination as its goal."

"The colonial and dependent countries of the world are waging a struggle for national liberation against the colonial powers headed, directed, and incited by the United States."

"The downfall of capitalism is inevitable because of contradictions in the system."

"Progress of the USSR in economic development is faster than that of the capitalist countries."

"The United States is continually losing friends and soon will be isolated politically and diplomatically."

Methods, Techniques, and Tricks

In directing their propaganda to the Free World, the Kremlin propagandists exploit the human qualities, the weaknesses, and vulnerabilities of our imperfect societies. They trade upon our ideas of democracy, our fears of war, our political inertia, and our humane impulses. And they endeavor to disrupt and destroy any parliamentary body they cannot dominate.

Their techniques are far more complex than simple persuasion. In fact, they influence action more frequently through disorientation than by convincing the target audience. Confusion of issues, rationalization regardless of logic and consistency, repetition of statements until they are accepted as true through sheer weariness, the use of suspense to build up dramatic effect and of demagogy to bully sectors of society, and sheer falsehood and duplicity are drawn upon as readily as if they were listed in a book of propaganda projection instructions. Great ingenuity is employed in the timing of a propaganda action so that it makes the world's headlines without immediately being refuted or neutralized.

Probably the most effective play is accusing the other country of what they are up to themselves. In fact, this practice is so well understood now in the Free World that, when the United States is falsely attacked for taking some action, the leaders in the Free World try immediately to discover whether the USSR has already taken that action or is planning to do so.

The Kremlin endeavors to lay a basic frame of reference in its propaganda to confuse audiences on the key issue of right and wrong, in order to make them susceptible to its propaganda and impervious to Free World communications. With changes of political policy line, its slogans and arguments are modified, even reversed, and thus aimed toward the new objective.

These propagandists divert attention from an important issue to focus public attention on an insignificant detail, use artificial contrasts of ideas and arguments, direct one argument toward one group and a diametrically opposite, contradictory one toward a second group on the same issue, overwhelm the casual reader or auditor with complex "scientific" argumentation. They manipulate tenses to describe a situation which existed years ago and imply that it exists today.

Every opportunity is used to drive a wedge between groups, such as Europe vs. America, in the name of culture or "sovereignty," and America vs. Europe, in the name of "liberal democracy." The Kremlin propagandists try to trade on our moral sense—which, of course, they do not share—indulge in group flattery, and the Goebbels-type "Big Lie" and personality "smear." They promise the moon to the unwary and ignorant, try to take credit for the achievements of others, and claim to be first in all inventions.

They employ a half-truth or quarter-truth to "prove" an argument and use such phrases as "everybody knows," "as is well known," "the whole world knows," whenever they cannot document their points. The phony syllogism is also resorted to which runs along these lines: (a) John Doe heads the local United States Information Service; (b) information services gather information; so do spies; (c) John Doe, therefore, is a spy. And they frequently hang a "dirty" adjective around an expendable noun with such phrases as "skyrocketing profits" and "mercenary press."

Tricks with words are sprinkled through all Kremlin propaganda and can be picked out of any official statement. "Aesopian language" has been in vogue since Lenin was working under the tsars as a revolutionary. It consists of using a particular word to convey one meaning to the initiated and another to those who are to be fooled. Whenever "reform" was used in one of Lenin's published pieces it meant "the revolution" to his followers. In fact, this practice has led to the development by the Kremlin of a series of false labels which today constitute an entire vocabulary of upside-down language. This produced what is now termed "logocide." It is of particular significance to us from the standpoint of propaganda conflict when our symbols are stolen and turned against us, as has been done, for instance, with "Iron Curtain" and "creation of tensions." But when they use "democratic" to identify groups of dictatorially ruled Kremlin communists they have gone farther, penetrated more deeply into the foundations of our society. They have taken a serious step through semantics to destroy the ideals of humanity for which we stand.

A Typical Speech

To show that many tricks of the propaganda trade are applied in one single major address, Khrushchev's speech of September 23, 1960, before the United Nations General Assembly has been chosen. The element of *timing* is important in this instance: Khrushchev emphasized the need for continued "struggle" against colonialism precisely at the time when delegations from numerous African countries were being seated; he also professed love of peace at the time of neutralist pressure for the resumption of disarmament talks. The whole effort illustrates the "thief-calling-others-thieves" technique. Ignoring the fact that the Congo had been granted independence by Belgium, the Kremlin boss pretended to believe that the Congo's independence was being threatened by the Belgian "colonialists" and their friends, although it was clearly the Kremlin that was trying to gain a foothold in the former colony by means of promoting chaos and backing its local agents as the "legitimate" government.

His reliance on elements such as *revolutionary parliamentarianism, demagogy, repetition,* and *confusion* is fairly obvious throughout the speech. Only slightly less obvious is the dictator's use of devices such as *group flattery; exploitation of the West's political naïveté; exploitation of fear, of humane qualities of the Western world, of free society rivalries,* and *of inertia* as shown in the following excerpts:

> 1. The new, more progressive, more equitable has established itself. Our epoch is one of the rapid emergence of new forms of the existence of human society, of an unprecedented upsurge to domination over the forces of nature, of an unparalleled upsurge to a more progressive social order.

(Takes for granted that *communism is the wave of the future;* professes the *scientificized belief* it cannot be stopped; Kremlin communism is tacitly identified with "progressive social order.")

> 2. No one can dispute the fact that the Soviet Union has never spared any effort to make international relations continue further to develop in this gratifying direction. However, the sinister forces who profit by maintaining international tension cling hard to their positions. These are a small handful of people, but they are fairly influential and greatly affect the policies of their states.

(Uses the stock phrase, "No one can dispute the fact." It is *sinister* forces—supposedly controlling the Free World—which prevent the peoples of the world from enjoying a Kremlin-sponsored era of brotherhood and peace. *Exploitation of political naïveté; artificial contrast; promising the moon.*)

> 3. Like a deep source of dangerous infection in an organism these bases destroy the normal political and economic life of states upon which they have been imposed. They block the establishment of normal relations between these states and neighboring countries. Indeed,

what kind of normal relations can there be if the people in these neighboring countries cannot sleep in peace?

(Trying to weaken Free World military might by *exploiting fear, political naïveté; confusion.*)

4. Courageous Cuba has become the object of all kinds of attacks, intrigues and subversion, economic aggression, and, finally, poorly concealed threats of intervention.

... For years the fruits of the Cuban people's labor were used not by themselves but by the American monopolies.... Cuba's purported guilt consists in that the freedom-loving and brave Cuban people wanted to live an independent life.

(Covers up for taking over Cuban revolution by branding Washington as exploiter of weak nations, colonialist, servant of "Wall Street." Fostering image of Kremlin as champion of weak nations. *Artificial contrast; confusion; thief calling others thieves.*)

5. The young Republic of the Congo already on the third day after the proclamation of her independence fell victim to aggression. Before the eyes of the whole world the Belgian government attempted to deprive that country of its freedom, to take back what the Congolese people have been selflessly fighting for over decades.... Armed aggression against the Congo has been condemned by the whole of Africa, by world-wide public opinion. ... The colonialists decided to get a puppet government created which, posing as an "independent" government, would, in fact, be obedient to the will of the colonizers.

The colonialists tried to bring this about by crude methods and direct interference, as they always do in such cases. Unfortunately, in the case of the Congo they have been doing this unseemly work through the United Nations secretary general, Mr. Hammarskjold, and his staff.

Lumumba is certainly no communist, but he is a

patriot of his country and honestly serves his own people in their struggle for liberation from the colonial yoke. . . .

The Soviet government has welcomed and is welcoming now the struggle of the colonial peoples for independence and will do its utmost to render moral support and material assistance to the colonial peoples in their just struggle. . . .

The Assembly should give a rebuff to the colonialists and their stooges and call Mr. Hammarskjold to order so that he should not abuse his position as secretary general and should discharge his duties in strict conformity with the provisions of the United Nations Charter and the decisions of the Security Council.

(Puts Kremlin in role of protector of colonial peoples, of all "honest patriots" against exploitation by "imperialists" and their alleged servants in the United Nations. *Double false assumption:* "armed aggression" has been committed, and it has been "condemned by world-wide opinion." *Revolutionary Parliamentarianism:* tries to destroy Hammarskjold and United Nations, when it is clear Kremlin cannot dominate them.)

6. There is no need here to describe in detail the impoverished state of over 100,000,000 human beings deprived of their rights, who are still languishing under colonial bondage. . . . What is happening in those countries and regions justly evokes profound indignation and revulsion among all honest people on earth. . . .

Look what is happening in the colonies today. Africa is boiling and swirling like a volcano. The Algerian people have been waging a heroic selfless struggle for national independence for about six years. Ever greater resolve is being manifested in the struggle for their rights by the peoples of Kenya, Tanganyika, Uganda, Ruanda Urundi, Angola, Mozambique, Northern Rhodesia, Southern Rhodesia, Sierra Leone, South-West Africa,

Zanzibar, as well as West Irian, Puerto Rico, and many other colonies.

It should be clear to all that the struggle of the peoples for their liberation cannot be checked by any means of force, because this is a great historic process which is going on with ever growing irreversible force. The domination of this or that state over another can be prolonged by a year or two but, just as in the past the bourgeois system came to replace feudalism, and just as today the socialist system is replacing capitalism, the slavery of colonialism will yield to freedom. Such are the laws of human development, and only adventurers can expect that mountains of corpses and millions of victims would stop the arrival of a radiant future.

(Again posing as *champion of colonial peoples,* the Kremlin propagandist adroitly reiterates the Marxist concept of *"immutable laws of history,"* which make the *ultimate victory* of communism a certainty. *Scientificized argument.* Stock phrase: "It should be clear to all." The height of effrontery: the ruler of the biggest colonial empire in the world mentions *Puerto Rico* as a colony struggling for its rights. *Big lie; group flattery; demagogy.*)

7. The colonialist policy with all its atrocities is supported by the allies of the colonial powers in aggressive military blocs. . . .

The Soviet Union faithful to the policy of peace and support to the struggle of oppressed peoples for their national independence which was proclaimed by V. I. Lenin, the founder of the Soviet state, is urging the United Nations to raise its voice in defense of the just cause of liberating the colonies, and to undertake prompt action toward the complete elimination of the colonial regime of administration.

(Images of Kremlin defense of peace and justice and of colonial "liberation" are made more vivid by the technique of *manipu-*

lating the tenses, i.e., speaking of colonial "atrocities" as if they were being committed now, rather than perhaps a generation or more ago. *Exploitation of humane qualities of the West.*)

8. I will not disclose a secret by saying that we entertain no liking for capitalism. But we do not want to foist our system upon other countries. So let those who determine the policy of states whose social system differs from ours also abandon their fruitless and dangerous attempts to dictate their will. It is high time for them, too, to admit that the choice of a way of life is the internal concern of every people. Let us build up our relations taking into consideration the actual facts of reality. This will mean peaceful coexistence.

... Whether they want it or not, but even those states whose governments still do not want to voice their approval of the ideas of peaceful coexistence, are forced to practice them in many respects. ...

If one is to speak about the actual shape of peaceful coexistence one might point to the relations maintained by the socialist countries with the new states of Asia, Africa, and Latin America which have set themselves free from the oppression of colonialism and embarked upon the path of independent policy. Typical of such relations are friendship, great mutual sympathy and respect, economic and technical assistance to less developed countries without any political or military strings attached. The relations of the countries of the socialist camp with neutral capitalist states such as, for instance, Finland, Austria, Afghanistan, Sweden, and others can also be cited as another good example.

... The Soviet Government is ready to go on doing its best to improve relations between our country and the United States of America.

(Reiterates the theme of peaceful coexistence. Reassures the world that the USSR does not want to impose her system on others, without explaining that he means the USSR government only, not the Kremlin international communist conspiracy. Again, he is not bothered by the illogic of expressing the wish for improved relations in the same speech in which he attacks the United States government. *Exploitation of inertia, naïveté; repetition; confusion; demagogy; group flattery.*)

> 9. The executive body of the United Nations should reflect the actual situation that obtains in the world today. The United Nations includes states parties to the military blocs of the Western powers, socialist states, and neutralist countries....
>
> We consider it reasonable and just for the executive body of the United Nations to be constituted not as one person—the secretary general—but as three representatives of the states belonging to the three basic above mentioned groups who could be invested with the lofty trust of the United Nations. The crux of the matter is not even in the name of this body but in that this executive body should represent the states parties to the military blocs of the Western powers, the socialist states, and the neutralist states. This composition of the United Nations executive body will create conditions for a more correct implementation of the decisions taken.
>
> ... Then the United Nations executive will really be a democratic body, it will really safeguard the interests of all United Nations member states irrespective of the social and political systems of the various states making up the United Nations.

(Idea of USSR bloc respectability is plugged, together with the suggestion that the USSR wants the United Nations to be really representative, i.e., not a supposed servant of the Western powers. *Semantic juggling; confusion; repetition; saturation.*)

> 10. ... Practice shows, however, that the United States restricts and curtails the rights of the representatives of

various states. Facts are known, for instance, of the representatives of young African and Asian states being subjected to racial discrimination in the United States and, moreover, to attacks by gangsters.

... I can declare in all responsibility that if it should be considered expedient to house the United Nations Headquarters in the Soviet Union we guarantee the best possible conditions for its work, complete freedom, and security for the representatives of all states irrespective of their political or religious convictions, and of the color of their skin, since in our country the sovereign rights of all states, the equality of all nations, big and small, are held in high esteem.

(Tries to lower the prestige of the United States; *driving a wedge* between Free World countries by trading on resentments of former colonial nations against the white man in general, and on sensibilities about national sovereignty and prestige. As a by-product, Khrushchev is trying to maneuver the United States into silencing anti-Kremlin demonstrators in New York. The demonstrators are labeled "gangsters" in accordance with the *false-label* technique. *Exploitation of rivalries; confusion; repetition; group flattery; threats.*)

CHAPTER 5.

Prescription for the American Propagandists

IT IS more difficult for a country with a democratic form of government to compete against one with a dictatorship in a cold propaganda war than in a hot shooting war. In both kinds of conflict reins of government must be drawn up sharply in centralized, concentrated control to organize the total resources of the community against those already centralized and organized by the opposition. But in a propaganda war the threat to physical security is not so evident to the public, so their cooperation is not spontaneous. The delicate problem confronting the United States in entering the propaganda conflict against the USSR consists in accomplishing this maneuver without sacrificing the freedoms we are fighting to preserve.

This problem is so difficult and so fundamental and important to our society that only the President can possibly try to solve it. It may possibly affect our way of life, modify the structure of our federal government organization, and alter the present operations of a number of government departments in Washington. And President Kennedy on April 20, 1961, declared that he was preparing to do just that when he said "we intend to re-examine and reorient our forces of all kinds; our tactics and our institutions here in this community. We intend to intensify our efforts for a struggle in many ways more difficult than war. . . ."

To show that Kremlin propaganda was a threat to the world's and our security and therefore of bipartisan national concern, former Vice President Nixon augmented President Kennedy's statement on May 6, 1961. He said that USSR strategy rules out world war but aims to pick off smaller nations without war if possible, and is willing to risk war if necessary. He observed that there was no easy way to meet this threat—not alone by economic assistance, moral support, military hardware, or "a giant propaganda offensive to make people understand us and like us better. . . ." Then Mr. Nixon suggested developing new programs "that can deal more quickly and decisively with the political, subversive, and para-military tactics" of the Kremlin communists.

Propaganda vs. Information

From his experience in the Eisenhower administration, the former Vice President knows this has not been done so far. For instance, in 1959 the United States Advisory Commission on Information, in a reappraisal of the United States Information Agency and its work, recommended the adoption of three basic principles designed "to establish through widespread understanding a broad base of people in foreign countries who will themselves resist and who will influence others to resist the misrepresentations about the United States which are circulated by communist propaganda and other sources of misinformation."

The three principles were:

(1) In informing others about ourselves, we must not try to remake them in our image, or to persuade them to swap their way of life for ours.

(2) Information must be presented in the indigenous foreign idiom and couched in language that will have meaning to the foreign audience. The presentation, but not the facts, must therefore vary from area to area.

(3) Programs must emphasize the basic identity of the national needs and interests of individual target countries with those of the United States. The story of the United States must be told in relation to the background, the history, and problems of the different audiences.

While the objective and its underlying principles were sound and timely in their emphasis, they did not go far enough into the political aspects of propaganda. They could apply to friendly countries, and allied countries such as Great Britain but by themselves offered no serious competition to the Kremlin. They were the information man's guide to information, but not the propagandist's guide to propaganda.

The same group might now, in cooperation with the review boards appointed to investigate para-military operations following the Cuban fiasco, draw up a plan for American propaganda projection which would coordinate the efforts of all government agencies operating in the foreign field and make recommendation about where the policy and operation of this work should be located.

Open Diplomacy and Open Propaganda

When De Tocqueville said "The Anglo-American relies on personal interest to accomplish his ends and gives free scope to the unguided exertions and common sense of the citizens: the Russian centers all authority of society in a single arm," he provided us with a clue to a successful approach to establishing a viable propaganda apparatus. Our national character, our society, our type of government are founded on frankness and forthrightness. We would be defeated if we attempted to use delusion as a method of operation. In fact, every time we pretend that something is not so when it is, and vice versa, we end by making fools of ourselves. As a practical measure we should not attempt to beat the Russians at their own game—but attempt to change the game and make them compete with us in ours.

By employing an "open-diplomacy" policy and open propaganda it would be possible to insist that the USSR do the same. We should not go in for subversion and we should acknowledge, as we did in the case of Cuba, that we help freedom fighters. But at the same time we should show that we are fighting subversion by the USSR, that it is the Kremlin which has first committed aggressive acts for purposes of political conquest, and we who are retaliating.

In one way or another we must capture the propaganda initiative as soon as possible. We must take the offensive against the

USSR and drive it over the air waves deep into the USSR and all her possessions. We must agitate overtly and support those states, organizations, and individuals who are prepared to raise their voices to choose freedom over servitude.

When the United States government feels it cannot, for diplomatic reasons, speak out directly, when the Kremlin communist attacks cannot be answered on a state-to-state basis, private groups should undertake to mount propaganda campaigns on their own.

Propaganda Policy and Organization

The American propagandists—both governmental and private—need to have the political objectives spelled out for them specifically in regard to conflict with the USSR in third countries and to dealing with the situation in the USSR herself. Once this is accomplished, propaganda or psychological warfare targets can be determined and each operational unit can set up its own programming.

It is essential in this process that psychological factors be given serious consideration at the planning stage in formulating foreign political policy. Also, it is of equal importance that policy be planned for propaganda and psychological warfare with just as completely defined objectives as those for foreign political policy. The issues to be dealt with, the timing and tailoring for different audiences all over the globe, should be worked out in advance of all policy implementation.

Under the Eisenhower administration, the National Security Council was assigned the task of all-over policy formulation, and the Operations Coordinating Board the function of implementing it. However, the policy did not come out definitely, clearly, or quickly enough to be effective. And the implementation function turned largely into a liaison exercise with the various government departments concerned. The OCB was eliminated when the new administration assumed office.

At the time of this writing, the Administration is reviewing the general situation of para-military activities into which propaganda in the Kremlin sense now falls. From its conclusions the Administration will decide what new machinery should be created or what old machinery might be retooled to deal with this problem.

Our Propaganda Formulation

American propagandists need a number-one spokesman, a focal point around which they can fashion their formulations. There is only one individual who can serve in this capacity and compete successfully with the Kremlin and Khrushchev; that is the President of the United States. If he not only steps into this number-one position but is himself propaganda-minded, American propagandists will have a truly effective champion—and inspiration—to wage psychological warfare.

These propagandists need to be told specifically that the primary target is the USSR, the state, which threatens world security, and not some ideology such as Kremlin communism, some social doctrine or way of life. In fact, our propagandists need to be told that ideological competition is Khrushchev's favorite red herring for Americans, that in fighting the theory of communism we give it a dignity and value it does not merit, and that in doing so we fail to expose it as a technique of delusion of a would-be world dictator.

American propagandists also need the backing of the American public so they can have a firm foundation from which to project their product. And the national point of view should be a realistic one. Our propaganda conflict with the USSR cannot be viewed as a sports contest in which, for instance, the side placing a man in space first is necessarily going to win the propaganda war. The conflict is not one simply of immediately competing images of prestige; it is long-range, and the cumulative effect on world opinion is the one that counts. If the USSR beats us by a few months but hides her failures in secrecy, suppresses the information about the number of human beings sacrificed in the process, and we admit all our failures and show our real concern for the human beings involved, we will ultimately leave the better image and will inspire the greater trust.

American propaganda with respect to the USSR breaks down into two sections: showing ourselves just as we are and, of course, emphasizing our good points; and exposing the fraudulence of the USSR claims, lies, and subversive operations, without, however, belittling the progress the people have been able to achieve in the face of hardships.

In revealing ourselves, we should show that we are fighting for what we consider a civilized life: to be able to *enjoy* the maximum amount of personal liberty feasible without threatening or destroying our traditional system of government. Personal liberty comes first, and we try to find for ourselves and others the security enabling people to breathe freely, to work and *play*, and indulge themselves in human emotions, and to enjoy the products of their efforts as just rewards.

We should emphasize our humanitarianism; we have more generosity of spirit, more concern for the other person, for any one single individual than has any other society. We should make this known all over the world. Also, our democracy, our liberty for the individual, our free enterprise system, our industrial society we built from scratch. The basic concepts which enabled us to do it, and would enable others to follow this example, should be revealed particularly to the emerging, presently underindustrialized peoples of Asia and Africa.

We should tell third countries over and over again the truth about our intentions toward them. We are in favor of any kind of economic system they follow as long as it is subject to popular control, to checks by periodic free voting. We do not wish to impose our way of life on other countries, but we are determined not to allow the USSR to inflict her totalitarian domination on them either. We do not seek to exploit third countries the way the USSR has done with the captive nations of eastern Europe.

If we have taken a holier-than-thou attitude in the past, we should stop it completely. We are not finer people than the

Russian people, the Germans, the French, or the Congolese. But we have a point of view about government and consumer goods and social benefits, about the free functioning of different political philosophies and expressions of dissent which we consider better than that of the Kremlin. In fact, our society which was literally constructed here by foreigners is the living protest against the single-arm rule in any society, a rule for which the current Bolshevik regime in the USSR stands.

In exposing Kremlin techniques of aggression and subversion we should point out that it slanders the United States in order to break down confidence in us and thereby our power to stand in its way of world conquest. We should explain how its propagandists endeavor to undermine the institutions in our country and misrepresent our true image to its own subjects.

We should expose the roles of Kremlin agents, witting and unwitting, who serve in so-called communist parties in the Free World and in "front" groups, and of diplomatic representatives in the never-ceasing campaign for totalitarian control of the world.

The warmongering of the USSR (since the Suez Crisis Khrushchev has threatened twenty different countries with USSR missiles on one hundred and thirty occasions) should be continually brought to the world's attention. And the two-faced fraud of "peaceful coexistence" should be relentlessly denounced. The methods of political domination and economic exploitation of third countries practiced by the USSR should be listed in detail. And above all the disregard for suffering, the lack of compassion, the cheapness with which a human life is held should be highlighted on every pertinent occasion.

The actual annexation of the countries of eastern Europe should be referred to constantly, and on appropriate anniversaries of the take-overs, full reviews should be made of the methods and the steps employed to subjugate the peoples. And the glorious, hopeless revolt of the Hungarians against the USSR occupation should be kept alive in the world's conscience until freedom is restored.

To document this Kremlin drive toward reducing the entire

world to totalitarian servitude we should cite the experiences of
the nationality groups in the USSR, the captive nations of eastern
Europe, the developing experiences of Castro's Cuba. These experiences should be exposed so they will be a warning to all
peoples—and leaders—who contemplate succumbing to USSR
propaganda encroachment. It is impossible, we should repeat, to
embrace Kremlin communism without becoming subservient to
the USSR.

We should keep on hammering away at the significance of
Tito's break with the Kremlin, pointing out that he would not
remain under servitude on an international basis, although he
favored a communist domestic system. We should show that the
USSR does not have a monopoly of the communisms, but seeks
only a monopoly of imperialist control.

To peoples in third countries we should explain how the Kremlin propagandists create the trappings of democracy but withhold
the reality, how those trappings are the ruse for capture. We
should at every opportunity reveal the tricks of the Kremlin
propaganda trade of delusion and upside-down language.

To the peoples of the USSR we should expose the disservice
done them by the current Bolshevik regime in the Kremlin. We
should demonstrate how this regime deliberately maintains—at a
high pitch—tensions of war, threats of war, and propaganda conflict in the world. We should explain the regime's purpose which
is to focus attention on a phony threat to internal security so as
to justify continued oppressive controls and the maintenance of
the present group in power. We should state plainly that the
continued aggression of the adventuristic Khrushchev may trigger
an all-out world war which could destroy the results of decades
of backbreaking labor of the peoples of the USSR.

All of the USSR vulnerabilities, including the chafing of the
different nationality groups under Kremlin oppression, should be
exploited in our propaganda to the peoples of the USSR as fully
as indicated by our foreign policy objectives. Since Marxism-
Leninism is the philosophy of the "have-nots" and the peoples of
the USSR are now in a position to be the "haves," we should

suggest to them that they deserve a more positive forward-looking social doctrine to produce freedom for the individual, to spur initiative, to provide free enterprise, and secure for each citizen his equitable share in the enjoyment of consumer goods. Taking the propaganda attack aggressively to the peoples of the USSR herself as our target number one should constitute the core of our propaganda-psychological warfare effort. Until and unless the Bolshevik regime in the Kremlin changes its foreign policy or is ousted there will be no peace and no security in the world.

Techniques

In devising their techniques, American propagandists have much to learn from their opposite numbers in the Kremlin. The lessons can be studied simply by substituting truth for lies and partial truths, and concentrating on means for inducement to action, for agitation toward political objectives, on framing phraseology with political twists. Ideas can be obtained, too, from Madison Avenue and from the sociologists as guides for the wording of the output. These will not substitute for policy plans, however, which have to determine the content of the output.

Repetition, saturation, timing, suspense, and dramatization can all be drawn upon, just as they are in the field of advertising and promotion in this country. Direct confrontation, such as calling Khrushchev a liar when he is lying or accusing him of duplicity when he tells different stories to different audiences, or exposing his contradictory statements, should not be shied away from for diplomatic reasons. Ridicule, satire, and humor are particularly effective against the pomposity of Kremlin agents: for it they have no defense—and no offense.

It must be kept in mind that propaganda does not have to be fresh and catchy to be effective; it must bore its way into the consciousness of the individual and remain there for future reference, influencing action. It cannot be objective in the informational sense, that is, simply projecting the news of the day without discrimination; propaganda must emphasize those points which are to be impressed on the audience. It cannot claim to put out "all the news that's fit to print" but must "sell," like TV commercials, in a highly competitive political market.

To accomplish their mission, the American propagandists must not only dramatize on top of the news but be dull where there is no news peg readily at hand. They must be patient and aggressive and not meet every accusation by the Kremlin with abject explanations. Ignoring the charges is often a most effective way of dismissing them, but they must not allow the Kremlin to play this same trick on us.

Like the Kremlin, American propagandists must use, when necessary, power and the threat of power to make propaganda impressions stick. But as suggested by Mr. Nixon, we must be prepared as a matter of foreign policy to take the actions we imply if called upon to do so.

In dealing directly with the USSR and Kremlin propaganda, American propagandists would do well to seek advice from former citizens of the USSR and former officials of the captive nations of eastern Europe who have professional experience in conducting state-to-state relations with their neighbors. These people are prepared to help and can offer insights which Americans can hardly aspire to.

Help, too, is needed by the American propagandists from the professionals in the communications media of the United States. They might have useful suggestions to make as to how Kremlin propaganda can be countered. They might also be wary of being put to use by the Kremlin propagandists for their own purposes and find ways of presenting balanced impressions so as to offset the delusion of Kremlin propaganda.

There is nothing in the American character or form of government to prevent us from waging a successful propaganda war against the USSR. What is needed is a total cooperative effort of all the citizens. And to produce this effort, the people—at all levels of personal and professional interest—need a basic education in political propaganda. From mass media and general-information programs to courses in universities and in government, our people must be alerted to and tutored in the techniques of

Kremlin propaganda and the responsibilities we have to shoulder to counter them.

Once aroused, Americans will rise to the demands of a propaganda war in the same aggressive spirit they respond to the demands of a shooting war. They will follow the President when he says, "We intend to intensify our efforts for a struggle in many ways more difficult than war. . . ."

APPENDIXES

1. Glossary of Kremlin Communist Upside-Down Language

AGGRESSION—Determined armed opposition to military or political actions of the Kremlin or its local agents.

AGGRESSIVE CIRCLES—People, particularly in the United States, who distrust the Kremlin and say so.

AGGRESSOR—Anyone opposing Kremlin imperialism.

AGRARIAN REFORMER—Alias for "communist," to be used in propaganda in Free World to make a revolutionary venture in rural areas look respectable.

ANTI-COLONIALISM ⎫
ANTI-FASCISM ⎬—communism
ANTI-IMPERIALISM ⎭

ANTI-PARTY—A handy term for the current Kremlin ruler to use against rivals in the party.

CHAUVINISM, BOURGEOIS—Non-Russian nationalism, which is bad.

CONCILIATIONISM—Belief that differences between Kremlin communists and heretical communists may be resolved, which is bad as long as the current Kremlin ruler says it cannot be done.

COOPERATION—Arrangement whereby the Free World is required to let the Kremlin do what it wants, and even help it in getting what it wants.

COSMOPOLITAN—Citizen of a USSR bloc country who, at the wrong moment, notes some positive values in noncommunist countries; often simply a Kremlin subject who has aroused the ire of the Kremlin.

COUNTERREVOLUTION—Revolt for liberation from Kremlin communism.

CULT OF PERSONALITY—Counterproductive overdose of terroristic rule by the Kremlin's boss; by definition, only a past ruler, never the current one, may be accused of indulging in it.

CULTURE, SOCIALIST—Idea, not necessarily connected with culture, that arts and sciences must be subservient to Kremlin communist ideology.

DEFENSE OF FREEDOM—Attempt to install or maintain Kremlin communist dictatorship.

DEMOCRACY—In its "ideal" state, a Kremlin communist dictatorship.

DEMOCRATIC—Kremlin communistic or, outside the USSR bloc, eager to serve the interests of the Kremlin.

DEMOCRATIC CENTRALISM—Concept, first spelled out by Lenin, which assures the Kremlin communist party leadership of the unquestioning obedience of lower-echelon leaders and the party rank and file; in other words, not democracy, but dictatorship.

DEVIATIONIST—One of the worst names a Kremlin communist could be called: it accuses him of not toeing the current party line or, if he is outside the USSR, of not fully acknowledging the undisputed right of the CPSU to call the tune.

DICTATORSHIP OF THE PROLETARIAT—Dictatorship of the communist party, which in turn means dictatorship of the Kremlin.

DISARMAMENT—Weakening of the military preparedness of nations outside the USSR bloc.

DIVERSIONIST—Kremlin communist who has disagreed with the ruler on a point of policy and is being thrown to the wolves.

DOGMATIST—Kremlin communist who is not nimble enough in following the zigzags of the party line when "interpreting" Marxism-Leninism.

ELECTION—Kremlin technique of forcing the ruled to endorse their rulers.

ENEMY OF THE PEOPLE—Anyone who does not take orders from the Kremlin.

FASCIST—Free World leader whom the Kremlin considers dangerous; current target of Kremlin's big propaganda guns.

FORMALISM—Artist's aberration of thinking too much of his art and too little of Kremlin propaganda.

FRACTIONALISM—Crime charged against top-level cliques which have lost out in the struggle for power in the party.

FREEDOM OF SPEECH—In the USSR bloc countries, obligation to praise the regime; in the Free World, opportunity to disseminate Kremlin propaganda.

ILLEGAL—Not arranged for, desired by, or in the interest of the Kremlin.

IMPERIALISM—Any policies of a powerful state which, when its national security is at stake, is willing and able to oppose the Kremlin.

INNER-PARTY DEMOCRACY—Right of party members to criticize others or themselves, when they know the Kremlin ruler wants them to do so.

INTERNATIONALISM—Right and duty of people outside the USSR to defend and support the Kremlin by every means.

KULAK—Any peasant opposing Kremlin communist agricultural policies.

LAYING THE FOUNDATION OF SOCIALISM—Physical extermination of individuals or groups to facilitate establishment of a Kremlin communist dictatorship.

LIBERALISM—Ideological aberration resulting from the survival of bourgeois morality within the USSR bloc, but an admirable idea outside the USSR bloc if it serves Kremlin policy or propaganda.

LIBERATION—Establishment, through the use of force, of a Kremlin-controlled regime.

MARXISM-LENINISM—Communist ideology approved by the current Kremlin dictator.

MILITARISM—Proposed or actual building up of military defenses by governments not controlled by the Kremlin.

MONOPOLIST—Free World industrialist, particularly a successful American industrialist.

MORALITY—View that everything must be done to strengthen the Kremlin's regime and to destroy Free World regimes.

NEGOTIATION—Tactical maneuver to get something in a pleasant way which otherwise would have to be taken by force; diplomatic phrase in the relentless war on the Free World.

OBJECTIVISM—Serious aberration consisting of seeing in the historical process anything that might justify a non-Kremlin communist system; in other words, an ideological propaganda sin of commission or omission.

OPPORTUNISM—Crime of believing that social advances may be achieved without a Kremlin communist revolution.

PACIFISM—Failure, on the part of someone in the USSR bloc, to recognize the need of USSR orbit countries to be armed to the teeth.

PATRIOTISM—In the USSR, Russian nationalism, guided by the Kremlin, which is good; in the rest of the world, willingness to follow the Kremlin lead.

PEACE LOVING—Any policies pursued by USSR bloc regimes or any other government accepting Kremlin domination.

PEACEFUL COEXISTENCE—Khrushchev's version of the "Cold War"; based on the promotion of class dissension and struggles and civil strife in states outside the USSR bloc.

PEOPLE, THE—Kremlin communists, their collaborators and sympathizers in other countries.

PEOPLE'S DEMOCRACY—Far from denoting democracy, the term describes a regime, controlled by the Kremlin, which is trying to turn its country into a copy of the USSR as quickly as possible.

POPULAR—Kremlin communistic or deserving of the Kremlin's support.

PROGRESSIVE—Kremlin communistic; anyone supporting Kremlin policies.

PROLETARIAN INTERNATIONALISM—Idea that the Kremlin has to be supported by labor organizations throughout the world and that, conversely, the USSR regime has the right to meddle with labor movements throughout the world.

PROLETARIAT—Those members of the working class who, through their organizations, support Kremlin policies.

REACTIONARY—Opposed to "progressive" (i.e., Kremlin communist) ideas or actions.

REFORM—Kremlin-led or -inspired revolution in its initial stage, when it still depends on noncommunist support.

REVISIONISM—Criminal theory holding that Kremlin-approved Marxist-Leninist ideology may not be infallible.

REVOLUTIONARY—Unquestioningly obedient to the current Kremlin ruler.

SLANDERER—Anyone criticizing the Kremlin system, its leaders, or its actions.

SELF-DETERMINATION—Duty of nations within the Soviet orbit to stay in it, and of those outside the orbit to allow themselves to be swallowed up by it.

SEPARATIST PROPAGANDA—Treasonable expression of a desire for national independence on the part of people in any country subservient to the Kremlin.

SOCIALIST NATIONS—Countries controlled by the Kremlin.

SOCIALIST REALISM—Idea that life should not be represented as it is but as it should be according to Kremlin communist doctrine.

STATUS QUO—Arrangement by which no one may interfere with the domination of the Kremlin over its satellites.

TRAITOR—Anyone opposing the Kremlin, particularly a former party member who has turned against Kremlin subversion.

UPRISING—Kremlin-led revolution which is camouflaged as a spontaneous occurrence.

VANGUARD ROLE—Assumption by Kremlin communists of leadership in subversive activities.

WAR, JUST—Any war fought by or for the Kremlin communist regime.

WAR, UNJUST—Any war which the Kremlin says is not a just war.

WARMONGERS—Synonymous with "aggressive circles," particularly today in the United States.

2. Kremlin Propaganda Stratagems

EXPLOITATION OF HUMAN QUALITIES IN FREE SOCIETIES [1]

The following are some of the characteristics of Western peoples Kremlin propagandists seek to exploit:

Democratic Orientation of the West

Since democratic government hinges on the consent of the governed, party politics are an essential part of the democratic process. Kremlin communists use this political activity not to participate in the democratic way of life, but as a means of subverting the system that gives them this opportunity.

Fear

By means of rocket rattling and other threats, Soviet propaganda seeks to frighten the timid and tries to persuade leading men in critical areas of political and government activity to make a deal with the Kremlin in the expectation that the Kremlin would be ruthless in victory and the Free World tolerant.

Inertia

Kremlin propaganda is designed to induce
- A) "Conservative" thinkers to believe Kremlin diplomacy is the same as diplomacy of other countries.
- B) "Advanced" thinkers to believe the economy of the USSR has no equal.
- C) "Liberal" thinkers to believe the Kremlin stands for ideas of the left: for workers, for progress, for economic rationality, social justice, the independence of peoples.

[1] Acknowledgment is made of the substantial contributions made by Robert S. Byfield,*The Fifth Weapon,* Bookmailer, 1954, and by Suzanne Labin, *The Technique of Soviet Propaganda,* A Study presented by the Subcommittee to Investigate the Administration of the Internal Security Act and Other Internal Security Laws of the Committee on the Judiciary United States Senate Eighty-sixth Congress Second Session; United States Government Printing Office, Washington, D.C., 1960.

Because many people in the West favor quietude and are lazy, they like to eliminate the necessity of giving special thought and treatment to USSR actions. Consequently, they prefer to have faith in the Kremlin's assurances, its treaty offers, and its diplomatic representations. But to the Kremlin, diplomatic adjustment is not an end, while propaganda is. A treaty is an expedient, transitory in nature, according to Lenin.

As for the Kremlin's economic claims, we cannot check the accuracy of their statistics: open inspection is not permitted.

And in regard to ideology, the Kremlin is digging the earliest grave for the leftists: they are the easiest to liquidate, having been appointed to positions in the first front government of a country subverted and taken over.

Humane Impulses of the West

The humane aspects of Western society are exploited by Kremlin propagandists to weaken Western morale and military power:

A) Uneasy conscience: for past sins of imperialism and colonialism.
B) Pacifism: to make firmness look like warmongering.
C) Tolerance: to allow establishment and activities of communist parties.
D) Objectivity: to incite neutralism by striking a balance between United States "faults" and USSR "faults."
E) Humor: to persuade audiences of the simplicity, sincerity, and humaneness of Kremlin leaders.
F) Liberals' mistrust of government power: to weaken Western governments and paralyze Western unity.

METHODS OF OPERATION

Conquest by stages: A country or institution is taken over piecemeal. No slice is large enough to arouse the victim into organizing resistance. For instance, in Romania, propaganda attacks were made first on some "mistakes" in American foreign policy, then successively on its foreign policy as a whole, on certain personalities and leaders, on American character and intentions, on local American operations, on local American representatives, until finally the United States Information Office was closed by the regime and the legation was reduced to a very small complement of officers and clerks.

Corruption from within: Key points are taken over in advance of complete conquest with the help of the Trojan-horse device.

In Romania, the Ministry of Information was one of the first taken over by members of the local Kremlin communist party after the installation of the fellow-traveling premier. It held control of a vast majority of the opinion-molding institutions in the country and played a leading role in the "softening-up" campaign leading up to the forced abdication of the King and the end of independence for Romania.

Revolutionary parliamentarianism: This is The System's name for the tactic of using forums and discussions for ulterior purposes other than reaching agreement.

Kremlin communist members of Parliament in democratic countries have traditionally obstructed orderly exchanges of views; they have consistently tried to procrastinate, to disrupt debates. Their purposes are first of all to hit the front page with their propaganda; secondly to harass and embarrass the opposition. In so doing they are trying to lower the prestige of the Parliament as an institution. These same practices can be observed today in all international organizations in which Kremlin communists participate. The forum the USSR cannot control, it attempts to destroy.

PROPAGANDA TECHNIQUES

Rationalization: Consistency and logic, as we know them, play no particular role in Kremlin propaganda. Kremlin propagandists find that the requirements of logical procedure cramp their style. Instead of arriving at a conclusion inductively, i.e., step by step, they like to start by stating a pseudo-generalization—which really is an assumption—and, through "deduction," to arrive at a "conclusion." This is what their so-called deductive method amounts to. An example would be: "The goal of USSR policy is peace; in a war between the USSR and Finland, Finland is of necessity the aggressor, since we know that the USSR cannot pursue a policy of aggression."

Saturation: The very amount of propaganda poured on the Free World wearies many people, besides confusing them. This weariness frequently induces men or governments to make believe that the problems posed by the USSR do not exist, thus allowing the Kremlin to proceed unopposed.

Confusion: By making misleading statements as to their intentions, by alternating warlike threats with sweet reasonableness, the Kremlin has managed to bewilder many people in the Free World. As a result, governments have sometimes been unable to make policy decisions on the basis of a realistic evaluation of the Kremlin's policy objectives.

Repetition: The number of times a statement or an allegation is repeated has a direct bearing on its general acceptance as genuine, truthful, or significant. The intrinsic truth value of the item has relatively little to do with the phenomenon. According to a Russian saying "Repetition is the mother of learning."

If the repetitive method is used, for instance, in order to assassinate somebody's character, enough doubts will be raised in the course of time to undermine his relationships with a number of people.

Timing: The Kremlin times its actions and propaganda releases to influence the situation on the diplomatic front, to catch an adversary off guard, and to grab the headlines to influence public opinion.

Khrushchev and Bulganin got off their threatening or cajoling letters to leading statesmen in time to make an impression on public opinion just when some important Western conferences opened. *Lunik,* the successful shot to the moon, was timed to catch the headlines on the eve of Khrushchev's trip to the United States. Major statements by Khrushchev are released on Western holidays or over weekends when reaction in the Western press cannot be published before Monday morning and leaders cannot be reached for comment.

Suspense: The Kremlin has been particularly successful in keeping the world on edge, wondering whether it would take some action that might disturb the peace. The Berlin crises have frequently served this purpose in the last few years as did the build-up of the U-2 incident until the fate of pilot Powers was decided at his Moscow "trial."

Demagogy: The emotions of people the world over, and in all sectors of society, have been cynically played upon by Kremlin propaganda. This exploitation of sensitivities, bias, prejudices is trying to achieve, on a global scale, what heretofore has frequently been tried by rabble-rousing politicians on a national scale.

The Kremlin's play upon the yearnings for independence of the Algerians; on the resentment by Negroes of racial discrimination in the United States; on the anti-Israel sentiment among Arabs.

Falsehood and duplicity: The Kremlin propagandists do not shrink from telling downright lies or misleading people or governments, if such action is likely to further Kremlin objectives. Anything that helps to divide, paralyze, or mislead target audiences is good propaganda, according to Kremlin standards.

A typical example is the "germ-warfare" charge made by Kremlin propagandists against the United States at the time of the Korean War, with all the fanfare they could muster.

PROPAGANDA TACTICS

Constructing new frames of reference: Basic to Kremlin propaganda is
the attempt to build up, through communication, frames of reference
among its audiences which will induce them to absorb the Kremlin's
"message." For this purpose concepts and language are designed to confuse audiences about what is right and what is wrong, and ultimately
to make them impervious to Free World communications.

The following table summarizes the main modifications in criteria and
attitudes which are surreptitiously fed to Free World audiences by
Kremlin auxiliaries:

	Concerning the Soviet Regime	Concerning Western Regimes
Frame of reference adopted for judging	Dialectic	Ethics
Terms of reference used for judging	The future	The past
	The historical process	The blemishes of the present
	Ends	Means
Elements considered valid for judging	Promises	Achievements
	Doctrines	Abuses
Attitude adopted	Deterministic	Purist
Intellectual standards	Dialectical weaving (to evade contra-dictions)	Logical rigor (to em-phasize contradic-tions)
	Scruples (to obstruct censure)	Polemics (to speed up censure)
Key words thrown into speeches	The people	Money
	Progress	Stagnation
	Work	Exploitation
Style of approval	Vibrant	Stiff
Style of criticism	Stiff	Vibrant
State of mind culti-vated	Open	Guilty

Changes of the line: With changes of the policy line by the Kremlin,
slogans and arguments are made to fit the new situation. A slogan such
as "The Roosevelt Peace Policy" was used in connection with confer-

ences at Teheran, Yalta, and Potsdam, until the political war started in earnest. Then "The Wise Stalin Peace Policy" was substituted for it. During the war and lend-lease we were called "democratic" and "peace loving"; now we are "fascist" and "warmongering."

Aggression by irrelevance: This aims at diverting attention from an important issue; the propagandized are expected to ease up in dealing with an issue that may seem important to them but is really irrelevant to the point involved. For instance, political opponents are frequently attacked and, if possible, destroyed by Kremlin communist regimes, on grounds of alleged "treason to the country" or involvement in "crimes." The real reason—their opposition to Kremlin communism—is not mentioned.

Artificial contrasts: The USSR is shown as the saint, with halo, and the United States as the devil, with horns. Their wars are "just wars," wars of "liberation," because giving Kremlin communism to the world justifies all means. The wars of the "imperialists" are "unjust," because they are "fought for profit" and are "the last desperate acts of a decaying system."

Driving a wedge: Creating or aggravating conflicts among groups or nations that oppose the Kremlin is one of the most frequently applied tactics.
Samples of such incitement are:

Town vs. country, because bread is too expensive
Country vs. town, because grain is too cheap

Government officials vs. tradesmen, in the name of planning
Tradesmen vs. government officials, in the name of initiative

Germany vs. France, in terms of nationalism
France vs. Germany, in terms of "peace"

Europe vs. America, in the name of culture or "sovereignty"
America vs. Europe, in the name of "liberal democracy."

Taking advantage of its own turpitude: Attempts will be made to force the opposition to do something it does not want to do because of its sense of decency or morality, then to take propaganda advantage of the opponent's pangs of conscience. At the end of World War II the USSR rearmed while the United States disarmed. Today the propagandists attack the "military circles" for our defense program and some of our citizens are deluded through the effect made on their consciences.

Contradicting arguments: This means using whatever line of persuasion is considered necessary to induce the propagandized to act, regardless of whether the argument given to one group is completely inconsistent with that given another.

Radio Moscow has told its audience in France that the United States was aiding the Algerian rebels in order to take over French oil interests in the Sahara; on the same day it broadcast to the Algerian rebels allegations that the United States was shipping arms to the French to enable them to quell the uprising.

Scientificized argumentation: The Kremlin propagandists give deliberately complicated and confusing "explanations" to make the unwary believe The System is a true science.

The Kremlin's approach to life is given the high-sounding name of "science of society," pretending to "prove" the contentions of Kremlin communist ideologists. Capital is made of the ignorance of the propagandized. Khrushchev's speeches, for instance, regularly refer to the "laws of history" which supposedly make the final victory of Kremlin socialism "an absolute certainty."

Manipulation of tenses: The Kremlin propagandists will mention a situation which existed years ago in a context which implies it continues to exist today. The outstanding example of this is quoting Marx on capitalism as it existed a century ago, while discussing present-day conditions.

Group flattery: This means the tactic of influencing intellectual groups, particularly in underdeveloped countries, by referring to historical events which allegedly prove that, unlike any of the Western powers, the USSR or Russia has always been on their side. "Neutralist" countries such as Indonesia and the UAR are the targets of such endeavors. Also, on an even larger scale, leaders of Negroes all over the world are told that throughout modern history the Russians have always been the friends of the Negro race.

The big lie: This is a demogogic "smear," calculated to reduce the prestige of the victim. There is not even a fraction of truth in the accusation.

A Kremlin agent said after the war, "The United States has built up by far the biggest empire in the history of the world ... the combined war conquests of Hitler, Mussolini, and Hirohito did not equal those of Wall Street."

A thief calling another person "thief": This is another "smear" tactic which is fundamental in Kremlin propaganda. Its use is particularly intense among the peoples of Asia and Africa. To divert attention from the Kremlin's own imperialism, it systematically accuses Free World nations, and particularly the United States, of imperialism and colonialist exploitation.

General Romulo of the Philippines has pointed out, in a speech before the United Nations General Assembly, that Kremlin charges against West ern countries usually forecast its own intentions. And General Mark Clark has warned that Kremlin accusations of germ warfare against us might indicate its willingness to use this weapon.

Promising the moon: By oversimplifying issues and circulating terse slogans, the Kremlin holds out the promise of the moon to the unwary and ignorant. The propagandists know their promise cannot be fulfilled quickly, directly, or simply, or at all.

Illusions are merchandised in slogans such as "Ban the Bomb," "Let's Make West Berlin a Free City," "Complete Disarmament within Four Years." And, of course, the hidden joker in the deal is that the USSR herself refuses to find common ground for negotiation and agreement.

Free ride on another's achievements: Moving into a situation which has been created by somebody else and claiming credit for its benefits is a cheap way to obtain results.

In the early days of Marshall Plan aid shipments the American ambassador to Italy had to be at the dockside to have his picture taken welcoming the ship. Otherwise local communist officials would appear and have their pictures snapped, taking credit for the food shipments in the name of the USSR.

The partial truth: Use of the half-truth, quarter-truths, or fractions of truths is another trick of Kremlin propagandists. In attacking the bogey of Wall Street, the Kremlin has stated that "corporate profits in the United States have been the largest in recent history of the country."

The other part of the truth is that gross national product, national income, wages, salaries, etc., have been highest, too, so the implied exploitation is just not present.

One point has been lifted out of context to "prove" their argument.

Double false assumption: By using the phrases "everybody knows," "as is well known," "the whole world knows," and then adding something such as "that the United States refuses to conclude a peace pact, while the Soviet Union pursues the conclusion of such a pact" (Malenkov to XIX CPSU Congress), the Kremlin propagandist implies two central premises. The first is that sometime, somewhere, somehow a plebiscite has been held or at least wide groups have seriously discussed the fact; and the second is that the votes cast determined Malenkov's conclusions about those of the United States.

Phony syllogism: Something along the following lines:
  a) John Doe heads the local United States Information Service.
  b) information services gather information; so do spies.
  c) John Doe, therefore, is a spy.

(In reality, the United States Information Service dispenses information about the United States and the USSR Information Service gathers intelligence.)

"Albatross" and false identity: Hanging a dirty adjective around the neck of an expendable noun, like the Ancient Mariner's albatross: "skyrocketing profits," "monopoly capitalism," "mercenary press." Closely related to this is the practice of word contamination through systematic association with a universally disliked symbol. Thus "profiteer" discredits "profits" when used in close connection; "trust" or "cartel" contaminates "corporation."

The straw man of Wall Street: This straw man has been selected with great care. It is the symbol of evil in American lore, handed down from the nineteenth-century stage of capitalist development.

Because we value the free enterprise system but don't like to dwell on the role of social benefits in our society for fear of the stigma of "socialism," the Kremlin propagandists are able to get much mileage out of "Wall Street." This symbol is a straw man aimed at scaring the public both in the United States and elsewhere in the world.

Aesopian language: It was the Greek slave Aesop who developed the technique of hiding political and moral criticism behind superficially innocent stories and coined such telling expressions as "sheep in wolf's clothing," and "sour grapes."

A similar technique was utilized by Lenin to circumvent censorship by the Tsar. "The reform" meant "revolution" in his writings.

When Khrushchev speaks of "peaceful coexistence" it means "live and let live" to the uninitiated and "political war short of Kremlin military attack" to the agents of The System.

False labels: This is a practice of turning definitions of words upside down and is related to Aesopian language. The Kremlin propagandists have evolved an entire vocabulary which is aimed at upsetting the concepts of the Free World, attempting to shake society at its foundations, undermine governments. Confucius said that disorder in language would lead to bad government.

Mr. Chauvel, the French delegate at one time to the Security Council, told Mr. Malik, the Russian delegate, "You point to a table and call it a chair."

(See Glossary of Kremlin Communist Upside-Down Language, p. 209.)

Symbol stealing: Just as the Kremlin propagandists have taken over our own rather antiquated fearsome symbol "Wall Street," so have they appropriated certain words and phrases we have coined to meet the situation of political warfare. "Iron Curtain," "Cold War," "Brinkmanship," and "Creation of tensions" have been stolen and turned against us in their propaganda.

Logocide: This stands for the corruption of ideas by the Kremlin to mislead target audiences. People become familiar with ideas and concepts through the use of established word symbols. It is one of the Kremlin's most brazen tricks to change the idea but to keep the word. A notorious example is its use of the word "democratic" to identify groups of dictatorially-ruled Kremlin communists.

3. Examples of Contradictions in Kremlin Propaganda

The following quotations, taken from statements by Kremlin spokesmen or from materials carried by Soviet mass media, show that Kremlin propaganda will condemn today what it praised yesterday, and vice versa. The only constant element in Kremlin propaganda is not truth or consistency, but the design to further the Kremlin's interests, as defined by the current dictator.

APPRAISAL OF THE UNITED STATES

To the United States

Soviet scholars have the same serious approach to current developments in American history that they have to those of the past. They stress the similarity of interests of the two peoples and show how peaceful collaboration between them has always proved mutually beneficial.

—*USSR* (magazine published by the Soviet embassy in Washington) No. 7, 1958.

Propaganda of amorality and misanthropy is being carried on with particular intensity in the USA Army. The Wall Street bosses need not only mercenary government officials and cabinet members but also corrupted soldiers and officers. The aims of the war which the American and British imperialists strive to unleash are hostile to the interests of the peoples, including the interests of the American and British peoples, and, therefore, these aims are criminal and incompatible with the concept of justice. In order to turn their soldiers into blind tools of aggressive policy and a predatory war, into men capable of killing everybody, regardless of sex and age, who resists aggression and defends freedom and independence of his motherland, the American bourgeoisie kindle among the troops chauvinism, bestial hatred toward other peoples and base passions.

—*Marksizm-Leninism o Voyne i Armii* (*Marxism-Leninism on War and the Army*), Moscow, 1957, pp. 67–68. This volume forms part of a collection called "The Officer's Library."

UNITED STATES CLERGY

Khrushchev Praises

Permit me to express my sincere gratitude to Bishop John Wright...
I am also sincerely grateful to the minister who read the prayer at the
beginning of our dinner here.... Our priests, mullahs, and rabbis, like
your priests and bishops, pray to God that there should be peace on
earth and friendship between people.

—Khrushchev speech at a dinner in Pittsburgh, September 24, 1959.

Soviet Radio Blames

Religion plays an important role in the ideological deception of
American servicemen.... Religion is one of the basic supports of the
reactionary policy of the United States whose aim is world domination.
Chaplains prepare servicemen for aggression and concentrate religious
propaganda upon making them hate the Soviet Union and the other
countries of the socialist camp....

The defense of capitalist society and praise of the American way of
life play an important part in religious propaganda. American servicemen, who in the vast majority come from the working masses of the
population, are told by the chaplains that the capitalist system and the
American way of life represent the height of perfection and that servicemen must be interested in strengthening and preserving the bourgeois
system. The chaplains, in their efforts to conceal the discrepancy between exploiters and exploited, ascribe Godlike origins to capitalism....

American chaplains give particular attention to the propaganda of
the strength of American forces in Europe and the propaganda of atomic
and hydrogen weapons. American chaplains are ardent propagandists
of militarism and colonialism. Chaplains justify the aggressive policy of
the United States in the Middle and Near East....

—Radio Volga broadcast to Soviet Armed Forces, August 11, 1959.

"WE WILL BURY YOU"

Denial

Such assertions by Mr. Lodge do not tally with facts.... The words
which Mr. Lodge insists were said by Mr. Khrushchev on November 17,
1956 "We will bury you"—are the fruits of idle talk by those who are

instructed to handicap the improvement of Soviet-American relations in every way.

—Statement by the Soviet delegation to the 12th United Nations General Assembly Session, TASS, October 5, 1957.

Confirmation and Apology

I really spoke about that, but my statement was deliberately distorted. What I meant was not physical burying of anyone at any time, but a change in the social system, in the historical development of society.

—Khrushchev, answer to a question at the National Press Club, September 17, 1959.

UNITED STATES AND ALGERIA

United States Refuses to Aid French Algeria

Judging by press comments, Debré's statement was coolly received in London and Washington, which are in no hurry to formulate their stand on this question. As reported by the Associated Press, "authoritative quarters" in Washington made it understood that the United States cannot satisfy France's request for aid in Algeria. According to the *Manchester Guardian* one of the reasons behind this unwillingness to support the French in the Algerian question is fear of "repulsing a considerable part of Africa and Asia from the West."

—Moscow, TASS to Europe, August 18, 1959.

United States Aids French in Algeria

It is easy to sound the real opinion of a country on the problem of liberating African peoples by noting its recognition of the right of peoples to manage their own affairs. For example, whom do the United States and West Germany back in the Algerian war? For whom are United States arms and the NATO arsenal earmarked—for the French expeditionary corps or the Algerian army of national liberation? On whose side are the 40,000 West German legionnaires fighting? The answers to these questions make it clear that West Germany's anti-colonialism is nothing but a word game, a smoke screen covering the real nature of the inveterate enemies of African peoples.

—Moscow radio broadcast to Africa, same day.

INSTALLMENT BUYING

Capitalist Evil

But nowadays in the capitalist countries, particularly in the United States, credit buying has degenerated into a system of unscrupulous robbery of the consumer, and has netted many millions in extra profits for the banks and credit organizations. . . . Millions of American families live in the shadow of "repossession," always haunted by fear that sickness, wage cuts, or layoffs might deprive them of their worldly possessions.

—I. Lapitsky, "Life on the Installment Plan," *New Times*, No. 35, 1959.

We Have It Too

In the near future, Comrade Radio Listeners, you will be able to buy articles you require on credit in many towns. Buying on credit is a very convenient form of trade, the cost of the articles being paid by you in installments spreading over several months. . . . It appears that this trade is profitable not only to customers but also to the stores. It is profitable to the store because goods being sold through installments are in very large supply in the Univermag (Department Store).

—Moscow radio broadcast, August 27, 1959.

THE PRESS

Genuine Freedom

The Soviet press is truly free and a genuine press of the people. Therein lies its fundamental difference from the bourgois press.

—Moscow radio broadcast, November 12, 1959.

Twilight of Evening Moscow

The editor of the newspaper *Evening Moscow* has been fired for a major journalistic oversight—he did not get around to printing the news of the launching of the Soviet rocket that hit the moon last September.

"This serious political mistake was not accidental," said the monthly magazine *Soviet Press* in reporting the incident. "The editorial board of the newspaper has not displayed the necessary operativeness and sharpness in reflecting events of domestic and international life."

—*Washington Post*, November 16, 1959.

GOLF

Not Played

The educational significance of golf is not great. The game is mostly played in England and America. In the USSR it is not cultivated.

—*Large Soviet Encyclopedia*, first edition, Vol. XVII, Col. 533.

Hoot Mon! We Invented It!

Lately the game of golf is becoming more and more popular in the USSR. There are already several golf courses in the Crimea. Near Moscow they will be laid out in the spring of 1960. President Eisenhower will be able to try out the game he fancies at the time of his visit to the USSR. As reported by *Pravda,* golf was a game which the Caucasian shepherds played with enthusiasm almost a thousand years ago.

—*Slowo Powszechne,* November 20, 1959.

WAR

Advocacy of War Impossible, Khrushchev

No communist party anywhere, if it is really communist, has ever said that it hopes to achieve its aims through war. Nor, indeed, could it say so.

—Khrushchev, speech at the Hungarian Communist Party Congress, December 1, 1959.

Renunciation of War Absurd, Lenin

We are not pacifists . . . we have always declared it to be absurd for the revolutionary proletariat to renounce revolutionary wars that may prove necessary in the interests of socialism.

—Lenin, *Selected Works* (International Publishers, New York, 1943) Vol. VI, p. 16.

RELIGION

Freedom of Conscience

We consider the question of religion in our country to be of interest to all our friends abroad who have never visited the Soviet Union to see

for themselves the fact that freedom of conscience for citizens is fully
assured in the Soviet Union.

—Soviet radio broadcast in Armenian, January 19, 1960.

But No Religion for Children

Freedom of conscience for parents who are believers must not be
turned into a denial of the freedom of the public and the state to inter-
vene positively in questions of family training. Our public and legal
organs must enter into the defense of children subjected to spiritual
and moral mutilation on the part of parents.

—*Molodoi Kommunist*, No. 10, October 1959.

Freedom of Worship

Freedom of worship is guaranteed by the constitution of the Soviet
Union under section 124, and there are people practicing many different
kinds of religion in the country.

—Moscow radio broadcast, January 26, 1960.

But Not to Teach

The Reverend Priest [Petr Lieypniyek] set up something not unlike
a seminary for the children.

It was established at the trial that Petr Lieypniyek, both in the church
and in his own home, instructed young children in fundamental Catholic
dogmas. There were fifteen to twenty persons in the groups organized
by him. But perhaps the Reverend did not know about the existence
of a law in our country concerning the separation of church and state.
... The guilt of Petr Lieypniyek was completely proved.

—*Sovetskaya Latviya*, September 17, 1959.

SUMMITRY—SOVIET STYLE

Slanderous Assertions

The attempts to misconstrue the Soviet position will not mislead
public opinion. The cries about a Soviet ultimatum are worth no more
than the slanderous assertions about the Soviet threat. The language of
ultimatums and diktats is alien to our foreign policy.

—*Pravda*, May 17, 1960.

Of Ultimatums and Diktats

We are holding a summit meeting. This is why we came to Paris. But this requires the United States Government's admission that an aggressive intrusion into our country has been committed, its condemnation of this intrusion, and an assurance that such actions will not be repeated and that the guilty will be punished.

—Khrushchev remarks at Paris press conference, May 18, 1960.

Moral Principles of Communism

I am telling you frankly: If an ally of ours had acted this way, we would have plucked up courage and said that this is not the way to act. But if the thing has been done, you should apologize. However, these are the moral principles of communism; the capitalist countries have different moral principles it would seem.

—Khrushchev remarks at press conference, Paris, May 18, 1960.

Defined

We consider moral that which benefits the construction of communism and strengthens the power of the Soviet Union and the socialist camp.

—Kishinev, Moldavia, radio broadcast, April 14, 1960.

OVERFLIGHTS

Never

New York Times correspondent: Has the Soviet Union ever carried out unauthorized flights over United States territory or that of countries allied with it?

Answer: The answer to this question is simple. The very thought of the possibility of such action contradicts the policy of the Soviet Union.

—Gromyko at press conference, May 11, 1960.

Maybe—But We Apologize

If there have been any individual instances of our planes inadvertently violating the air space of other countries—this has happened on our frontier with Turkey and Iran—we have apologized to those countries and punished those responsible for such violations.

—Khrushchev remarks following press conference, May 11, 1960.

Without Foundation

According to the information of relevant Soviet bodies, the assertions contained in this Note of the Ministry on alleged violation by Soviet aircraft of Iranian air space are devoid of any foundation. As already reported to the Ministry in Embassy Note No. 64 dated May 2, a check carried out by appropriate Soviet bodies has established the unfounded nature of the information of the Iranian Foreign Ministry that Soviet aircraft violated Iranian air space.

—Soviet Note to Iran, May 31, 1959.

ANTI-SEMITISM IN THE USSR

Gross Lies Invented by Imperialists

The Soviet Constitution guarantees freedom of conscience to everybody. In particular, Jewish believers have every opportunity to practice their religious rites, but in spite of that, imperialist and Zionist propaganda invents gross lies about the imaginary anti-Semitism in the USSR and persecution of the Jewish religion.

—*Science and Life*, No. 4, December 1959.

Confirmed in the Soviet Press

Usury with the blessings of Jehovah! ... This charge made all the more clear the picture of the greedy faces of these synagogue servants, the faces of moneygrubbers who are without conscience and without honor. ... In the present case, the means of punishment is not important. It was important that the people ... saw before them not unselfish "servants of God" but a flock of black crows picking the bones of both the living and the dead. ...

Draznin and Teper denied the majority of the accusations brought against them: participating in teaching prayers to school students, conversations of doubtful political virtue which had no relation to religious ceremonies. ...

The public prosecutor, physician Labunsky, said angrily in his address that such operations [circumcisions] were a barbaric custom from pagan times and formerly were one of the acts of sacrifices to a god and were now incompatible with the principles of socialist humanism and morality.

The speech of another public prosecutor, Comrade Karger, manager of the Interkolkhoz Construction Trust, was heard with great interest. ... Comrade Karger said that the Jewish religion basically was not only reactionary but also nationalistic. . . . Then he suggested measures of punishment for the accused.

—Soviet Moldavia, April 28, 1960.

NEUTRALITY

It Is Good to Be Neutral

It is not without reason that a policy of neutrality is now being pursued by states on whose territories a quarter of the world's population live. . . . Furthermore, neutral states can do much to ease international tension and strengthen world peace.

—Khrushchev, speaking in Finland; TASS, September 3, 1960.

But Not too Neutral

There is between the policy of the West and the socialist countries a gap which cannot be narrowed or bridged by a theory. As to the theory, "Neither the East nor West," it is one which serves the interests of the imperialist and only aims at depriving the young states of the East of the strong support which they receive from the socialist countries.

—Moscow Radio broadcast in Arabic, August 31, 1960.

4. "Peaceful Coexistence" by Lenin, Stalin, and Khrushchev

LENIN:

1916: Every "Peace Program" Is a Deception

Every "peace program" is a deception of the people and a piece of hypocrisy unless its principal object is to explain to the masses the need for a revolution, and to support, aid, and develop the revolutionary struggle of the masses that is starting everywhere. . . .

April 1916.

1918: A Conflict Is Inevitable

International imperialism . . . could not under any circumstances, on any condition, live side by side with the Soviet Republic because of its objective position and because of the economic interests of the capitalist class which are embodied in it. . . . In this sphere a conflict is inevitable.

March 7, 1918.

1918: There Is No Middle Course

Either the Soviet government triumphs in every advanced country in the world, or the most reactionary imperialism triumphs. . . . Anglo-American imperialism which has perfectly mastered the art of using the form of a democratic republic. One or the other, there is no middle course.

—"Valuable Admission of Pitirim Sorokin," 1918.

1919: One or the Other Must Triumph in the End

We are living not merely in a state, but in a system of states, and the existence of the Soviet Republic side by side with imperialist states for a long time is unthinkable. One or the other must triumph in the end. And before that end supervenes, a series of frightful collisions between the Soviet Republic and the bourgeois states will be inevitable.

—At 8th Party Congress, 1919.

1920: We Must Take Advantage of Contradictions

The fundamental thing in the matter of concessions, from the standpoint of political considerations . . . is the rule which we have not only

232

mastered theoretically, but have also applied practically, and which will, until socialism finally triumphs all over the world, remain a fundamental rule with us, namely, that we must take advantage of the antagonisms and contradictions between two capitalists, between two systems of capitalist state, inciting one against the other.

—November 26, 1920.

STALIN:

1927: Struggle for Possession of the World Economy

Thus in the course of further development of international revolution two centers will form on a world scale; a socialist center, binding to itself the countries that gravitate to socialism, and a capitalist center, binding to itself the countries that gravitate to capitalism. The struggle between these two centers for the possession of the world economy will decide the fate of capitalism and communism in the whole world.

—September 9, 1927.

1927: Must Maintain Peaceful Relations Until Capitalism Ripe for Downfall

We cannot forget the saying of Lenin to the effect that a great deal in the matter of our construction depends on whether we succeed in delaying the war with the capitalist countries, which is inevitable but which may be delayed either until proletarian revolution ripens in Europe or until colonial revolutions come fully to a head, or finally, until the capitalists fight among themselves over the division of colonies. Therefore, the maintenance of peaceful relations with capitalist countries is an obligatory task for us. The basis of our relations with capitalist countries consists in admitting the coexistence of two opposed systems.

—December 2, 1927.

1928: Peace Is Another Form of Fighting Capitalism

The peace policy of the proletarian state certainly does not imply that the Soviet state has become reconciled with capitalism.... This policy is the Leninist policy of the proletarian dictatorship. It is merely another, and under present conditions a more advantageous, form of fighting capitalism; a form which the USSR has consistently employed since the October Revolutions.... There is a glaring contradiction between the imperialists' policy of piling up armaments and their hypocritical talk about peace. There is no such contradiction, however, between the Soviet government's preparations for defense and for revolutionary war and a consistent peace policy. Revolutionary war of the proletarian dictatorship is but a continuation of revolutionary peace policy "by other means."

—Theses of the VI World Congress of the Communist International (1928).

KHRUSHCHEV:

1955: Let's Compete in Raising Living Standards

Let us prove in practice whose system is better: This is our appeal to the statesmen of capitalist countries. Let us compete without war. . . . We stand, and shall always stand, for the kind of competition which helps raise the people's welfare, their standard of living.

—November 26, 1955.

1955: No Ideological Disarmament

If certain people regard as a violation of the "Geneva spirit" our conviction that victory will be on the side of socialism, of the Marxist-Leninist teaching, these people obviously do not understand the "Geneva spirit" correctly. They should remember that we have never renounced and will never renounce our ideas, the struggle for victory of communism. They will have to wait forever for us to disarm ideologically!

—December 30, 1955.

1956: Want Normal Relations, Not Mere Absence of War

We are setting ourselves the task not only of avoiding war, but also of creating conditions in which there may be normal development of trade, cultural and scientific relations, the mutual exchange of tourists; the task of doing everything necessary for the peaceful coexistence of the two systems, of eliminating the possibility of an outbreak of war, and of deciding all questions which arise patiently, in a spirit of mutual understanding and cooperation among states.

—August 1, 1956.

1958: Peace Needed for Propagation of Communist Ideas

It is not an army but peace that is required to propagate communist ideas, disseminate them, and establish them in the minds of men.

—February 15, 1958.

1958: Must Rise Above Ideological Differences

Our point of departure is that in the present circumstances every government which correctly realizes its responsibility for the future of peace must put itself above ideological differences.

—April 13, 1958.

1958: Show Us

Representatives of the capitalist countries: If you capitalist gentlemen are certain that your system is firm, that it is unshakable, then let us have peaceful competition. Show in practice the advantages of your capitalist system and we shall show the advantages of the socialist system. Whichever system provides the best conditions for man's life will win. If you are sure that you will win this "combat" then let us test our strength in peaceful competition.

—July 22, 1958.

1959: Economics Is Focus of Competition

Economics is the main field in which the peaceful competition of socialism and capitalism is taking place, and we are interested in winning this competition in a historically brief period of time.

—January 27, 1959.

1959: Demonstration of Communism's Superiority Will Conquer Capitalism

The moral-political unity of Soviet society, the friendship of peoples, Soviet patriotism, socialist internationalism—such are the inexhaustible founts of the strength of Soviet society. We are confident that we shall conquer capitalism. We shall conquer it not by war, but by demonstrating practically to all the working people the superiority of communism over capitalism.

—March 7, 1959.

1959: No Concession on Ideology

But one must not confuse mutual concessions in the interest of peaceful coexistence with concessions of principle, in matters that concern the actual nature of our socialist system, our ideology. In this there cannot be any question of concessions or any adaptation.

—October 31, 1959.

1959: Fight for Marxism-Leninism to Continue

We have looked and will look for ways that would be acceptable to both the capitalist and the socialist states in the solution of disputes, in order to prevent war. But we shall never, of course, forego our ideological principles. We are fighting and will fight implacably for Marxist-Leninist ideology, for the triumph of the lofty ideals of communism.

—December 1, 1959.

1960: Active Cooperation Wanted

We must strive that peaceful coexistence shall be transferred from a mere absence of war into active cooperation among all states in the sphere of economics, culture, and science.

—March 24, 1960.

5. Carrot and Stick Statements from the Kremlin

The following is a compilation of the more important peaceful and belligerent utterances emanating in alternating sequence from the Kremlin in the period of March 1957–July 1960.

Stick

The destructive potential of modern weapons is such that blows struck to suppress the aggressor bases will inevitably devastate large areas around them, which would spell a catastrophe even for a country with a larger territory than Norway. This is obvious if only due to the fact that tests have shown that one hydrogen bomb can cause destruction within the range of hundreds of kilometers. The question arises: what will happen if several such bombs are used?

—Khrushchev, TASS, March 25, 1957.

... the United States, barring the Civil War and the small campaign against Mexico, still does not know what war means. If war is not averted, the Americans will experience the most devastating war ever known by mankind. It will rage not only in Europe and Asia, but with no lesser fury in the United States.

The United States is seeking to preserve its overseas military bases, regarding them as advanced outposts. But these bases do not lie in the desert. They are situated in the most densely populated areas. What are these bases? They are the territories of Britain, France, West Germany, Norway, Denmark, Italy, Spain, Turkey, and some other countries. These bases are close to us for a blow against the Soviet Union and the other socialist countries, but they are also close for a counterblow. It is to be believed that the Germans in West Germany, the French, the Italians, the British, the Turks, the Spaniards, the Dutch, and others will finally realize that should American imperialists use their territory for an attack on the Soviet Union and the other peaceful countries, counterblows by the Soviet Union will follow. The people will realize this and will, of course, lift their voices in protest.

—Khrushchev, interview with Henry Shapiro of UP, November 14, 1957.

Carrot

Let us, for instance, compete in the output of corn. I have talked much on this subject with the American expert, Mr. Garst, and he presented me with a sample of his corn. It was much more pleasant to talk about corn than about the intercontinental missile. The American public and press can do a good turn for the people if they promote competition precisely in this peaceful direction.

—Khrushchev, interview with Wm. R. Hearst, Jr., November 22, 1957.

We believed, and believe, that at a conference of representatives of socialist and capitalist countries positive results can be achieved. What is needed for this? First, to refrain from considering at such a conference questions on which there are ideological differences.... Second, it is necessary to recognize the coexistence of socialist and capitalist countries, not to interfere in each other's affairs, not to have recourse to cold-war methods, and to give up attempts to change the existing situation by force.

—Khrushchev, TASS, December 21, 1957.

Stick

Yet now the USSR has launched, on the basis of the intercontinental ballistic rocket, an artificial earth satellite. And when this satellite started to orbit around the earth and everybody was able to see it—provided he was capable of seeing—by glancing at the sky, our enemies became silent.

—Khrushchev, addressing Byelorussian workers, *Pravda,* January 26, 1958.

Carrot

It can safely be said that though certain circles in the imperialist countries are feverishly clinging to the bankrupt positions of strength policy, the prospects for the relaxation of international tension and the development of economic cooperation and scientific cultural exchanges between countries with different social systems have become more favorable at present. Take, for instance, the agreement on the development of cultural contacts concluded between the Soviet Union and the United States. It is a big step forward.

—Khrushchev, interview with Trybuna Ludu, March 10, 1958.

We stand resolutely for liquidation of the cold war. We stand for comprehensive development of trade relations and cultural ties with all countries, and for easing the international tension. In brief we stand for peaceful coexistence and peaceful competition among all states.

—Radio Moscow, March 14, 1958.

Stick

They (the United States) will need very many satellites the size of oranges in order to catch up with the Soviet Union.

—Khrushchev, commenting on launching of Sputnik III, *New York Times,* May 16, 1958.

Carrot

The peoples of our countries are deeply interested in genuine peace in the world. They threaten nobody, they conduct a constant struggle for peace and against war and war threats. War is alien to the very nature of the socialist countries who are the champions of freedom and independence of peoples and the standard bearers of peace.

—Khrushchev in Bulgaria, TASS, June 7, 1958.

Stick

We know that the United States has atomic and hydrogen bombs; we know that you have an air force and navy. But you are also well aware that the Soviet Union, too, possesses atomic and hydrogen bombs, an air force and navy, plus ballistic missiles of all types, including intercontinental ones.

—Khrushchev letter to Eisenhower, TASS, July 19, 1958.

Carrot

What else then do we need? We need peace. Representatives of the capitalist countries: If you capitalist gentlemen are certain that your system is firm, that it is unshakable, then let us have peaceful competition.

—Khrushchev, TASS, July 22, 1958.

We declare once again, just as we have declared in the past, that our armed forces will not be used anywhere or at any time for predatory purposes, which are alien to the very nature of our social system. We shall never settle controversial problems in relations between states by means of war. We shall endeavor to solve problems of this kind peacefully, by negotiation.

—Khrushchev, November 14, 1958.

Stick and Carrot

On the day that *Lunik* was launched, Khrushchev addressed the following New Year's message to the American people:

... at the present time there is no dispute or unsettled issue that could not be solved by peaceful means, provided, naturally, all parties concerned genuinely desire to do so. On our part we can say that we do have such a desire.

—Khrushchev, January 2, 1959.

The rocket—*Lunik,* the Russians are calling it—passed the moon last night and headed for orbit around the sun. It was unquestionably the greatest achievement of the Space Age and its psychological impact upon the world was profound. It emphasized the steady widening of the horizons of the cold war. In that struggle the Soviet feat came at a time of growing communist challenge to the West—not only in the realm of space but also in the military, diplomatic, and economic fields.

Lunik made plain that the Russians still hold the lead over the United States in the space competition. The American program has had major successes and is gathering momentum, yet it is now demonstrated that the Russians have more powerful rockets—and therefore greater capacity to deliver intercontinental missiles.

—*New York Times,* January 4, 1959.

Stick

I think it is high time for the American strategists to come out of their fool's paradise that in the event of a military conflict the territory of the United States would remain invulnerable. For a long time now this has not accorded with reality and has been nothing more than wishful thinking on the part of America's generals. In point of fact, the Soviet Union today has the means to deliver a crushing blow to the aggressor at any point of the globe. After all, it is not a mere figure of speech when we say that we have organized serial production of intercontinental ballistic missiles.

—Khrushchev, February 5, 1959.

Carrot

Let us reach an agreement that our armies should pull back while the diplomats should advance and realistically estimate the balance of power and, this is the main thing, take account of the people's striving for peace and find solutions that would insure peaceful coexistence.

—Khrushchev, speech in Berlin, March 2, 1959.

The Soviet State did not, does not have, and cannot have, any annexationist intentions with regard to other countries. . . . The only and invariable aim of our foreign policy is to prevent war, to assure peace and security for our country and for all other countries.

—Khrushchev, TASS, April 9, 1959.

Stick

I give you our solemn pledge that we will never, never, never start a war against any country any time. . . . I have told Americans: you have missiles that can send up oranges. We have missiles that can send up tons. Imagine the kind of bombs that could be contained in our missiles compared with . . . yours.

—Khrushchev, speech in Poland, *New York Times*, July 19, 1959.

As a result of World War I, Soviet Russia became a socialist country. As a result of World War II, twelve other countries became socialist countries. As a result of a third world war, should it ever be launched by the imperialists, capitalism will be eliminated. We are convinced of this. We hope that the imperialists also understand this and will not play with fire.

—Khrushchev, speech boadcast by Radio Moscow, July 30, 1959.

I hope you would not say that I am trying to frighten you if I remind you that the Soviet Union has rockets in a quantity and of a quality unequaled by any other country in the world. This can be confirmed by the launching of our sputniks and cosmic rockets. Under these conditions to settle disputable questions in the way the militarist-revanchist quarters of West Germany apparently want—by war—is tantamount to suicide, to destruction of one's country.

—Khrushchev in letter to Adenauer, August 18, 1959.

Carrot

Jokingly I said to Mr. Lodge: If fate should cast me, a representative of the working class and the CPSU, and him, a representative of the capitalist world, on a desert island, then we apparently would find a common language, and would insure peaceful coexistence on that island. Why, then, cannot states with different social systems insure coexistence? Our states are also on a kind of island, since the means of modern communications which have drawn the continents closer together makes our earth appear a small island indeed. We must realize this. Having realized the necessity of coexistence, one must pursue a peaceable policy and live in friendship not by rattling weapons but by destroying them.

—Khrushchev's speech on returning from the United States, Radio Moscow, September 28, 1959.

But it is unreasonable to be eager for war as a cock is eager for a good scrap. If you and I understand that war can bring terrible calamities to the people, I told Mr. Eisenhower, why should we not agree on joint actions in the interests of peace? Let us reach agreement, the President said.

—Khrushchev, speech at Vladivostok, broadcast by Radio Moscow, October 8, 1959.

More than once we have made proposals on measures to make the European atmosphere less tense and to insure security of all peoples living in that area. We are prepared both for farreaching steps in that direction and for any sensible partial measures. We only wish this matter to progress, the situation in Europe to be improved, so that the European now should not remain entangled and tightly drawn.

—Khrushchev speaking before Supreme Soviet, broadcast by Radio Moscow, October 31, 1959.

Naturally such coexistence of states with different social orders presupposes that they make mutual concessions in the interest of peace. One may say that a realistic approach is required, a sober appraisal of the true state of affairs, mutual understanding, and consideration for each other's interests.

—Khrushchev addressing Supreme Soviet, Radio Moscow, October 31, 1959.

Stick

I am proud because these means are in the hands of the most peace-loving state in the world, in the hands of the communist party, in the hands of our people, which is championing the cause of peace. Consequently, they are a support in the struggle for peace. . . .

Let those people abroad learn that I am not hiding anything. In one year the factory we visited made 250 hydrogen rockets on the production line. That is many millions of tons, if we figure in terms of ordinary explosives. You can see that if such a deadly weapon were to be exploded over a country, there would not be anything left there at all.

—Khrushchev, addressing Soviet journalists, *Pravda*, November 18, 1959.

After the launching of Soviet artificial satellites and cosmic rockets, which demonstrated the possibilities of modern technology, the fact that the United States is now in no way less vulnerable militarily than any other country has firmly entered the minds of the American people. I believe that nobody will suspect me of trying to intimidate anybody by such words. No, this is the actual state of affairs, and it is evaluated in this way not only by us but also by Western statesmen, including statesmen of the United States itself.

—Radio Moscow broadcast, January 14, 1960.

War would begin in the heart of the warring countries; moreover, there would not be a single capital, not a single major industrial or administrative center, not a single strategic area which would not be subjected to attack, not only during the first days, but during the first minutes of the war.

Should the aggressors unleash a new war not only would it be their last war, but it would be the death of capitalism, because the peoples would clearly understand that capitalism is a source for starting wars, and would not further tolerate this system which brings suffering and calamity for mankind.

—Khrushchev, speech to USSR Supreme Soviet, Radio Moscow broadcast, January 14, 1960.

Carrot

Analyzing the atmosphere which has arisen in the world in relations between peoples and governments, I am firmly convinced that all the conditions now exist for the preservation and strengthening of peace. Not only I myself but all my friends who have made a realistic assessment of the international situation think so. I repeat—we consider that it is now favorable for the struggle for peace, for the preservation of peace.

—Khrushchev in speech to Soviet-Indian Friendship Society, Calcutta, broadcast by Radio Moscow, March 4, 1960.

The alleviation of tension in Europe would, in our opinion, be greatly promoted by a nonaggression pact between the two alignments of states. The conclusion of such a pact would constitute the first concrete step along the road toward eliminating existing military alignments.

—Khrushchev speaking in Paris, TASS, March 25, 1960.

Stick

Those countries which have bases on their territory must get it into their heads that if they are going to permit people to fly from these bases over our territory, we shall strike at those bases.

—Khrushchev speaking at Czechoslovak embassy reception, Moscow, May 9, 1960.

(If the United States) wishes to unleash a war, we shall be compelled to fire rockets which will explode on the aggressor's territory in the very first minutes of the war.

—Khrushchev speaking at U-2 exhibit, May 11, 1960.

We shall shoot these planes down, administer shattering blows at the bases whence they come and at those who have set up these bases and actually dispose of them.

—Khrushchev at Paris press conference, May 18, 1960.

The Soviet Union has the means to punish the ones who commit aggression.

—Khrushchev at Kremlin press conference, June 3, 1960.

We are going to make the imperialists dance like fish in a saucepan!

—Khrushchev speaking in Bucharest, June 25, 1960.

We consider whether it would be possible at the same time as the Bundestag is meeting in West Berlin to arrange the signing of a peace treaty with the GDR. In that way the situation would be such that all members of the Bundestag would be forced to ask comrade Grotewohl for a visa to get out of Berlin.

—Khrushchev at press conference in Vienna, July 8, 1960.

The presence of . . . foreign rocket installations in northern Italy, if they should be used against the socialist countries, would constitute a violation of Austrian neutrality.

—Khrushchev speech, July 9, 1960.

The United States is certainly aware of the consequences its policy of deliberate provocation against the Soviet Union may entail. . . . The position of the Norwegian government is, to say the least, unwise and dangerous for the Norwegian people.

—Khrushchev at press conference, July 12, 1960.

Britain, too, has become an accomplice in this aggressive act (RB-47 flight). The British people . . . must seriously ponder this.

—Khrushchev at press conference, July 12, 1960.

6. News and Propaganda Distribution

TASS, OFFICIAL NEWS AGENCY OF THE USSR

The Telegraphia Agency of the USSR (TASS) is an official instrument of the Kremlin communist party and the government of the USSR. In its 1954 report on TASS, UNESCO notes that the agency's "director-general and his deputy are appointed by the USSR Council of Ministers. They stand very high in the state hierarchy."

The far-flung operations of TASS include not only news reporting, but also domestic and foreign propaganda, censorship, agitation and political organizing, courier services and espionage.

As an important bureau in The System TASS holds the monopoly of distribution within the USSR of both domestic and foreign news. Distribution of official USSR news—and all news from this totalitarian country must be official—throughout the world has also been channeled through TASS as a monopoly. In the Kremlin-controlled bloc, TASS plays the dominant role as coordinating and directing agency for all the official news agencies of the member states.

TASS reports are generally considered reliable indicators of the current Kremlin line. However, a factor not to be overlooked in analyzing that line is TASS's practice of distributing different versions of politically important items, to serve Kremlin objectives in different target areas.

The propaganda concept governing TASS operations was spelled out by its director, N. G. Palgunov, in a lecture at Moscow University in 1956:

"News must be organized; otherwise it is news of mere events and happenings. . . . News is agitation via facts. In selecting the subject, the author of the report must above all proceed from the realization that the press should not simply report all the facts and just any events. . . . News must be didactic and instructive."

A higher level of objectivity is maintained in a special news file prepared by TASS for members of the party and the USSR government. Marked "For Official Use Only," it contains items of military, political, and economic intelligence gathered in foreign countries.

As a special service for the highest members of the party hierarchy, TASS also prepares a secret daily summary of intelligence highlights. It is usually referred to as "Red TASS."

It is standard practice for TASS to censor accounts of speeches made by USSR or foreign representatives; sections which do not accord with the Kremlin line of the moment are either deleted or rephrased.

TASS representatives abroad reveal the official nature of their organization by using diplomatic and communication advantages enjoyed by the diplomatic missions of the USSR. However, in order to take advantage of news—and information—gathering facilities customarily extended to members of the foreign press, TASS representatives request regular accreditation as foreign correspondents, as well.

On numerous occasions in the past, including the Petrov case in Australia and the Gouzenko case in Canada, TASS representatives have been publicly exposed as members of the Kremlin's secret-police organization.

It is routine procedure for TASS to serve USSR propaganda abroad. A frequently practiced deception is the following: TASS supplies specially prepared propaganda articles to foreign publications controlled by Kremlin agents or sympathizers; then it follows up by carrying, in its world-wide news service, extensive quotes from the same articles, presenting them as genuine expressions of local opinion.

WEEKLY HOURS OF INTERNATIONAL BROADCASTING BY THE USSR, 1959

WEST EUROPE

	Hours
English	31:30
French	28:00
German (to Austria)	14:00
German (to Germany)	40:15
Italian	24:30
Spanish *	19:15
Danish	8:45
Dutch	8:45
Finnish	21:50
Norwegian	8:45
Portuguese	7:00
Swedish	10:15
Music	39:50
W. EUR. TOTAL	262:40

* Includes some Catalan.

Source: Simon Costikyan, *Twelve Years of Communist Broadcasting, 1948–1959* (Office of Research and Analysis, United States Information Agency, Washington, D.C.)

Hours

EAST EUROPE

Albanian	14:00
Bulgarian	7:45
Czech/Slovak	5:00
Hungarian	7:00
Polish	13:30
Romanian	10:30
Music	0:30
E. EUR. TOTAL	58:15

YUGOSLAVIA

Macedonian	7:00
Serbo-Croat	15:15
Slovene	6:00
Music	0:55
YUGO. TOTAL	29:10

EUROPE TOTAL	350:05

NEAR EAST, SOUTH ASIA AND AFRICA

Arabic	49:35
Greek	17:30
Persian	49:35
Turkish	32:10
English	36:45
French	17:30
Bengali	17:30
Hindi	12:15
Tamil	3:30
Urdu	24:30
Azerbaijani	7:00
Tadzhik	14:00
Pushtu	10:30
Music	0:30
NEA TOTAL	292:50

Hours

FAR EAST

    Cantonese   —
    Mandarin   14:00
    Mongolian   8:45
    Uighur (to Sinkiang)   —
    Burmese   10:30
    Indonesian   19:15
    Vietnamese   10:30
    Japanese   31:30
    Korean   21:00
    English   3:30
    Music   —
        FAR EAST TOTAL   119:00

LATIN AMERICA

    Portuguese   14:00
    Spanish   35:00
        L.A. TOTAL   49:00

NORTH AMERICA

    English   84:00
    Ukrainian   21:00
    Yiddish   —
    Music   —
        N.A. TOTAL   105:00

OTHER

    Armenian   19:05
    Ukrainian   17:30
    Estonian   2:00
    Latvian   —
    Lithuanian   5:30
    Russian   15:10
        OTHER TOTAL   59:15

WORLD TOTAL   975:10

ENGLISH-LANGUAGE KREMLIN PERIODICALS PUBLISHED IN MOSCOW AND DISTRIBUTED IN THE UNITED STATES

Name	Weekly or Monthly	Published or Printed by	Editions in Other Languages
Culture and Life	M	Union of Soviet Societies for Friendship and Cultural Relations with Foreign Countries.	Russian, French, German, Spanish, Polish, Czech, Romanian.
International Affairs	M	Soviet Society for the Popularization of Political and Scientific Knowledge.	Russian.
Moscow News	Tabloid, twice a week.	Union of Soviet Societies for Friendship and Cultural Relations with Foreign Countries.	
New Times	W	Trud [central organ of the trade unions of the USSR].	Russian, French, German, Spanish, Polish, Czech, Romanian.
Soviet Film	M	Sovexportfilm.	Russian, French, German, Spanish, Arabic.
Soviet Literature	M	Union of Soviet Writers.	German, Polish, Spanish.
Soviet Union	M	Pravda [central organ of the Communist party of the USSR].	Russian, Chinese, Korean, Hindi, Urdu, Arabic, Vietnamese, Hungarian, Serbo-Croat, French, German, Spanish, Finnish, Japanese, Romanian.
Soviet Woman	M	Soviet Women's Committee and the Central Council of Trade Unions of the USSR.	Russian, Chinese, German, Hindi, Hungarian, Japanese, Korean, Spanish.

USSR MAGAZINE

USSR, an illustrated monthly magazine, is officially sponsored by the government of the USSR. In accordance with a reciprocal agreement—which was confirmed in an exchange of notes in September 1955 between the governments of the United States and the USSR—the government of the USSR has the right to distribute in the United States an informative, nonpolitical monthly magazine describing life in the USSR in exchange for the right of the United States government to do the same in the USSR. (The Russian-language magazine produced by the United States government for distribution in the USSR is called *Amerika.*)

USSR is published by the embassy of the USSR in Washington, D.C. Printed by a commercial printing concern in the United States, it has a standard format of 64 pages, with black-and-white, two-color, and four-color printing.

The current agreement provides for a distribution of 50,000 copies through commercial channels every month. In addition, the embassy of the USSR has the right to distribute 2,000 complimentary copies of every issue.

The magazine is available at newsstands at 20 cents a copy. The annual subscription rate is $1.80.

7. Exchanges U.S.A.-USSR Bloc

EXCHANGE PROJECTS (AND NUMBER OF VISITORS)
JANUARY 1–JULY 1, 1960

	U.S. Projects (and visitors) to Bloc	Bloc Projects (and visitors) to U.S.
I. USSR		
a. Scientific and Technical	19 (339)	32 (169)
b. Cultural	5 (79)	9 (82)
c. Academic	9 (23)	1 (3)
	33 (441)	42 (254)
II. POLAND		
a. Scientific	2 (4)	8 (21)
b. Cultural	6 (16)	3 (3)
c. Academic	2 (7)	6 (98)
	10 (27)	17 (122)
III. CZECHOSLOVAKIA		
a. Scientific and Technical	2 (2)	5 (9)
b. Cultural	1 (7)	0 (0)
c. Academic	0 (0)	0 (0)
	3 (9)	5 (9)
IV. HUNGARY		
a. Scientific and Technical	0 (0)	5 (8)
b. Cultural	1 (1)	0 (0)
c. Academic	2 (2)	3 (3)
	3 (3)	8 (11)
V. ROMANIA		
a. Scientific and Technical	1 (1)	0 (0)
b. Cultural	1 (1)	0 (0)
c. Academic	0 (0)	1 (1)
	2 (2)	1 (1)

VI. BULGARIA

a. Scientific and Technical	0 (0)	1 (0)
b. Cultural	2 (2)	0 (0)
c. Academic	0 (0)	0 (0)
	2 (2)	1 (0)
TOTALS	53 (484)	74 (397)

Source: "Report on Exchanges with the Soviet Union and Eastern Europe," No. 15, July 1, 1960, Department of State, Washington, D.C.

8. Kremlin "Fronts"

INTERNATIONAL KREMLIN-CONTROLLED "FRONT" ORGANIZATIONS AND THEIR PUBLICATIONS

"Fronts"	*Periodical Publications*
World Peace Council	*Horizons* (Monthly) *World Council of Peace Bulletin* (Biweekly)
Subsidiary: International Institute for Peace	
World Federation of Trade Unions	*World Trade Union Movement* (Monthly) Department bulletins
World Federation of Democratic Youth	*World Youth* (Monthly) *Information Service* (Biweekly bulletin) *WFDY* (Monthly news-sheet)
International Union of Students	*World Student News* (Monthly) *IUS News Service* (Biweekly bulletin)
Women's International Democratic Federation	*Women of the Whole World* (Monthly) *News in Brief* (Newsletter) *Information Bulletin* (Bimonthly) *Radio-Press Bulletin* (Weekly news release)
Subsidiary: Permanent International Committee of Mothers	
World Federation of Teachers' Unions	*Teachers of the World* (Monthly) *Quarterly Review*
International Association of Democratic Lawyers	*Information Bulletin* (Monthly) *Review of Contemporary Law* (Irregular)

"Fronts"	*Periodical Publications*
World Federation of Scientific Workers	*WFSW Bulletin* (Irregular) *Scientific World* (Semi-annual)
International Organization of Journalists	*The Democratic Journalist* (Monthly)
International Medical Association	*Living Conditions and Health— A Quarterly Medical Journal*
International Radio and Television Organization	*Documentation Review* (Monthly) *Information and Documentation Bulletin* (Quarterly)
Committee for the Promotion of International Trade	*CPIT Bulletin* (Monthly)

OFFICIAL KREMLIN DIRECTIVE FOR "FRONT" ORGANIZATIONS

The following is an excerpt from a speech by Willi Muenzenberg before the Sixth Congress of the Communist International in Moscow, July 20, 1928.

"Front" organizations have been created for the following reasons:

1. To arouse the interest of those millions of apathetic and indifferent workers ... who simply have no ear for communist propaganda. These people we wish to attract and arouse through new channels, by means of new ways.
2. Our sympathetic organizations should constitute bridges for the nonparty workers ... who have not yet mustered the courage to take the final step and join the communist party, but who are nevertheless in sympathy with the communist movement and are prepared to follow us part of the way.
3. By means of the mass organizations we wish to extend the communist sphere of influence itself.
4. (To provide) the organizational linking up of the elements in sympathy with the Soviet Union and with the communists....
5. We must build up our own organizations in order to counteract the increasing efforts of the bourgeois and social-democratic parties in this respect....
6. Through these sympathetic and mass organizations we should train the cadres of militants and officials of the communist party possessing organizational experience.

HOW TO IDENTIFY A KREMLIN "FRONT" IN THE UNITED STATES

The following is an excerpt from the testimony of J. Edgar Hoover before the House Committee on Un-American Activities on March 26, 1947:

For the most part, front organizations assumed the character of either a mass or membership organization or a paper organization. Both solicited and used names of prominent persons. Literally hundreds of groups and organizations have either been infiltrated or organized primarily to accomplish the purposes of promoting the interests of the Soviet Union in the United States, the promotion of Soviet war and peace aims, the exploitation of Negroes in the United States, work among foreign-language groups, and to secure a favorable viewpoint toward the communists in domestic, political, social, and economic issues.

The first requisite for front organizations is an idealistic-sounding title. Hundreds of such organizations have come into being and have gone out of existence when their true purposes have become known or exposed while others with high-sounding names are continually springing up.

There are easy tests to establish the real character of such organizations:

1. Does the group espouse the cause of Americanism or the cause of Soviet Russia?
2. Does the organization feature as speakers at its meetings known communists, sympathizers, or fellow travelers?
3. Does the organization shift when the party line shifts?
4. Does the organization sponsor causes, campaigns, literature, petitions, or other activities sponsored by the party or other front organizations?
5. Is the organization used as a sounding board by or is it endorsed by communist-controlled labor unions?
6. Does its literature follow the communist line or is it printed by the communist press?
7. Does the organization receive consistent favorable mention in communist publications?
8. Does the organization present itself to be nonpartisan yet engage in political activities and consistently advocate causes favored by the communists?
9. Does the organization denounce American and British foreign policy while always lauding Soviet policy?
10. Does the organization utilize communist "double talk" by referring to Soviet-dominated countries as democracies, complaining

that the United States is imperialistic and constantly denouncing monopoly capital?

11. Have outstanding leaders in public life openly renounced affiliation with the organization?

12. Does the organization, if espousing liberal progressive causes, attract well-known honest patriotic liberals or does it denounce well-known liberals?

13. Does the organization have a consistent record of supporting the American viewpoint over the years?

14. Does the organization consider matters not directly related to its avowed purposes and objectives?

Source: *Guide to Subversive Organizations and Publications,* Revised and published as of January 2, 1957 (85th Congress, 1st Session; House Document No. 226).

Suggested Reading List on Soviet Propaganda

American Strategy for the Nuclear Age edited by Walter F. Hahn and John C. Neff. Garden City, N.Y.: Doubleday and Company, Inc., Anchor Books, 1960.

Background Information on the Soviet Union in International Relations. Report of the Foreign Affairs Committee. Washington, D.C.: U.S. Govt. Printing Office, 1959.

Battle for the Mind by William Sargant. Garden City, N.Y.: Doubleday and Company, Inc., 1957.

"Big Sell in the Cold War" by David Finn. *Saturday Review of Literature,* October 10, 1959, p. 13.

The Blowing Up of the Parthenon or How to Lose the Cold War by Salvador de Madariaga. London: Pall Mall Press, New York: Frederick A. Praeger, Inc., 1960.

Blueprint for World Conquest (As Outlined by the Communist International). Human Events, Washington–Chicago, 1960.

Bolshevism: An Introduction to Soviet Communism by Waldemar Gurian. Notre Dame, Ind.: University of Notre Dame Press, 1952.

Brainwashing by Edward Hunter (The Story of the Men Who Defied It). New York: Farrar, Straus and Cudahy, 1956.

A Century of Conflict by Stefan T. Possony. Chicago: Henry Regnery Co., 1953.

The Communist Conspiracy (Strategy and Tactics of World Communism). Part I, Communism outside the U.S.
    Section A. Marxist Classics Foreword and General Introduction.
    Section B. The USSR 5/29/56.
    Section C. The World Congresses of the Communist International.
    Section D. Communist Activities around the World.
    Section E. The Comintern and CPUSA.

The Communist Party of the Soviet Union (A Study) by Alan Braith.

Communist Psychological Warfare (Brainwashing). Consultation with Edward Hunter. House Un-American Activities Committee, 85th Congress, 2d Sess., March 13, 1958. Washington, D.C.: U.S. Govt. Printing Office.

Contradictions of Communism. Report by the Subcommittee to Investigate the Administration of the Internal Security Act and other Internal Security Laws to the Senate Judiciary Committee, 86th Congress, 1st Sess. Washington, D.C.: U.S. Govt. Printing Office, 1959.

Control of the Arts in the Communist Empire. Consultation with Ivan P. Bahriany. House Un-American Activities Committee, 86th Congress, 2d Sess., June 3, 1959. Washington, D.C.: U.S. Govt. Printing Office, 1959.

Democracy Is Not Enough by John Scott. New York: Harcourt, Brace and Company, 1960.

Facts on Communism (2 Vols.).
    Vol. I, *The Communist Ideology* by Gerhart Niemeyer.
    Vol. II, *The Soviet Union from Lenin to Khrushchev* by David Dallin. Prepared for the House Un-American Activities Committee. Washington, D.C.: U.S. Govt. Printing Office, 1960.

The Fifth Weapon by Robert S. Byfield (Notes on the Kremlin's Concept of Total Coordination of all Weapons). New York: 1954.

For Victory in Peaceful Competition with Capitalism by Nikita S. Khrushchev. New York: E. P. Dutton and Co., Inc., 1960.

The Foreign Policy of the Soviet Union edited by Alvin Z. Rubinstein. New York: Random House, 1960.

A Forward Strategy for Americans by Robert Strausz-Hupé, William R. Kintner and Stefan T. Possony. New York: Harper and Brothers, 1961.

From Lenin to Khrushchev by Hugh Seton-Watson. New York: Frederick A. Praeger, Inc., 1960.

A Guide to Communist Jargon by Carew Hunt. London: Geoffrey Bles, 1957.

Handbook on Propaganda by Oliver Carlson. Vol. II, No. 1, Winter 1953. Studies of the Foundation for Social Research, San Jacinto, Cal.

International Communism (The Present Posture of the Free World). House Un-American Activities Committee, 85th Congress, 1st Sess., October 21, 1957. Washington, D.C.: U.S. Govt. Printing Office.

International Communism (Revolt in the Satellites). House Un-American Activities Committee, 84th Congress, 2d Sess., October 29-30, November 1, 17, 20 (1956). Washington, D.C.: U.S. Govt. Printing Office.

International Propaganda by John Martin. Minneapolis, Minn.: University of Minneapolis, 1958.

Investigation of Un-American Propaganda Activities in the U.S. (The Communist Party of the U.S. as an Agent of a Foreign Power).

House Un-American Activities Committee, 80th Congress, 1st Sess., April 1, 1947. Washington, D.C.: U.S. Govt. Printing Office.

IPI SURVEY (The Press in Authoritarian Countries). Published by The International Press Institute, Zurich, 1959.

Khrushchev's Strategy and Its Meaning for America. Prepared for the Subcommittee to Investigate the Administration of the Internal Security Act and other Internal Security Laws, Senate Judiciary Committee, by the Foreign Policy Research Institute, University of Pennsylvania. Washington, D.C.: U.S. Govt. Printing Office, 1960.

Language as a Communist Weapon. Consultation with Dr. Stefan T. Possony. House Un-American Activities Committee, 86th Congress, 1st Sess., March 2, 1959. Washington, D.C.: U.S. Govt. Printing Office.

Neither War Nor Peace by Hugh Seton-Watson (The Struggle for Power in the Post-War World). New York: Frederick A. Praeger, Inc., 1960.

Neurosis on a Global Scale by George F. Sutherland, M.D. Reprinted from *The Humanist,* 1959, Vol. 19, No. 5. The American Humanity Association, Yellow Springs, Ohio.

Pavlov, A Biography by B. P. Babkin. Chicago: University of Chicago Press, 1949.

A Primer on Communism by George W. Cronyn. New York: E. P. Dutton Co., Inc., 1958.

A Primer on Communism (200 Questions and Answers). Washington, D.C.: U.S. Information Agency, 1956.

Problems of Soviet Foreign Policy (A Symposium of the Institute for the Study of the USSR) edited by Oliver J. Frederiksen. Proceedings of the 11th Institute Conference, Munich, July 24-25, 1959.

Propaganda by Lindley Fraser. London: Oxford University Press, 1957.

Propaganda Analysis by Alexander L. George. Evanston, Ill.: Row Peterson and Co., 1959.

Protracted Conflict by Robert Strausz-Hupé et al. New York: Harper and Brothers, 1959.

Public Opinion in Soviet Russia by Alex Inkeles. Cambridge, Mass.: Harvard University Press, 1951.

Readings in Russian Foreign Policy edited by Robert A. Goldwin. New York: Oxford University Press, 1959.

The Revival of the Communist International and Its Significance for the U.S. Staff Study by the Subcommittee to Investigate the Administration of the Internal Security Act and other Internal Security Laws, Senate Judiciary Committee, 86th Congress, 1st Sess. Washington, D.C.: U.S. Govt. Printing Office, 1959.

Scientific, Technical, Educational and Cultural Exchanges (Treaties and Other International Arts, Series 4362). Agreement between USA and USSR, Moscow, November 21, 1959, and Memorandum, Washington, D.C., November 24, 1959.

The Secret Name by Lin Yu Tang. New York: Farrar, Straus and Cudahy, 1958.

The Silent Language by Edward T. Hall. New York: Doubleday and Company, Inc., 1959.

Soviet Conduct in World Affairs. Compiled by Alexander Dallin. New York: Columbia University Press, 1960.

Soviet Total War (Historic Mission of Violence and Deceit). 2 Vols. Prepared for the House Un-American Activities Committee. Washington, D.C.: U.S. Govt. Printing Office, 1956.

Soviet World Outlook (A Handbook of Communism). Publication of the United States Department of State, Washington, D.C., 1959.

Speeches and Interviews on World Problems by Nikita S. Khrushchev. Moscow: Foreign Language Publishing House, 1958.

A Study of Bolshevism by Nathan Leites. Glencoe, Ill.: The Free Press, 1953.

A Syllabus on Soviet Communism by Konstantin Shteppa. New York: American Committee for Liberation, 1958.

Target: The World edited by Evron M. Kirkpatrick. New York: The Macmillan Co., 1956.

The Technique of Soviet Propaganda. A Study by Suzanne Labin. Presented by the Subcommittee to Investigate the Administration of the Internal Security Act and other Internal Security Laws, Senate Judiciary Committee, 86th Congress, 2d Sess. Washington, D.C.: U.S. Govt. Printing Office, 1960.

The Techniques of Communism by Louis F. Budenz. Chicago: Henry Regnery Co., 1954.

This Is the Challenge by William Benton. New York: Associated College Presses, 1958.

The Threat of Soviet Imperialism edited by C. Grove Haines. Baltimore: The Johns Hopkins Press, 1954.

To Win the Minds of Men by Peter Grother. Palo Alto, Calif.: Pacific Books, 1958.

Truth is Our Weapon by Edward W. Barrett. New York: Funk and Wagnalls Co., 1953.

Twelve Years of Communist Broadcasting, 1948-1959. Report prepared by Simon Costikyan. Office of Research Analysis, Washington, D.C.: U.S. Information Agency.

U.S. Foreign Policy with USSR and Eastern Europe. Study prepared at the request of Senate Foreign Relations Committee, by a Columbia–

Harvard Research Group under the Administration of Columbia University. No. i, February 14, 1960, 86th Congress, 2d Sess. Washington, D.C.: U.S. Govt. Printing Office, 1960.

The Weapon on the Wall by Murray Dyer (Rethinking Psychological Warfare). Baltimore: The Johns Hopkins Press, 1959.

What We Must Know About Communism by Harry and Bonaro Overstreet. New York: W. W. Norton & Company, Inc., 1958.

"Words That Divide the World" by Stefan T. Possony, *Saturday Evening Post,* July 9, 1960.

World Communism Today by Martin Ebon. New York: McGraw-Hill Book Co., Inc., 1948.

World Communist Movement Selective Chronology 1818-1957. Library of Congress Legislative Reference Service, Vol. 1. Washington, D.C.: U.S. Govt. Printing Office, 1960.

Worldwide Communist Propaganda Activities edited by F. Bowen Evans. New York: The Macmillan Co., 1955.

Year of Crisis edited by Evron M. Kirkpatrick. New York: The Macmillan Company, 1957.

Index

Acheson, Dean, undersec'y of state, attacked by Ehrenburg, 34
Adenauer, Konrad, German chancellor, and RFE, 76
agents: communists as, 179
training of, 5, 7
as US propaganda target, 202
Agerpress, 25
agitation, 168
and labor unions, 98
in Romania, 19
as US propaganda weapon, 183-84
See also propaganda
agitation-propaganda rallies, 58
Agitprop. *See* Section of Propaganda and Agitation
agrarian reform: in Cuba, 20, 21
in Romania, 20
allegiance, of communists, 12
Allen, George V., USIA: and library exchange, 138
and radio jamming, 148
Allied Control Commission, 32
American Air Force, and bacteriological warfare, 61
American Committee for Liberation from Bolshevism, 66, 149-51
American-Soviet Facts, bulletin, 93
Americans, as "imperialist spies," 46
Amerika, magazine, 92, 127, 141-42
Anglo-American espionage agency, 48
"Anglo-American imperialists," 31-32, 66
See also imperialists
"Anglo-American spies," 66
See also spies

annexation, of Eastern Europe, as US propaganda tool, 202-3
See also satellite nations
Antonescu Iron Guard regime, 20
Argentina, USSR propaganda in, 85-86
ARLUS. *See* Association for Strengthening Romanian-Soviet Relations
Armenia, as threat to USSR, 122-23
army, Cuban, and propaganda, 21
Association for Strengthening Romanian-Soviet Relations (ARLUS), 21
Aswan Dam, withdrawal of US aid to, 67
"Atlantic lie," 36
atom bomb, as propaganda, 77
attitudes, US democratic, as propaganda tool, 201-2
Australia, USSR propaganda in, 85
Austria, accused by USSR, 75
authoritarian character, of USSR, 122
Azerbaijan, as threat to USSR, 123

Bacon, Francis, quoted, 3
bacteriological warfare, charges of, 56-57, 58-62
behavior, USSR, as propaganda subject, 177, 181
Benton, William, US ass't sec'y of state: attack on USSR, 38-39
attacked by USSR, 39-40
calls Geneva reception, 44
"big lie," and Kremlin, 13, 187
"big smear" campaign, against Eisenhower, 132